HOW TO BE AN
INDEX INVESTOR

HOW TO BE AN INDEX INVESTOR

Max Isaacman

McGraw-Hill

New York   San Francisco   Washington, D.C.   Auckland   Bogotá
Caracas   Lisbon   London   Madrid   Mexico City   Milan
Montreal   New Delhi   San Juan   Singapore
Sydney   Tokyo   Toronto

Library of Congress Cataloging-in-Publication Data

Isaacman, Max.
   How to be an index investor / by Max Isaacman.
   p. cm.
   ISBN 0-07-135683-5
   1. Investments. I. Title.

HG4521 .I8 2000
332.6—dc21   00-021161

McGraw-Hill

*A Division of The **McGraw·Hill** Companies*

1 2 3 4 5 6 7 8 9 0 DOC / DOC 0 9 8 7 6 5 4 3 2 1 0

ISBN 0-07-135683-5

*This book was typeset in New Times Roman by Inkwell Publishing
Services. Printed and bound by R. R. Donnelley & Sons Company.*

This publication is designed to provide accurate and authoritative
information in regard to the subject matter covered. It is sold with the
understanding that the publisher is not engaged in rendering legal,
accounting, or other professional service. If legal advice or other
expert assistance is required, the services of a competent professional
person should be sought.
   *—From a declaration of principles jointly adopted by a committee
   of the American Bar Association and a committee of publishers.*

 This book is printed on recycled, acid-free paper
containing a minimum of 50% recycled de-inked fiber.

McGraw-Hill books are available at special quantity discounts to use
as premiums and sales promotions, or for use in corporate training
programs. For more information, please write to the Director of
Special Sales, Professional Publishing, McGraw-Hill, Two Penn
Plaza, New York, NY 10121-2298. Or contact your local bookstore.

CONTENTS

Foreword   *vii*

Acknowledgments   *xi*

Introduction   *1*

PART I
OVERVIEWS AND STRATEGIES

1   An Overview of Exchange Index Shares   *13*

2   Trading Exchange Index Shares   *31*

3   Individual and Professional Strategies for Using Exchange Shares   *51*

4   Behavioral Finance   *63*

5   The Electronic Index Investor and Trader   *69*

PART II
THE DIFFERENT CLASSES OF EXCHANGE SHARES

6   The Select Sector SPDRs   *85*

7   DIA   *95*

8   SPY and MDY   *105*

9   QQQ   *129*

10   WEBS   *137*

Appendix A: The Stocks of the Select Sector SPDRs   *183*

Appendix B: The Electronic Index Investor and Trader Research Source   *247*

Index   *253*

FOREWORD

When I began investing in the stock market in 1970, I made my first investment in a small-cap fund that was heavily advertised at the time in many top magazines. I relaxed and waited for the windfall. A bear market began in 1972, but I held on. The S&P 500 declined by nearly half over the next two years, and ended up underperforming lowly treasury bills for the next decade. But small-cap stocks put in a very stellar performance over the period, so much so that academics deemed them an asset class that long term should outperform all other equities. But my portfolio manager evidently didn't select the right stocks. In fact, in 1982 I sold the investment at a loss. That was my first lesson in one of the risks that was not explained to me in the investment texts of the time: the risk that the market segment will do very well and the fund manager will do very poorly.

Most experienced investors today, thanks to far better informed financial journalists and all the free information available on the Internet, know that there are few mutual fund managers who can walk on water for long periods. It's now commonplace that 75 percent of active managers underperform the S&P 500 over five-year periods and that almost all do so on an after-tax basis. If that's true, why do we see so many ads today in the media for funds that are beating the S&P 500? The most likely reason is that if the fund is beating an S&P 500 index fund on a long-term basis it is because the fund is using the wrong benchmark. An S&P 500 index fund is a growth and income fund. A fund that is beating it is very likely one that should be measured by the S&P/Barra 500 Growth Index or the Nasdaq Composite or an appropriate S&P sector index. This is the second lesson I have learned about investing that I didn't find in the textbooks: when an asset class outperforms—say small caps or midcaps or the technology sector—the best way to capture that outperformance is with an index fund that replicates that asset class or sector.

For the past 10 years I have been privileged to serve on the S&P Index Committee and to oversee the maintenance of S&P's indexes on a global basis. Three additional lessons I have learned in this activity are worth repeating. One is that markets are far more efficient than most investors realize until they have lost a good deal of money or underperformed the market for a long time. The next time you are in a busy grocery store notice how the lines quickly become the same length. Transactions markets are even more efficient than that. Second, diversification—many eggs in multiple baskets—is a very powerful tool that investors need to understand better. A risk-adjusted analysis S&P did of the returns of all stocks in the 500 index last year showed that while Cisco blew out the lights, the 500 index itself came in eleventh in risk-adjusted returns. That shows the power of holding a large list of stocks and also that the odds of picking the best performing stocks—ten chances in 500—for the risk taken are not very high compared to just picking them all. The third and final lesson is that most investors, myself included, like the "entertainment" benefit of the investment experience. Indexing through mutual funds will never qualify as an extreme sport deserving of a daily session on CNBC.

Is there no way to be an intelligent investor without surrendering all the fun to another party? Yes, finally there is. The explosion of new exchange-traded index funds, sector funds, country funds, value and growth funds, and—soon on an exchange near you—probably exchange-traded active funds, means a whole new era of opportunity for individual investors to tailor investments to suit their risks and preferences while profiting from the lessons that I enumerated above. And finally, as well, Max Isaacman has produced the first guidebook for this new adventure. *How to Be an Index Investor* is the only book I have seen that explains concisely and thoroughly how to invest in Spiders, Diamonds, Sector Spiders, WEBS, and all the other new vehicles soon to be launched to get the maximum benefit from indexing while preserving the opportunity to "entertain" oneself with some active trading around a core portfolio of indexed assets.

Isaacman explores the thought process that went into developing exchange-traded funds, why they are superior to plain vanilla index funds, and how to structure your own best portfolio using your brokerage account. If you are an airline pilot, for example, the S&P 500 may not have enough exposure to the energy industry to offset the risk you face if oil prices surge and stay high for years. Isaacman points out a simple way for you to "overweight" energy by adding the Select Energy Sector Spider, traded on the American Stock Exchange, to your portfolio. He makes it clear there is a new way to "personalize" your investing, to make "side bets" on stock sectors that catch your fancy, and to otherwise make investing entertaining without having to learn and relearn the lessons I mentioned earlier. Exchange-traded funds are destined to be one of the most innovative financial instruments of the new century both in the United States and abroad. Isaacman has your passport for this venture.

I urge you to buy this book, study it, and understand how these exciting new products can work for you, whether you are an investor or a trader.

James Branscome
Managing Director, Investment Analysis
Standard & Poor's

ACKNOWLEDGMENTS

First of all, I'd like to thank my wife, Joyce Glick, whose never-ending "urgent itineraries" kept me hopping around the country garnering information. Special thanks to my publisher at McGraw-Hill, Jeffrey Krames, whose guidance in putting this book together was invaluable, and to his assistant, Laura Libretti, who was there whenever I needed her. Also, thanks to my editor, Ela Aktay.

Many people volunteered their time and professional insights, and I am most appreciative: John Downes, Jordan Goodman, James Clunie, John Jacobs, Sue Crosby, Jim Branscome, Charles Proses, Carl Gargula, Tomas N. Rzepski, Peter Yuen, Dan Dolan, John Prestbo, Jon Isaacman, Dan Hubbard, Tom Taggart, Burt G. Malkiel, Amy Schioldager, Jack Hanson, Ed McCartin, Doug Holmes, Jay Baker, Kevin Ireland, Gary Gastineau, Rich Hogan, Jim Ross, Mike Schwartz, Tony Denninger, Greg Friedman, Diane Paul, Michael Babel, Terry Odean, Keith Grogan, Dan Noonan, Robert Angle, Gerry Kusschuk, Meir Statman, and the partners at East/West Securities in San Francisco, Dr. Charles Chen (a two-time winner of the U.S. Trading Championships) and Leslie Harris.

Also, our daughters, Carrie Edel Isaacman and Danielle Kaplan, deserve recognition for their help.

Max Isaacman

INTRODUCTION
THE INDEX REVOLUTION

T ruly, there is a revolution sweeping Wall Street, changing the Street as it has never changed before. Main Street really *has* taken over Wall Street. Moreover, it's a twofold revolution. With her computer, an investor today can manage her portfolio on the Internet and simulate sending orders directly to the floor. The trader is aided in this by the research available today, which is unprecedented in its availability and low cost to those who invest and trade online.

The second aspect of the revolution is the availability of exchange traded index shares. For the first time, investors and traders can, at the click of a mouse, buy an entire sector. If an investor or trader wants to buy a stock that tracks the market in Switzerland, the energy sector of the U.S. market, a basket of fast-growing NASDAQ companies, or some other index, he can do it quickly, cheaply, and at any time the markets are open. What's more, a trader or investor can short the indexes on a downtick or a zero downtick; trade in 1/64ths, which is a very tight market; buy or sell or short very close to the bid/asked quotes; trade in huge volume, as hundred-thousand shares are routinely done at the bid/asked; or trade in small pieces. And there are many other things you can do, all of which this book covers.

These developments made this book imperative. We needed a resource that would simultaneously describe today's online trading developments, give insights and instructions on the basics of trading over the Internet, and explore exchange traded shares and offer strategies for using them, all explained in a way and bolstered by examples useful to both individuals and experienced professionals.

WHY BOTHER WITH INDEXING?

Indexing is a method whose time has come. It is radically changing the way people invest their money.

Institutions have used index investing for years. Its use derives largely from one simple conclusion: On average, active money managers do not beat the indexes. Institutions have known this for years. So now, individual investors are reasoning that if managers can't beat the indexes, why not just buy the indexes? Why not, indeed? Using exchange index shares, it is an easy thing to do.

Basically, there are two types of investment managers. Active managers develop and follow their own strategies, trying to find stocks they think will go up in value, or in the case of hedge funds, stocks that will go down. Index managers structure portfolios to replicate or optimize an index.

The Dow Jones Industrial Average and the S&P 500 index are the two best-known indexes. Even in the extended bull market we are currently experiencing, it is estimated that some years about 75 percent of active managers do not beat the indexes. In fact, many money managers lose money. One analysis concluded that over the past three years, an astounding 96 percent of money managers did worse than the S&P 500 index.

Table I.1 shows returns from the average general equity mutual funds from 1988 to 1998. The S&P index did about 3 percent better per year than the average equity fund.

TABLE I-1   Mutual Funds Versus the Market Index

	Total Return	
	Ten Years Ended June 30, 1998	
	Cumulative	Annual Rate
Standard & Poor's 500 index	+448.88	+18.56
Average general equity fund	+313.05	+15.24

Source: Malkiel, Burton G., *A Random Walk Down Wall Street*, New York: Norton.

Figure I-1 makes the case another way. The illustration shows what $10,000 invested in an S&P fund in 1969 would have been worth in June of 1998. The value would have grown to $311,000. The chart also shows that same $10,000 invested in the average actively managed stock fund. That investment would have grown to $171,950. The investor would have been far better off in the S&P 500 fund.

Then there's the expense issue. Professional money managers have to make trips to see companies, attend investment seminars, and otherwise spend vast sums in their research and due-diligence activities. They create glossy brochures to send out to prospects and customers that extol their virtues, degrees, and successes. Many multibillion-dollar institutions have teams of analysts and portfolio managers and assistants and research people . . . and often don't beat the indexes or barely make money or have a losing year. The investor pays for all this. And almost always, these costs increase the active manager's expense ratio above that of the index manager, who simply follows index guidelines.

Take a look at Figure I-2. Again, we see how active management stacks up against the S&P 500 index. This chart, courtesy of Barclays Global Investors (BGI), compares active and indexed portfolios, both operating in the institutional sector, against the S&P 500 benchmark. In the time period between 1987 and 1997, the S&P benchmark outperformed the active port-

FIGURE I-1   The Value of $10,000 Invested in 1969

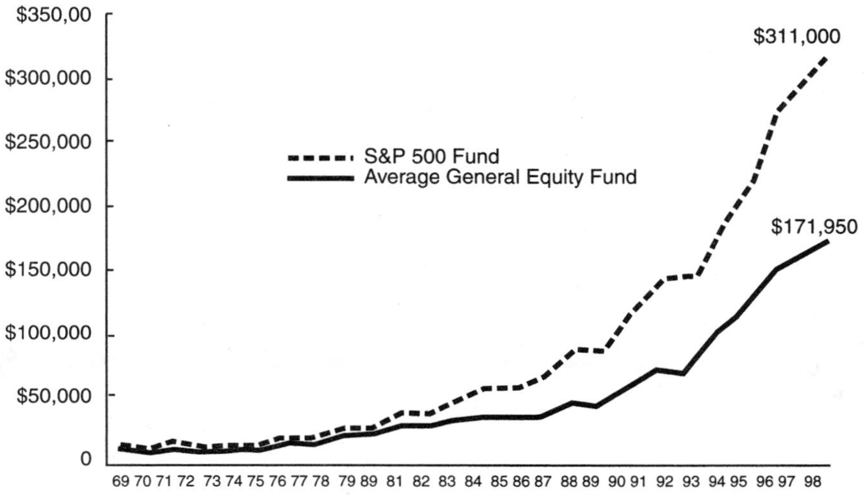

**FIGURE I-2   Relative Returns for the U.S. Large-Cap Institutional
Sector (1987–1997)**

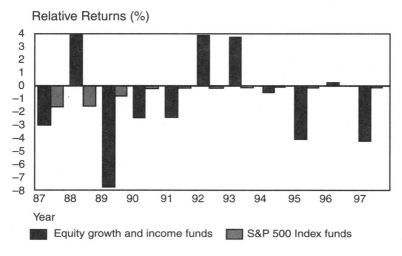

folio by about 1.2 percent a year. The index portfolio matched the index, as
it should have. Callan Associates and Frank Russell, two major consulting
firms, also report an underperformance of managed accounts over a 10-
year period. Frank Russell reports a 0.5 percent underperformance. The
Callan Associates' figure is 0.8 percent.

This is not intended to be a blanket indictment of active management.
There are times when a given manager can and does beat the indexes. Also,
active managers can be effective in a certain segment, gold or silver, for
instance, where an index is not available or cannot perform as well as a seasoned professional.

Institutions put money into indexing as a low-cost way to get broad
market exposure. Look at Figure I-3. Indexing has grown dramatically in
the institutional segment. The chart presents data on U.S. tax-exempt international assets. The numbers are drawn from Pension & Investments
Annual Surveys.

There is a time and place and proportion for all investments. But for the
core portion of portfolios, for those funds that should be invested for broad
market exposure, including international investments, the position of this
book is that exchange index shares are the lowest-cost and most flexible
way to get there.

FIGURE I-3   Growth in Indexing of U.S. Tax-Exempt Institutional Assets (1975–1996)

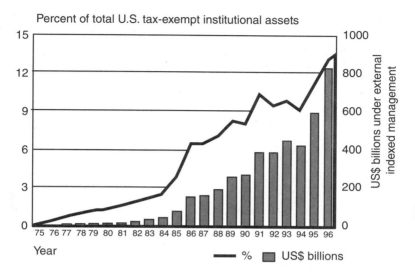

The amount of individual stocks that you want to trade, both U.S. and foreign, and how much you want to leave with an active manager is up to you: Regardless, this book can be used as an adjunct to your investment and trading strategies.

THE PROBLEM OF STOCK PICKING

Some studies show that about 80 percent of investment success lies not in market timing or stock selection but in sector selection. The problem with individual stocks is that you can be right on the sector, such as energy or technology, and still not profit if the stocks you select, for whatever reason, don't perform. You can pick the right country, such as Japan, and still lose money on your investment if your stocks are not the right ones. Stocks can and do blow up, sometimes for reasons that you don't, and can't, foresee.

For example, if you want representation in a fast-growing industry like technology, you can simply purchase shares of Microsoft or another major company in the technology sector. But Microsoft might run into trouble and not perform, as happened with the government antitrust suit. If you buy the Technology Sector SPDR, you get Microsoft and the other companies in the SPDR. Some of these companies can grower *faster* than Microsoft, plus, it spreads your risk, possibly without lowering your profit potential.

So with indexing, you make an investment over a group of stocks in a sector or in a country, reasoning that if you are right on the sector or country, even if one or a few stocks get into trouble, you will still emerge with a profit.

Also, through the use of options, which are covered later in the book, you can better manage your risk.

Here's as an example of how it works. You can simultaneously buy a put on the Dow Jones Industrial Average and DIA (DIA is the symbol for *Diamond*, the exchange share that tracks the Dow Jones Industrial Average; it is explained in more detail later). The price you pay for the put will depend on market conditions and volatility, but let's say you pay about 10 percent. In this way, you limit your risk of holding DIA to about 10 percent over a two-year period. You give up none of your upside over that period of time, but you limit your loss—all for a 10 percent premium cost.

This "married put" method can be used with the other exchange shares as well.

Later on, I'll outline some simple and easy-to-use strategies that can help you invest on a global basis. Exchange traded shares makes this investing easy and low cost. Stock markets around the world move independently of each other. Opportunities may abound in one market, while another market stands on the brink of disaster. Today, the U.S. stock market has the highest ratio of market capitalization to gross national product ever recorded: 140 percent. For perspective, the ratio in 1929, just before the great depression, was 81 percent. This doesn't mean a crash is imminent. But it does point up the wisdom of international diversification as a way of hedging your investments.

Although exchange shares have become available only recently, they have broken records for their acceptability as a new product. Although new products will continue to flood into the market, this book will stay relevant. The information on how the shares are structured, how they work, and strategies to utilize them fully should not become obsolete in the near future, and the techniques covered here can be adjusted to meet any new class of shares.

THE EVOLUTION OF INDEXING

Barclays Global Investors (BGI), located in San Francisco, is a major institutional investor. They manage about $600 billion. Along with its predecessor, Wells Fargo Bank, Barclays initiated the era of quantitative investing with the first indexed fund in 1973. Since then, indexing has grown rapidly, now accounting for an estimated 23 percent of institutional equity investing in the United States. In the United Kingdom indexing started taking off in the 1980s. It has expanded quickly, however, now accounting for an estimated 20 percent of U.K. institutional mandates.

With its popularity and acceptance among institutional investors, indexing is now spreading to individuals. This is largely attributable to the efforts of two people.

Dr. Burton G. Malkiel, Professor of Economics at Princeton University, is author of *A Random Walk Down Wall Street*, in which he explores the limitations of active professional management. Malkiel's conclusion is that it is difficult, if not impossible, for an average active manager to consistently beat the index.

A Random Walk Down Wall Street was *not* a welcome addition to financial literature—not from the perspective of Wall Street. After all, brokers, analysts, portfolio managers, and other financial professionals pride themselves on and make big money at extolling their understanding of the logic and rationality of the stock markets.

Malkiel exploded this myth. An academician, he used his scholarly tools to show that individual stock prices often move randomly. In the short term, at least, price movements are unpredictable. He reasoned, therefore, that investors would probably be better off buying an index of stocks rather than having their money actively managed or trying to manage the funds themselves through common stock selection.

The second person, John C. Bogle of Vanguard Investing, made that possible. Bogle was instrumental in creating the first index fund to be marketed to individual investors.

The rest is history. Not only institutional funds have flown into indexing. Figure I-4, using data is supplied by Reuters Limited 2000, illustrates the growth of stock funds that track the S&P 500 index. From 0.4 percent of retail equity funds in 1984, the funds grew to 3.3 percent in 1997.

Active management can get complicated too. Even if a person wanted to invest in active management, which funds should he choose? Funds that do well in one time period may not do well in another. Table I-2 shows that the fund rankings from the 1970–1980 era did not carry over into the 1980–1990 time frame.

FIGURE 1-4   U.S. Retail S&P 500 Indexed Equity Funds Under Management

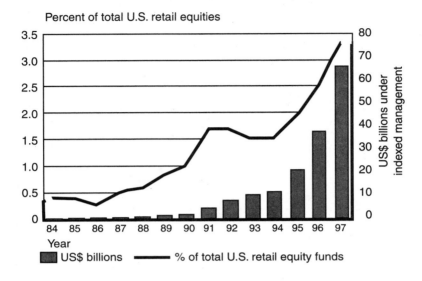

TABLE I-2   How the Top 20 Equity Funds of the 1970s Performed During the 1980s

Fund Name	Rank 1970–1980	Rank 1980–1990
Twentieth Century Growth	1	176
Templeton Growth	2	126
Quasar Associates	3	186
44 Wall Street	4	309
Pioneer II	5	136
Twentieth Century Select	6	20
Security Ultra	7	296
Mutual Shares Corp.	8	35
Charter Fund	9	119
Magellan Fund	10	1
Over-the-Counter Securities	11	242
American Capital Growth	12	239
American Capital Venture	13	161
Putnam Voyager	14	78

TABLE I-2 (*Continued*)

Fund Name	Rank 1970–1980	Rank 1980–1990
Janus Fund	15	21
Weingarten Equity	16	36
Hartwell Leverage Fund	17	259
Pace Fund	18	60
Acorn Fund	19	172
Stein Roe Special Fund	20	57
Average annual return:		
Top 20 funds	+19.0%	+11.1%
All funds	+10.4%	+11.7%
Number of funds	177	309

Table courtesy of Malkiel, Burton G., *A Random Walk Down Wall Street*, New York: Norton.

Another angle can be seen in Table I-3. Note that the top funds in 1978–1987 did not repeat as top funds in 1988–1997. This table also shows that if you had just been in the S&P 500 index all of those years, you would have done almost as well as the funds listed, which were the top ones, not the average funds.

TABLE I-3   How the Top 10 Equity Mutual Funds of 1978–1987 Performed During 1988–1997

Fund	Average Return 1978–1987 (%)	Average Return 1988–1997 (%)
Fidelity Magellan	30.93	18.88
Federated Capital Appreciation A	26.08	15.60
AIM Weingarten A	23.35	16.68
Van Kampen American Capital Pace A	22.24	15.30
Alliance Quasar A	22.08	15.83
AIM Constellation A	21.47	20.36
Spectra	21.08	21.78
IDS New Dimensions A	20.62	18.66
Smith Barney Appreciation A	20.48	15.25

TABLE I-3 (*Continued*)

Fund	Average Return 1978–1987 (%)	Average Return 1988–1997 (%)
Growth Fund of America	20.00	16.65
MFS Growth Opportunities A	19.94	14.79
Mutual Shares Z	19.93	17.37
American Capital	19.80	15.27
Janus Fund	19.65	18.34
Stein Roe Special	19.52	17.31
Van Kampen American Capital Comstock A	18.77	16.56
AIM Charter A	18.49	16.45
Van Kampen American Capital Enterprise A	18.29	17.63
Fidelity Congress Street	18.27	17.40
Van Kampen American Capital Emerging Growth A	18.15	19.06
Average	20.95	17.26
S&P 500-Stock Index	15.18	18.04

Source: Mutual funds data from Morningstar, Inc. Includes all domestic diversified stock funds.

I'll also be exploring here the new and fast-growing field of behavioral finance, which examines how and why we invest and trade the way we do, not how we think we do. The section on behavioral finance determines who the best investors are, and why. You may be surprised. You will for sure gain insights into many investing and trading myths, and that will help you understand your own trading and investing characteristics. This section sheds further light on why index investing makes sense, at least for a portion of your funds.

At the present time I own the German WEBS and the Midcap Spyder. I many not own these securities at the time this book is published. Also, my customers own QQQ, DIA, MDY, and other securities that may not be owned by them at the time this book is published.

OVERVIEWS AND STRATEGIES

CHAPTER

1

AN OVERVIEW
OF EXCHANGE
INDEX SHARES

LISTED INDEX SECURITIES—WHAT THEY ARE;
WHAT THEY'RE NOT

At first glance, there wouldn't seem to be any difference between exchange index securities and stocks. But exchange index securities are not stocks. They are either unit investment trusts, or they are open-end mutual funds. But regardless of the form in which they are structured, the securities track a specific area of the market. It could be an index, an industry group, a specific stock group, or a country index.

A unit investment trust is a portfolio of stocks that is fixed and unmanaged, meaning that the securities are not actively changed. A mutual fund is an investment company that is designed to meet specific investing goals or that specializes in a particular class of stocks. Mutual funds are governed by the Investment Company Act of 1940, which protects investors against unfair activities by investment companies. This makes a difference in the investing practices of WEBS, as we shall see.

Exchange index securities, listed index securities, exchange shares, or exchange traded funds (ETF) all mean the same thing, and are unique investments that give the holder ownership in a sector or country or area of the stock market; the securities comprising the index are represented by one share of the security. Put another way, you can buy an entire index just by purchasing a single share of the index securities on the American Stock Exchange (ASE). Trading is easy. You call your broker, or click on your mouse to trade through your online broker.

During the day, as the markets move up and down, you can trade the index securities as you would individual stocks, taking advantage of rallies and dips. Because you are trading an index, you are not subject to the vicissitudes of just one company. If you are right on the country or sector or index, you will have the right result.

THE INDEX SECURITIES TRADING ON THE ASE

Diamonds (symbol DIA): These securities track the Dow Jones Industrial Average. The Dow is the oldest market gauge of the New York Stock Exchange (NYSE). It is narrow in scope, covering only 30 stocks. Each DIA share represents ownership in the 30 Dow Jones blue-chip stocks.

Standard & Poor's (S&P) Depositary Receipts, SPDRS (SPY): Called "spiders," these securities track the companies in the S&P 500 index. This benchmark has for years been the key barometer for institutional investors and is now becoming popular with individual investors as well.

MidCap SPDRS (MDY): These spiders track the companies in the S&P MidCap 400 Index, which is made up of smaller capitalized companies. You can calculate the market capitalization (market "cap") of a company by multiplying the number of outstanding shares by the market price. For example, if a company has 10 million shares outstanding and the market price is 50, the company's market cap is $500 million.

Select Sector SPDRS: These spiders allow you to buy and sell particular sectors or groups of industries in the S&P 500. Think of it as unbundling the index. Introduced in December 1998, this type of index security is a very important tool. Some experts estimate that 80 percent of an investor's profit is made by being in the right sector of the market. The select SPDRS make it possible for you to focus on a sector. The sectors covered and symbols are as follows:

Basic Industry	XLB
Consumer Services	XLV

Consumer Staples	XLP
Cyclical/Transportation	XLY
Energy	XLE
Financial	XLE
Industrial	XLI
Technology	XLK
Utilities	XLU

Nasdaq-100 (QQQ): The newest securities are the Nasdaq 100 shares. One share of QQQ represents 100 stocks, the largest and most actively traded companies listed on the Nasdaq stock market. The Nasdaq market is for unlisted shares, or over-the-counter (OTC) trading. In the Nasdaq market, a market maker quotes firm buy and sell prices for securities. Usually, market makers have a position in the stocks they trade, either a long or short position. They risk their own or their company's money. This method of trading differs from listed trading on one of the other exchanges. On the exchange, a member specialist is charged with maintaining an orderly market in assigned securities. Basically, the specialist buys and sells stocks for himself and others to maintain a liquid and fair market. QQQ opened for trading in March 1999 and set a first-day trading record with 2.6 million shares changing hands.

World Equity Benchmark Shares (WEBS): Introduced in April 1996, these shares offer a simple and quick way to invest internationally. WEBS track the Morgan Stanley Capital International (MSCI) country indexes. Through WEBS, you can buy stocks in the markets in mature countries as well as in emerging markets. The symbols and countries are as follows:

Australia	EWA
Austria	EWO
Belgium	EWK
Canada	EWC
France	EWQ
Germany	EWG
Hong Kong	EWH
Italy	EWI
Japan	EWJ

Malaysia	EWM
Mexico	EWW
Netherlands	EWN
Singapore	EWS
Spain	EWP
Sweden	EWD
Switzerland	EWL
United Kingdom	EWU

As far as the structure of the index securities, it makes little difference. No matter what the structure, all of these securities trade just like stocks. Incidentally, SPY, MidCap SPY, DIA, and QQQ are structured similarly to unit trusts; select SPDRS and WEBS are mutual funds.

Exchange shares today cover almost all investor needs, but this is just the beginning. The concept is so popular that the ASE plans many more classes of shares in the near future. There could be as many as 100 classes trading within the next year.

FOLLOWING YOUR LISTED INDEX SECURITIES
You can keep up with your securities by reading *Barron's*, *The New York Times*, or *The Wall Street Journal*. If you live in a big city, your local newspaper will probably list all the shares. Smaller city newspapers may give only a partial listing of the ASE, but the listed index securities are so popular, they are almost always included.

Figure 1-1 on pages 18–19 is a listing from *The New York Times*, which pictures offering quotes of the index securities and an explanation of the codes.

HOW ARE INDEX SECURITIES MANAGED—AND BY WHOM?
There are different management processes for different products. For the typical index securities, which excludes WEBS, there really is no active, decision-making portfolio manager. Actively managed portfolios employ portfolio managers, who buy and sell stocks based on the manager's strategies. The index securities have their systems in place to track indexes, and the activities of the index managers have more to do with creating and redeeming exchange shares.

Index portfolio management is different from active portfolio management. The index managers are charged only with replicating an index and do not use the tools of active management, such as charting, asset allocation, and market timing. Make no mistake, however; indexing has its own set of required quantitative skills and disciplines.

The day-to-day activity of an index manager has little in common with active portfolio management. In fact, index managers usually have little experience in traditional portfolio management. There is no need for that type of experience. From time to time, however, index managers do have to exercise a degree of sophistication. Managing WEBS, for example, involves a strategy known as portfolio optimization.

WEBS attempt to come up with a portfolio that has the same kind of responsiveness to economic variables as the overall index that is being tracked. The optimized stock portfolio tracks a country index, using fewer issues than the index contains. WEBS do not try to outperform the MSCI indexes, however. The WEBS manager simply creates an algorithm, the goal of which is simply to come up with industry and factor weights in the portfolio to create a subset of the stocks in a particular MSCI country index. Although the WEBS stock portfolio will not necessarily match the stocks in the MSCI index portfolio, in creating this subset, WEBS attempt to replicate the performance of the MSCI index. Having fewer stocks also makes it cheaper to create and redeem shares and lowers transaction costs.

These are very stable portfolios, unlike more aggressive optimization strategies in which the algorithms can lead to unstable portfolios. Once built, the WEBS portfolio doesn't change much unless there is a significant change in the composition of the index that is being tracked or in the business of the companies in the index.

COMPANY CHANGES IN THE INDEX
Even in a straight index fund, there are times when sophisticated techniques must be used, such as when there are company changes. Company changes are more frequent in straight index funds than in most WEBS because there are more companies represented in the straight indexes.

FIGURE 1-1 Example of ASE Listing from *The New York Times*

The high and low of the exchange share for the last 52 weeks

The dividend rate

The yield at that rate

Diamonds

The day's sales volume

The last trade and the difference from the prior day

52-Week High	52-Week Low	Stock	Div	Yld %	P/E	Sales 100s	High	Low	Last	Chg
1 13/16	3/16	AquaAll wt	...	...	...	2	3/16	3/16	3/16	- 1/8
7	5 5/8	ArizLd	.40e	6.4	15	10	6 1/4	6 1/4	6 1/4	+ 1/4
14 15/16	8 7/8	ArmorH	...	...	25	200	12 11/16	12 1/8	12 5/8	- 1/16
2 1/8	7/8	Arhyth	...	...	dd	45	1 1/4	1 1/4	1 1/4	...
20 1/4	2 7/8	AstLivng	...	...	24	822	3	2 7/8	2 15/16	...
3 5/8	1 3/4	AtlPrem	...	...	20	20	2 3/4	2 3/4	2 3/4	...
16 1/4	6 3/4	AtlTele	.60	6.9	3	9	8 3/4	8 9/16	8 11/16	...
9 3/4	5 3/4	Atlantis	...	...	11	89	9 3/4	9 3/8	9 3/4	+ 1/2
20 7/8	**3 3/8**	**AudioBC**	...	...	**dd**	**4816**	**14 3/4**	**11 7/8**	**14 11/16**	**+ 3 1/16**
7 7/16	3 5/8	Audvox	...	...	26	733	6 3/8	6 1/8	6 1/4	+ 1/8
8 5/8	13/16	AutoBond	...	...	dd	30	1 3/4	1 11/16	1 11/16	- 1/16
3 1/16	1 1/8	Autotote	...	...	dd	694	1 1/2	1 1/4	1 1/2	...
9 1/2	5 9/16	AvalonH n	...	...	dd	116	6	5 13/16	6	+ 1/4
6 3/4	1 5/8	AvenEnt	...	...	...	26	2 1/4	2 1/16	2 1/16	- 3/16
31 1/4	26 1/2	Axogen n	...	...	...	18	30 7/8	30 5/8	30 3/4	...
1 1/8	5/16	Azco	...	...	dd	134	11/16	5/8	11/16	...
9	1 3/4	B&HO	...	...	44	4	1 3/4	1 3/4	1 3/4	...
11	5 1/2	BFC Cns g	...	...	...	16	6 13/16	6 5/8	6 13/16	+ 1/16
2 3/8	1 1/16	BFX Hosp	...	...	dd	5	1 1/4	1 1/4	1 1/4	+ 1/8
145 5/16	102 9/16	BHC	1.00e	0.8	73	22	130	128	128 1/4	+ 1/4
5 1/4	1 13/16	BLC Fn n	...	...	11	151	2 1/8	2	2	- 1/16
40 5/8	25	BadgrM	.72f	2.4	14	37	30	29 1/2	29 1/2	- 1/4
10 5/8	6 3/16	Baker	...	...	dd	129	7 5/16	6 3/8	7	+ 3/8
9 3/4	2	BalCare	...	...	cc	152	2 1/2	2 5/16	2 1/2	+ 3/16
6 1/2	2 7/8	Baldw	...	...	5	646	3 1/8	3	3	- 1/8
26 7/8	19 7/8	BanFd	3.79e	16.4	q	24	23 1/4	23 1/8	23 1/8	...
28 3/4	16 1/4	BarHarb s	.68	3.5	5	4	19 1/4	19	19 1/4	...
16 3/4	10 7/8	Barnwl	...	...	dd	18	11 5/16	11 1/4	11 1/4	- 1/8
33 3/4	18 5/8	BayStBc	.05p	...	...	15	20 7/8	20 13/16	20 7/8	+ 1/8
7 3/8	2 3/8	BayCorpH	...	...	dd	47	3	2 7/8	2 7/8	- 1/8
9 3/8	2 5/8	Bayou	...	...	2	61	3 1/2	3 3/8	3 1/2	+ 1/8
5 15/16	3 1/4	BeardCo	...	...	dd	5	3 3/4	3 3/4	3 3/4	...
2 13/16	5/8	▼BemaGold	...	...	dd	2616	11/16	9/16	5/8	...
3 1/16	13/16	BentPh	...	...	dd	121	1 9/16	1 1/2	1 1/2	- 1/8
3/16	1/32	BentP wtB	...	...	...	240	1/16	1/32	1/16	+ 1/32
200	134 1/2	BergCa	10.75e	...	q	6	200	199	199 7/8	- 1/8
3 1/2	1 3/16	BethCp	...	...	7	2	1 13/16	1 13/16	1 13/16	- 1/16
13 3/16	3	BigCRad	...	...	dd	14	3 15/16	3 7/8	3 15/16	+ 1/16
50	11 1/4	BinkSame	...	...	dd	327	16 5/8	15 5/8	15 5/8	- 3/8
34 1/8	18 7/8	BioR A	...	...	12	99	23 1/8	22 7/8	23 1/8	+ 7/16
14	11	BlkBl09	.83	6.4	q	x13	13	12 7/8	13	+ 1/16
16 3/4	15 1/8	BCAIQ	.88	5.3	q	x10	16 5/8	16 5/8	16 5/8	+ 1/8
16	13 11/16	BFLIQ	.80a	5.3	q	x20	15 1/16	15 1/16	15 1/16	+ 1/16
33 5/8	15 1/4	BlairCp	.60	3.7	7	525	16 7/16	16 1/16	16 7/16	+ 3/16
4 1/4	1 3/4	Blimpie	.07	3.3	9	x146	2 1/8	2	2 1/8	+ [illegible]

52-Week High	52-Week Low	Stock	Div	Yld %	P/E	Sales 100s	High	Low	Last	Chg
			8	2.2	cc	34	18	17 5/8	17 5/8	- 1/8
			..	...	33	583	4 1/4	3 15/16	4	- 3/8
				...	...	1048	5/8	1/2	5/8	...
			..	...	dd	500	2 3/4	2 7/16	2 9/16	+ 3/16
		D E								
103 5/8	73 7/8	^DJIA Diam	1.68e	1.6	...	13109	104 9/32	103	104 1/8	+ 39/64
15 3/8	7	DRS Tech			16	1078	7 1/4	7 1/16	7 1/8	
4 1/2	2 3/8	DairyA	...	...	dd	315	3	2 5/8	3	+ 1/4
4 3/4	1 1/2	ecDallG	...	...	31	45	3 1/8	2 3/4	2 3/4	- 1/4
8	2 7/8	DanlHd	...	...	22	20	3 1/8	3 1/8	3 1/8	- 1/16
8 1/4	1 5/8	Darling	...	...	dd	101	1 7/8	1 3/4	1 7/8	...
2 11/16	3/4	Datamet	...	...	dd	87	1 7/16	1 3/8	1 7/16	...
10 7/8	5 1/8	Dataram s	...	...	8	75	7	6 3/4	6 7/8	...
15 7/16	11 1/2	Daxor	...	...	dd	85	14	13 13/16	14	+ 1/4
1 5/8	3/64	DaytonMn	...	...	...	8849	3/32	1/16	1/16	...
8 1/2	4 15/16	DeWolfe	.12e	1.7	8	1	7 3/16	7 3/16	7 3/16	+ 1/16
11 3/4	6	Decoratr s	.28	4.3	8	9	6 1/2	6 1/2	6 1/2	...
32 3/8	16	DelLab	.14	0.8	13	4	17 1/8	17 1/8	17 1/8	+ 1/8
13 9/16	6	Depomed	...	...	dd	74	12 15/16	12 1/2	12 1/2	- 3/8
7 7/8	**13/16**	**Depmd wt**	...	...	...	**150**	**7 5/8**	**7**	**7**	**- 7/8**
40 1/2	20 1/8	DevnE	.20	0.7	dd	2303	28 7/8	28	28 1/2	+ 1/2
17	9 3/4	DiaMetA	...	...	...	61	12 1/8	12	12	- 5/8
19 1/8	9 7/8	DiaMetB	...	...	...	7	14 1/4	14 1/8	14 1/8	...
17 1/4	5	DigiLava n	...	...	dd	3905	14 7/8	13	13	- 5/16
7 15/16	7/8	DigiLav wt	...	...	...	603	7 3/4	6 1/4	6 1/4	- 1/4
6 3/4	1 1/4	DigPwr	...	...	6	61	1 1/2	1 3/8	1 7/16	...
10	3 3/4	Diodes	...	...	9	56	4 5/8	4 3/8	4 1/2	...
14 3/4	3 9/16	DivCpRes	...	...	10	45	5 1/2	5 1/2	5 1/2	...
15 9/16	7 7/8	DixnTic	...	...	18	7	10 1/2	10 3/8	10 1/2	+ 1/8
46 3/4	28	DolAutEx	2.75	8.7	...	10	31 3/4	31 3/4	31 3/4	- 1/4
15 1/8	10 1/8	Drewlnd	...	...	9	76	11 5/8	11 5/8	11 5/8	...
10 3/4	9 1/2	DryCal	.56	5.7	q	20	9 13/16	9 13/16	9 13/16	+ 1/16
10 3/16	8 3/4	DryfMu	.53	5.9	q	134	8 15/16	8 7/8	8 15/16	+ 1/16
10 5/8	9 1/4	DryfNY	.54a	5.4	q	49	10	9 7/8	10	+ 1/16
14 15/16	9	EFC Bcp	.10p	...	...	59	10	9 5/8	9 5/8	- 1/4
7 5/8	4 3/8	EZEM B	...	...	10	60	5	4 3/4	4 7/8	- 1/4
28 1/2	20 3/16	EstnCo	.66f	2.9	11	169	22 5/8	21 15/16	22 5/8	+ 13/16
4 1/4	1 1/8	Easyridr n	...	...	...	83	1 5/8	1 1/2	1 5/8	...
15 3/8	15	EVCAMu n	.06p	...	q	65	15 1/8	15	15	- 1/16
15 7/8	15	EVFLMu n	.06p	...	q	208	15 1/2	15	15 3/8	+ 3/8
15 3/4	15	EVMIMu n	.06p	...	q	128	15 5/8	15 3/8	15 5/8	...
15 1/4	14 15/16	EVNJMu n	.06p	...	q	91	15 1/4	15 1/16	15 1/4	+ 1/4

52-Week High	52-Week Low	Stock	Div	Yld %	P/E	Sales 100s	High	Low	Last	Chg
3 1/8	1	Halsey	...	...	dd	776	1 3/16	1 1/16	1 1/8	+ 1/16
19 3/4	3 11/16	HalterM	...	...	13	2072	5 9/16	5 1/4	5 1/2	...
7 5/8	4 1/2	Hamptl	.72t	...	11	88	5 1/16	4 13/16	5	...
17 1/2	3 3/8	HanovCap	.44m	10.7	dd	96	4 3/8	4 1/8	4 1/8	- 1/8
3 3/4	1/64	HanovC wt	...	...	...	1960	3/32	1/64	1/16	- 1/32
3 13/16	1 7/8	HanvDir	...	...	dd	6067	3	2 3/4	2 13/16	...
6 5/8	1 5/16	Harken	...	...	...	1926	1 11/16	1 5/8	1 5/8	- 1/16
8 3/8	5 1/8	Harold	...	...	39	34	6 1/8	5 7/8	6	- 1/4
30 3/8	18 5/8	^Hasbro s	...	...	30	10274	30 13/16	29 3/4	29 15/16	- 5/16
3 1/2	1 1/2	HawAir	...	...	14	242	2 13/16	2 5/8	2 11/16	- 1/8
23	13 3/4	HaywdBcs	.64	4.6	...	2	14	14	14	- 1/8
2 1/8	7/16	HltPlanet	...	...	dd	29	3/4	11/16	11/16	- 1/8
18 3/4	11 7/8	Heartlnd	...	...	dd	10	15 1/4	15 1/4	15 1/4	- 1/4
17 1/2	3 7/8	HeartldT	...	...	5	3	4 3/8	4 3/8	4 3/8	...
1 11/16	1/2	Hearx	...	...	dd	1643	9/16	1/2	1/2	- 1/16
12 1/4	7 3/8	HectorCm	...	...	7	63	8 9/16	8 1/4	8 3/8	- 1/4
8 1/2	6 1/4	HeistC	...	...	14	46	6 3/8	6 3/8	6 3/8	...
3 3/4	**3/4**	**^Helmstr**	...	...	**dd**	**5880**	**9 1/2**	**4 5/8**	**6 1/4**	**+ 2 1/2**
13 3/16	2 5/8	Hemispx	...	...	dd	323	6	5 13/16	5 7/8	- 1/16
9	3/4	Hmisph wt	...	...	...	56	2 1/2	2 3/8	2 3/8	- 3/16
6 3/8	5 1/8	Hersha n	.31e	5.8	...	5	5 3/8	5 3/8	5 3/8	...
9 1/4	3 7/8	HiShearT	...	...	20	48	6 3/8	6	6 3/8	+ 1/8
33 3/8	12 1/4	HollyCp	.64	4.8	9	575	13 1/4	12 7/8	13 1/4	+ 5/16
16 3/4	7 3/4	HooperH s	.05f	0.3	36	820	16 3/16	15 1/2	15 1/2	- 9/16
16 1/4	4 3/4	HorizPhm	...	...	28	124	5 1/2	5 1/4	5 5/16	- 3/16
10 1/2	1 3/4	HospWwde	...	...	dd	475	3	2 13/16	2 7/8	...
5	1 9/16	HostFdg	...	...	dd	30	2 9/16	2 9/16	2 9/16	- 1/16
11 1/2	6	HovnEn	...	...	6	18	7 7/16	7 7/16	7 7/16	- 1/16
8 3/8	2 1/8	HungTel	...	...	dd	17	4 1/8	4	4	...
11 3/4	3 1/4	ICH Cp	...	...	9	93	10 7/8	10 1/2	10 1/2	+ 3/8
3 1/4	1 1/4	IGI	...	...	dd	81	1 7/8	1 5/8	1 3/4	- 1/8
7 1/16	1 1/4	ILX Resrt	...	...	4	174	1 11/16	1 5/8	1 11/16	+ 1/16
44 3/4	4 3/4	IPC Info s	...	...	dd	124	39	36 5/8	37 1/2	+ 1/2
10 1/4	4 7/16	Identix	...	...	cc	2488	8 1/8	6 1/2	7 1/4	+ 1/2
17 5/16	1 7/8	ImpacC	1.80a	35.1	dd	205	5 3/8	5 1/8	5 1/8	- 3/16
17 3/8	2 3/4	ImpacMtg	1.96	40.7	dd	810	5	4 5/8	4 13/16	...
19 3/4	13 3/8	ImpOil g	.74	...	...	377	19 1/2	18 15/16	19 3/16	+ 1/16
10 3/16	5 5/8	ImpSugar	.12	1.9	dd	161	6 1/2	6 1/4	6 3/8	- 1/16
19	10 3/16	IndepBk	.20	2.0	10	17	10 1/4	10 3/16	10 3/16	- 5/16
9 3/8	5 1/8	IndlData n	...	...	cc	238	7 5/8	7	7 1/4	
2 7/8	2 5/8	Innsuites n	...	...	...	15	2 13/16	2 11/16	2 13/16	
4 9/16	3/4	InSiteVis	...	...	dd	977	1	7/8	15/16	...
20 5/8	11 1/2	Instron	.16	0.9	10	200	17 1/4	16 3/4	16 7/8	- 1/16
2 9/16	1	Integra	...	...	dd	5	1 1/4	1 3/16	1 1/4	...
7 1/8	1 1/2	IntgOrth	...	...	dd	437	2	1 5/8	1 7/8	...

• • •

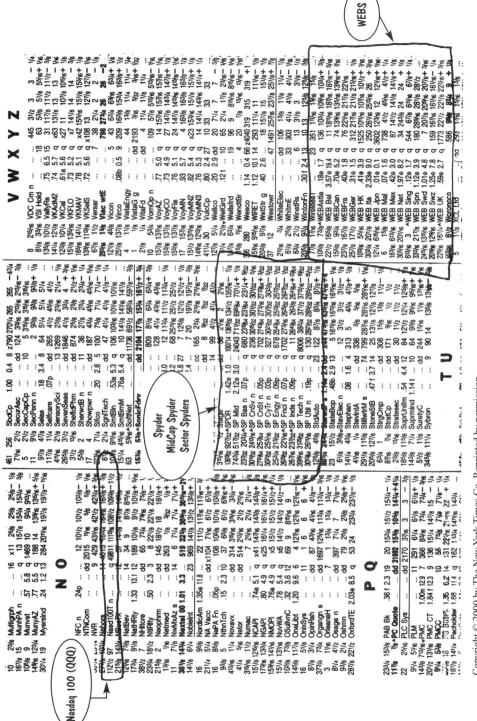

When stocks change in the index, those stocks must also be changed in the listed index security. Probably the most changes occur in the MidCap SPDR (MDY). Every time something falls out of the larger SPDR (SPY) as a result of a company being acquired or for some other reason, the replacement often is an MDY stock, necessitating a change in the index and listed index security.

The proprietor of the index announces when a change is to be made, along with the change date. The change date is always announced well in advance. Changes in the index security are always made at the close of the market day in which the change is made in the index.

Usually, index securities managers will enter "market on close" orders on the index change date. They sell the stock being dropped from the index or buy the stock being added. This takes some know-how to accomplish, but if done properly, there will be little or no variance in the degree to which the portfolio tracks the index.

Not all index managers make their changes the same way. Some will make all or part of their stock changes before the index changes. Some will hold off and make the transactions later. These strategy variations amount to speculation that prices will move higher or lower. For example, one manager's calculations may tell her that present prices leave too much on the table. This manager may think she can "scalp the market" and pick up additional profit.

DIFFERENT ACCOUNT STRUCTURES

Professional money managers can invest through different structures. They can set up *separate accounts*, for instance. A separate account is a portfolio kept in the name of the investor or joint investors. The investment performance is calculated for each account. Another structure is a *mutual fund*, a trust in which investors' money is pooled to buy stocks or other securities. An *open-end fund* is one in which more shares can be created by the fund when investors purchase shares. Shares are redeemed by the fund when holders of the fund sell their shares. Purchases and sales are executed at *net asset value*. Then there are *closed-end funds*, which are traded on an exchange or OTC. These funds trade at the *current market price*. Usually, closed-end funds trade at a discount or premium to their net asset value.

Open-end funds can be load or no-load. *Load* refers to a transaction cost, usually levied when a fund is purchased. Most of the load is a commission charge. Loads typically range between 2 percent and 8 percent.

Funds also charge a management fee. Fees for actively managed funds typically range from .50 percent to 2.0 percent of assets per year.

By professional, or institutional, investors is meant public sector pension plans, corporate pension plans, endowments, union funds, charitable trusts and foundations, insurance companies, and banks which invest their own assets or those held in trust for others. Pension plans include defined benefit and defined contribution schemes. The most important institutional segment in both the U.S. and the U.K. is the tax-exempt segment.

EXCHANGE SHARES EXPENSE ADVANTAGES

No matter how the products are structured, there are a lot of costs in managing money. Expenses detract from an investment's performance and diminish returns to the investor. A fund's expenses are referred to in terms of an *expense ratio*. An expense ratio is the percentage of the assets that were spent to run the fund. These expenses can include management and advisory fees, advertising and marketing costs, and all administrative costs associated with running the fund. Expense ratios do not include the fund's brokerage costs. The expense ratio is normally expressed in terms of basis points (bp). Ten basis points, for example, equals 0.10 percent; 18 bp would be 0.18 percent; 40 bp is 0.40 percent. This is a per-year expense. Expenses are net of current income, which means the investor does not pay out of pocket for the fund services.

In comparing the costs of listed index securities to other index investments, such as a conventional mutual fund, it is important to understand that SPY, the ASE's largest exchange share product in terms of asset size, is not designed to be a profit center. SPY was designed at the ASE to be traded there. The ASE receives remuneration from SPY and the other products being traded on the exchange. In fact, the way SPY is structured, it cannot spend more than it brings in. WEBS and sector SPDRs are not set up the same as SPDR, but their expense ratios are similar.

Expenses are very important, since a slight change in expenses can impact the performance of a fund. Also, higher expenses can be a tipoff. If a fund's management is careless regarding expenses, it could be less than efficient in its investment strategies and monitoring as well.

The SPDR expense structure can be compared to the Vanguard index fund. Vanguard is set up as a sort of cooperative organization. The funds own the management company. The management company is, in effect, a nonprofit organization. And it is the management company that employs the portfolio managers and provides other services to the fund.

The expense ratio of SPY is 18 bp. This is the same as the Vanguard 500 index fund. Various spending categories on SPY are capped, so that as a result of the growth in the assets coming into SPY, expense as a percentage of assets is kept low.

Usually, the assets at the end of the first year of an investment company will have risen appreciably above the level at the beginning of the year. SPY rose from a value of $4 billion in the trust at the beginning of 1998 to $12 billion at the end of 1998. Because there is a dramatic increase in the number of shares outstanding (as money comes into the trust, more shares have to be created), SPY has to pay a 24F2 fee. This fee is a charge by the Securities and Exchange Commission (SEC) for issuing more shares. It only has to be paid once. If SPY still had about the same number of shares outstanding at the end of the next year, there would not be a 24F2 fee for that year.

With larger funds, expenses can be amortized over more dollars. For example, SPY can charge 4 bp for advertising, marketing, and like items. SPY does quite a bit of advertising, spending about 3 bp presently. With assets of $12 billion, the amount for advertising is $3.6 million. This is a healthy budget, one in line with its growth phase. But as SPY grows, this expense, as a percentage, will go down. When SPY grows to $30.0 billion, for instance, it won't make sense to spend 4 bp. That would be $12.0 million a year for advertising.

So the higher the assets in a fund, the lower the expense ratio. Probably, by the end of the year, SPY will be able to reduce its expense rates by 1 or 2 bp.

This expense ratio is reasonable. If you invested $1000 in SPY, for example, your cost per year would be $1.80. If SPY lowered its expense ratio the next year, the expense per $1000 would fall to $1.70 or $1.60 per year.

MDY has a cap expense ratio of 30 bp. Presently, its expense ratio is 25 bp. MDY has grown rapidly and now has over $1.0 billion in assets.

DIA's expense ratio is capped at 18 bp. This trust has a market value of a little under $500.0 million. DIA has not grown as quickly as the other index products, and the ASE plans a marketing and advertising campaign to attract more capital.

In the prospectuses of the sector SPDRs, an expense ratio of 65 bp is shown. That is based on the assumption that all the sector SPDRs would have a combined value of about $1.0 billion. The sector SPDRs came out in December 1998 and have combined assets of over $1.2 billion—an impressive beginning. The expense ratio should stay where it is.

QQQ (traders on the floor call this trust "the Qs") has an expense ratio of 18 bp. The trust went to an impressive $1.2 billion in assets just five weeks after being introduced. The expense ratio is expected to stay at 18 bp.

We'll cover the WEBS expense ratios in the separate chapter devoted to WEBS.

It is clear that index funds are inherently cheaper to manage than actively managed funds.

As for other index funds, probably Vanguard 500, which tracks the S&P 500 index, has the lowest expense ratio, 18 bp. The ratios of other index funds go up from there. Many index funds charge in the vicinity of 30 bp.

Another cost advantage for index shares is their utilization of transfer agents. In the case of an open-end fund, a transfer agent, usually a bank, keeps track of the ownership of the fund shares. To accomplish this, the transfer agent maintains accounts. Each shareholder has a separate account for his or her shares in the fund. This is a necessary, but expensive process so that the fund can keep track of its shares and shareholders. Also, if there is a sales charge associated with a given transaction, the fund must keep track of which salesperson is linked to the customer and his or her fund shares.

However, in a listed index security the broker handles shareholder activity. There is a transfer agent function, but it is a much smaller one. It is more a matter of transferring ownership of the index shares into and out of the custodian. The customer sees purchases and sales of exchange shares as "book entry" transactions, an efficient and low-cost way of doing business.

By eliminating most of the transfer agent functions, depending on the nature of the fund, the exchange ratio of a small fund can be reduced by 20 bp, a large fund's by about 5 bp.

EXPENSE SAVINGS WITH SIZE

The beginnings of the subasset class Select Sector SPDRs started with the introduction of SPDRs on December 23, 1998. Between December 23 and the end of March 1999, the sector SPDRs collected $1.0 billion in assets. This is a very successful launch for exchange shares, and it is doubtful that a conventional fund could have raised this much. It is also questionable whether an open-end fund could have offered nine different industry classes as the sector SPDRs did. Even if a conventional fund did offer nine different funds, the management fees would be very high.

TRADING ADVANTAGES OF EXCHANGE SHARES OVER INDEX FUNDS

The ASE wanted to introduce index products that could be traded all day long. With peaks and valleys of the market occurring throughout the trading day, the thought was that the right index shares would allow traders to take advantage of market fluctuations. The initial SPY came out in 1993, and the whole concept of exchange shares has evolved into a trading niche.

A very important difference between listed index securities and conventional open-end index funds is that you can buy or sell the listed security any time during the trading day. The order will be executed at the market price when the order is transmitted to the floor. With a conventional open-end fund, no matter what time your order is placed, it gets priced at the 4:00 p.m. (Eastern time) net asset value of the fund.

Listed index share prices change throughout the trading day as the index changes. Also, every 15 seconds the ASE disseminates a number designed to show the approximate value of the listed shares vis-à-vis the index. Table 1-1 shows a comparison of two low-cost S&P 500 index funds.

This gives you great flexibility. Let's say the market is down in the morning and you think that this is a great time to buy. You can. You don't have to wait and receive a 4:00 p.m. price. Likewise, if you want out immediately, you simply call your broker or click on your mouse.

So a big advantage for individual investors is that they can buy a managed portfolio—of utility stocks or technology stocks or energy stocks, for instance—and hold them long-term or buy and sell them throughout the day.

Over the last few years, the market has seen intradays whipsaws, and many days the market ends unchanged after major price changes during the day. For nimble traders there are opportunities for swing trading, and this doesn't necessarily conflict with long-term investing.

If you want to buy and hold exchange index shares, you can. If you want to invest long-term and market-time with a portion of your assets, perhaps 10 percent or so, that can also be easily accomplished with the flexibility of the index shares. In this way, you can increase your portfolio's performance. There is also the risk that you could decrease your performance.

TABLE 1-1   A Comparison of Two Low-Cost S&P 500 Index Funds

		AMEX SPDRs	Vanguard Index Trust—500 Portfolio
1.	Net asset value per share, January 5, 2000	140.00	129.16
2.	Annual fees and expenses for individual investors	18 bp	18 bp
3.	Minimum cost to buy or sell	Negotiable commission +/− deviation from net asset value (see text)	Probable market impact at close on days of purchase and sale. Some investors may pay negotiable commissions if the fund is is held in a brokerage account.
4.	Holders protected from impact of purchases and sales (see text)	Yes	Yes
5.	Possible to invest or liquidate at intraday prices	Yes	No
6.	Times at which purchase or sale price may be set	9:30 a.m.–4:15 p.m. EST	4:00 p.m. EST
7.	Types of orders accepted	Market Limited price order At the close At the opening Not held Percentage order Scale order Sell "plus" or buy "minus" Stop order Stop limit order Switch order Time order	The equivalent of market at close orders only
8.	Dividend reinvestment	Limited	Yes
9.	Short sales possible	Yes	No
10.	Taxable capital gains distributions for 1998	None	$0.42/share

If you wanted to buy technology stocks for the long-term, you would have to wait until the end of the trading day to purchase. With exchange shares, you can try to buy at a low point during the day. Sometimes there are differences between the intraday high and low of 5 percent or more. If the shares were battered down in the morning and you wanted to buy, you could buy the technology sector SPDR and pay perhaps 5 percent less than waiting until the end of the day to buy the conventional fund.

TAX CONSIDERATIONS

Another advantage of listed index securities over conventional funds has to do with taxes. The listed index shares, because they are redeemed in kind, are a great deal more efficient than conventional funds. This is especially important for taxable accounts. By taxable accounts, I mean accounts that are taxed at long-term or short-term rates, such as individual accounts. Tax-exempt accounts apply for organizations such as registered charities and other nonprofit groups that hold tax-exempt status. Included among tax-exempt accounts are individual retirement plans.

Suppose a fund has grown in assets over many years, and that the stock that the fund holds has gone up in price and the cost basis of the shares in the fund is well below the NAV of the fund. For example, let's say the market price of the fund is the same as the NAV, which is $10.00 per share. The cost basis of the stocks held by the fund averages about $5.00. There is, then, a built-in short- and/or long-term gain in the market price of the fund.

If the fund starts to shrink, that is, if owners of the fund sell their fund shares, the fund may have to sell off some of the low-priced stock it holds to redeem the sellers. When the fund sells off the low-cost stock it holds, it will realize a capital gain. This capital gain will revert to fund holders as a capital gains distribution at the end of the year. So even if a holder bought and held the fund and did no other trading, she could find herself facing taxes on a capital gain distribution.

With listed index securities, any potential gain will be substantially less. If a regulated investment company, which the listed shares are, redeems securities in kind, the securities take their cost basis with them when they are redeemed out of the fund. So even if the cost basis of the shares is low and there is a big unrealized capital gain on the shares, that unrealized capital gain is minimized to the present holders when those securities are redeemed.

With the exchange share creation and redemption process, the tax burden is laid on the share owner who should be most responsible for paying the tax, the person who took the profit. This is not necessarily true with conventional index fund shares.

An example will help clarify this. Let's say a new open-end index fund is created today. The price is $100 a share. Your neighbor is the first person to buy and pays $100 a share. The fund does well, and then you come along and pay $200 a share.

After that, certain events occur: the market goes down; there are many sellers of the fund shares; the fund has to sell off low-priced shares of stock to pay for fund redemptions. When the fund sells off those shares, it takes a capital gain of $25 a share. You hold your shares. The fund collapses back to $100 a share. Your neighbor sells out there, breaking even.

Now, what about the capital gain that the fund manager had to take? It will have to be distributed, and the distribution will be to the present fund holders, of which you are one.

So you will receive a capital gains distribution of $25 a share, on which you must pay taxes, although your shares are now selling at half what you paid for them. The net result? A $100-a-share unrecognized loss, which has a limited tax benefit, and a taxable $25 gain.

This example is not that rare. One of the factors that makes a conventional index mutual fund so inefficient taxwise is that, usually, the size of the fund goes in cycles. The index fund gets popular and grows. Then it falls out of favor and shrinks in size. As we saw, when funds shrink in size, because more shares are being redeemed than purchased, the fund has to sell securities to pay for the redemptions. And if they have to sell securities that have a low tax basis, the fund will be realizing capital gains.

The creation and redemption process of exchange shares virtually eliminates this potential unfairness. With the tax liability buildup that a conventional fund can create, buyers can be punished for becoming long-term holders. Often, as the previous example shows, the conventional funds that come into vogue and are timely and popular as investments often have "hot money" flow in as traders flip in and out of the fund. If you are trading the exchange shares all day long, your profit and loss will be in your stock trading. The buildup in capital gains is minimal to nonexistent.

Another event could happen. A conventional index fund could have a large holding in a major industrial company, Chrysler, for example. The fund could have owned the shares for 20 years or so and have a huge unrealized gain. Then a foreign buyer comes along, say, Mercedes Benz. If this sounds familiar, it should be. Mercedes did buy Chrysler, in 1998.

The Chrysler buyout was a stock deal, but the index fund managers could not hold the surviving Mercedes stock because it was deleted from the index. This resulted in a huge capital gain that had to be taken by the fund and passed on to fund holders.

If a taxable investor bought the fund, she bought into a preexisting tax liability. Most of it was not expected to be realized soon, but there is always the potential for that gain to have to be realized.

Exchange shares can do better than this. As an example, SPYs have been out for about six years. Only about $.09 in realized capital gains has been distributed, and this in a roaring bull market.

The ASE feels that even this small amount is too much. There were nuances of managing the portfolio that the ASE hadn't totally prepared for, and this caused them to distribute this sum. They plan no more distributions for any of the exchange shares in the future. At the end of the 1998 fiscal year, SPY had a cost basis on the shares of the fund that was above the market price, so no capital gains distribution would be made.

Of course, if you make money trading the listed index securities, you don't avoid the tax; if you sell at a profit, you have to pay taxes. But the absence of capital gains distributions means that you can postpone any tax until you sell. You have the pretax assets working for you longer.

Also, if you hold index shares and their market price is well above your cost price and you die (which all of us must do, even if we're making money in the market), your heirs get a step-up in basis on those shares. They will not have to pay a capital gains tax. A step-up in basis means the acquisition price will become the market price at the time of death, not the price of actual purchase. That means letting your profits run is smart estate tax planning.

Exchange shares, then, help individuals and money managers to create tax efficiencies in taxable accounts. In a tax-exempt account, such as a retirement rollover or 401-k, this efficiency is not necessary.

EXCHANGE SHARE DIVIDENDS
Dividends are not much of a factor with most of the exchange shares: The dividend return on SPY, MDY, QQQ, and the sector SPDRs is negligible. What little dividend they do pay is paid quarterly. The utility sector SPDRs pay a decent dividend. Also, some of the WEBS pay a decent dividend. Dividend distributions are made to WEBS holders each August. DIA dividends are paid monthly.

MARGINABILITY OF EXCHANGE SHARES

A distinct difference between exchange shares and conventional index mutual funds is that all of the exchange shares can be margined, just like common stocks.

To margin securities, you must open up a margin account with your broker. This allows you to borrow funds to purchase stock from the broker, and the broker keeps your stock as collateral. You must deposit an initial margin when purchasing or selling short securities. Recently, the amount required on deposit has been 50 percent of the purchase, with a minimum of $2000. After that, you must maintain a minimum amount of equity in your account. This is referred to as *maintenance funds*. The amount needed for maintenance has recently been in the 25 to 30 percent range. It is advisable to know the details of your margin agreement. Usually, if your account falls below margin requirements, the broker issues you a margin call. The margin agreement stipulates that the broker can sell you out if you do not meet a margin call within a set time, often without notfication. Margin requirements can be met with stock or with cash.

The same rules apply when selling short, which can *only* be done in a margin account. When selling short, the broker must go out and borrow the shares to "protect" you; when you want to buy in to cover your short, the shares are available.

SHORT SELLING ON A DOWNTICK

With common stock, there is a Securities and Exchange Commission (SEC) rule requiring that short sales be done on an uptick or a zero-plus tick. The SEC is the government agency that oversees the securities industry. An uptick is a trade higher than the previous trade. If a stock last sold at 14⅞ and trades at 15, the 15 represents an uptick. You can short there. If the stock trades another time or two at 15, that is a zero-plus tick, and you may short there as well. If the stock then falls back to 14⅞, that is a downtick, and no short sale is permitted at that price. Index shares, however, are unique in that they can be sold short on downticks. So if the market is in a freefall and you want to short, you don't have to wait for an uptick.

SPY has roughly 100 million shares outstanding. Against that, in the recent past, there routinely have been 20 to 30 million shares borrowed for short-position buybacks. As previously mentioned, a broker must borrow shares to protect a customer's need to buy back shares when that customer initiates a short position.

These 20 to 30 million shares of borrowed securities represent about 20 to 30 percent of SPY's outstanding float. This is extremely high. It shows clearly how prominently shorting figures among those dealing in SPY. The other index shares also experience high levels of shorting.

2

TRADING
EXCHANGE
INDEX SHARES

TRADING CHARACTERISTICS

Many people trade the exchange shares rather than individual stocks because of the exchange shares' special features. There are different kinds of traders. *Chartists* use charts to decide at which point to buy or sell. *Technicians* use technical indicators, such as upside or downside volume, or up- and downside tick ratios. *Momentum traders* buy or sell or short whenever there are breakouts or breakdowns in a stock. And there are many other types of traders.

Any trader can use exchange shares. The nice thing about trading exchange shares is that they move, but they move rather slowly and orderly.

For instance, if you buy QQQ at, say, 100, and the market turns on you and suddenly starts down, QQQ doesn't abruptly drop to 99 bid. In a violent market, some stocks will drop a point, then another, then another, all on light volume. Exchange shares go down more systematically: down 1/32, down 1/32, down 1/32, each trade.

The same thing is true on the short side. All of the index shares are actively shorted. Since you can short the index shares on a downtick, in a free-falling market you can put an order in to short on the bid and probably get your order off.

Vast liquidity makes the index shares easy to short. Some people short as a speculation, some are hedging against mutual funds they are holding, and some are arbitraging the market price of the exchange shares against the value of the underlying shares.

The spread between the bid and asked prices on exchange shares is very narrow. The bid price is what people are bidding for shares. The ask price is what people are asking for their shares. A narrow bid/ask means that the difference between the two sides may be only 1/32 or 1/16. You can almost always sell or short your exchange shares on or near the bid price, and buy shares on or near the offer price.

Because of these factors, you can sit in front of your computer, see the market down 120 points, and if you think it is going lower, click on your mouse and short the exchange shares, probably getting done on the bid.

SPY, MDY, QQQ, and DIA all trade until 4:15 p.m. (Eastern time). This is because the S&P futures are open until that time. The stock markets cut off at 4:00 p.m. WEBS trade until 4:00, the sector SPDRs until 4:02 p.m.

Often, there is a lot of action in the futures market between 4:00 p.m. and 4:15 p.m.

The S&P 500 futures contract is traded by "master of the universe" types. Every major brokerage house, every major bank, insurance companies: all trade the S&P futures. Firms like Merrill Lynch, Citibank, and Bankers Trust are involved in a huge way. Also the multibillion-dollar sponsors, like state pension and retirement plans, use S&P futures in various ways, such as shorting them to hedge their long stock positions. Suffice it to say that the whole world trades the S&P futures.

For an example of what impact the S&P futures can have, imagine that Intel comes out with surprisingly negative earnings at 4:05 p.m. The futures are going to plummet between 4:05 p.m. and 4:15 p.m. The futures traders, through their stock-selling activities, are saying, "Hey, that 4:00 close of the S&P index is wrong; it should have been lower; the news that just came out shows things headed down." The SPY, DIA, MDY, and QQQ are probably all going to drop together, although in different degrees, reflecting the futures decline.

SPY trades at roughly one-tenth of the value of the S&P index. Sometimes, late in the day, SPY appears to be trading at a discount to the S&P index price. It really isn't. The SPY is trading lower because the futures sold off after 4:00 p.m., and the SPY is trading in relation to what happened in the S&P futures market. The S&P index closed with the other markets at 4:00 p.m.

Because of the trading power of the players in the futures market, odds are that the next trading day, the volume and direction of the S&P futures market will carry over into the other markets.

TRADING LARGE SIZE

Clearly, one of the advantages of trading index shares is their tremendous liquidity. When you enter the ticker symbols to bring these securities up on your screen, you will often see 999 × 999 on either the bid side or the asked side or both. The bid/ask size is usually located on your screen just after the last trade price. That 999 simply means that you can buy or sell up to 100,000 shares on the bid or offer. Check this out for yourself. Over the next several minutes or hours or days, bring the bid/ask up on your screen. Even when there is not a 999, there is usually real size on one or both sides of the bid/ask.

This is great for trading. When you're trading size and you can buy or sell 100,000 shares without moving a market, that is a real advantage; a major company like IBM is not out there all day with 100,000 shares up, *up* being the number of shares available to be bought or sold.

WHEN TRADING SMALLER PIECES

Except for WEBS, which trade in 1/16ths, the index securities all trade in increments of 64ths. Let's say, for instance, that QQQ is 100 last trade, and the bid/ask is 100 to $100\frac{1}{8}$, 999 × 999. Say you just want to buy 500 shares. Instead of buying the 500 shares at $100\frac{1}{8}$, put in an order to buy 500 shares at $100\frac{1}{64}$. You've improved the bid by 1/64; it is an auction market; therefore, the specialist has to reflect your bid by showing it. What might happen is that the specialist won't want to carry your bid because this would make the market $100\frac{1}{64}$ to $100\frac{1}{8}$, 500 shares x 100,000 shares. This 500 shares distorts the market. Now, the specialist cannot show 999 bid for at 100. Maybe it is an ego thing—and specialists are known for the size of their egos—or just good business, because this distortion is irritating and may keep the specialist from starting negotiations over a large trade.

The specialist probably does not want to buy 99,500 at 1/64 or higher. Many specialists have an arbitrage mentality. They deal with razor-thin profit margins. Consequently, if you bid 500 shares at $100\frac{1}{64}$, and the specialist doesn't want to raise her bid to compete with you, she may just execute your buy order at 1/64. Then she can drop her bid back to 100. If she had put her bid up, she might have gotten whacked by a 100,000 share block she'd have to buy at 100¹/64.

You can do the same thing on the sell side, that is, shave the offer by 1/64. You could offer 500, 1000, or even 2000 shares less 1/64 from the present offering, and maybe you would get filled all or partial.

In your trading, you can usually get into exchange shares near the last price, and using an online or other discount broker, you can keep your expense of trading down. There are brokers who execute trades for as low as $5.00 a trade for up to 5000 shares. When trading shares as high-priced as SPY, that amount comes out to less than one-tenth of $.01 a share; this is lower than large institutions usually pay for transactions. That $5.00 per trade applies only to market orders, however. Using a limit order, which was used in the prior example when agreeing to pay only 100¹/64, the brokerage charge goes up to $12.00. But buying shares 1/64th higher rather than paying 1/8th higher is worth the extra cost of a limit order. The difference between 1/64 and 1/8 saves more than the higher brokerage costs.

Many books on trading emphasize the importance of the size of the bid/ask spread. Traders grumble that they have to pay up to get in and take less to get out. Through the technique just discussed, you can shave in between the bid/ask price and trade in lower increments than the bid/ask, saving maybe 1/64 or 1/32.

Also, say you buy 500 QQQ at 100¹/64, and the market starts dropping. QQQ, like the other index shares, will not drop half a point or a point immediately. The market would have to drop really sharply for QQQ to go down a half point in a few trades. If you think to yourself, "Uh-oh, I goofed. I want out, right now!" you know you can sell. Almost always, there are 20,000, 50,000, or 100,000 shares bid for at close to the last trade, just as there is that kind of size on the offer side. You know you can get out unless, of course, you encounter that rare instance when there is a half-million or a million-share seller who also wants out. But even then, half-million-share orders are not that rare in exchange shares. After that seller or buyer, you can get your trade done.

Trading in smaller blocks of about 500 to 1500 shares, the smaller trader may have an advantage in getting in and out because of the tight spreads, the 1/64 trading increments, and the desire of the specialist to execute large trades.

Anytime you really want in or out and shaving 1/64th doesn't work, go ahead and try to shave 1/32 off of the shown bid/ask quote. Or shave up or down 1/16. What is the difference? When trying to complete or initiate a successful trade or cut a loss, 1/32 or 1/16 means very little.

MARKET MAKERS AND SPECIALISTS

The person who stands ready to buy or sell a round lot, usually a block of 100 shares, at her or his publicly quoted bid/asked prices is also charged with making an orderly market. This person is called a market maker in the OTC market and a specialist on the exchanges.

The role of the specialist is of interest because it shows how the prices of the exchange shares are held in place by arbitragers. Traders do not have to worry about the exchange share prices not reflecting the indexes. The market for the exchange shares cannot stray far from their market value, and the chances of overpaying for shares is lessened, because if the specialist is out of line with her quotes, she will be buried by arbitrage trades.

The specialist is the key individual in trading exchange shares. They perform functions that make trading activity much smoother. The specialist is charged with all of the functions necessary to create an orderly market in exchange shares. As such, he or she is located on the floor of the ASE.

Around the specialist, there is a group of market makers who trade in and out of the index shares all day long. Many in the crowd arbitrage between SPY and the S&P 500 futures. *Arbitrage* involves buying a commodity or security in one market for immediate sale in another market, profiting by locking in the price difference. If the SPY gets too cheap in comparison to the S&P future, the market makers will buy the SPY and sell the future, thereby locking in a profit. Arbitragers employ many variations of this profit-making strategy.

The arbitrage function ultimately benefits everyone. Anytime there is a deviation between the market price of SPY and its value in comparison to the S&P index, the arbitrage traders will come in and bid the exchange shares up or down, causing the deviation to go away.

Ordinarily, if the bid/ask on the exchange shares stays stable for an hour or so and the markets are fairly flat, the bid/ask will straddle the intraday net asset value of the fund. Arbitragers keep the market that tight. Sometimes, however, the market price of the exchange shares moves away from their net asset values. This is caused by traders bidding the shares up or down in the expectation that the price of the stocks in the index will move up or down. The stocks making up the index sometimes move less than the fund shares.

The symbol of the S&P 500 index is SPX, and its price changes throughout the day. The S&P index itself doesn't trade. S&P 500 index futures trade on the Chicago Mercantile Exchange. Futures prices extend out 24 months. The futures are considered commodities, and they are not to be confused with the actual S&P 500 index.

With the increase in the number of online brokers over the last several years, brokerage costs have declined sharply. The drop in costs has made it cheaper for the public to buy index securities. Professional traders have long been active in index shares, but now, with individual traders and investors using index shares, there is a much better mix between long-term investors and traders.

SPY still is the most popular index security for the professionals. It has been around the longest and usually has the largest daily trading volume. But although the volume of the index shares is huge, several million changing hands on any given day in any or all of the classes, many of these trades are small pieces, clearly being made by individuals. Particularly with the Qs, almost any day you will see trades of 500 shares, 300 shares, 1000 shares, 800 shares, and so on. These are not institutional-sized trades. Of course, there are small trades in SPY and in the other shares as well, but the Qs seem to have a greater proportion of small trades.

Besides trading, the institutions like to use SPY and DIA to equitize cash. Let's say a money manager finds herself with a large amount of cash, doesn't know what her next move will be, but the market is moving and she doesn't want to sit idle. Buying the DIA or the SPY is a great way to get broad market exposure for a short period of time until a longer-term strategy can be put into place.

Also, the money manager may be required to be fully invested in stocks, or to always have a percentage of her assets in stocks, say, 70 or 80 percent. Buying DIA or SPY is an excellent way to temporarily own stocks and still have great liquidity.

Individuals as well as institutions can equitize cash by buying the index shares. Any time market participation is desired and the individual issues are not yet decided on, money can be parked into the market using one of the exchange share classes. Since there is a variety of exchange shares to use, asset allocation is very important in the buying decision.

Alternatively, a manager can buy a clump of sector SPDRs, weighting in areas he favors, such as energy or utilities or technology. In this case the manager is getting broad representation in certain sectors without the risk of being invested in individual stocks. In addition, the manager could be conservative and buy DIA or be aggressive and buy the Qs, always with the great liquidity the exchange shares offer. When you want out, the shares are easy to sell.

These same tactics can be used by individuals as well, or by other institutions, such as small company profit-sharing plans.

There are times when an individual or institution experiences an unexpected influx of cash. Putting the cash in Treasury bills is an option. But if the person or institution thinks the market is headed higher and wants to capitalize on that market performance with a security that can be quickly sold, the exchange shares are a good choice.

Say you have $25,000, $50,000, or $100,000 invested in SPY. Suppose, too, that Internet stocks have collapsed and you think this is a good time to jump into them. You could peel off half of your SPY money and put it into Internet shares. That leaves half your funds in SPY, which gets you S&P 500 market performance, and half your funds in riskier, but potentially more rewarding, Internet stocks.

Here's another example. Let's say a money manager likes technology stocks, but after checking balance sheet numbers, earnings estimates, and charts, she still can't decide which specific issues to buy. She can buy the Technology Sector SPDR. Now, in effect, she owns the 80 major technology stocks listed in the S&P index, and she has time to keep doing research. Her sector SPDR will almost surely advance with that sector.

SPECIALISTS, MARKET MAKERS, AND THEIR ROLE IN EXCHANGE SHARES

The specialist is the key to swift and accurate executions of exchange shares, and fills a threefold role. The first role is executing principal and/or agency trades.

1. Principal trades are done for the specialist's own "book," for his own or his firm's account, and he trades for his own account at the same time he's maintaining a fair and orderly market.

2. Agency trades are those done by the specialist for customers. These are nonprincipal trades. The orders do not come exclusively from customers of the specialist firm. Agency orders can be from any individ-

ual or institution, and they are left with the specialist to execute in an orderly and fair market.

In today's market, orders flow to the specialist electronically from online brokers or from brokers on the ASE floor. Brokers drop off order tickets to the specialist. The specialist enters the order into his electronic book and executes it with the general order flow. If there are no other buyers or sellers, the specialist stands ready to buy or sell, to keep an orderly and fair market. This can put specialists at risk. In exchange, he or she receives certain privileges. Among them is the privilege of being an agent and principal trader in the same day for the same stock and, sometimes, being on both sides of the trade. No other members on the exchanges have that privilege. The other exchange members can trade either as agent or as principal, but not both at the same time.

Market makers are also present on the ASE floor, and in day-to-day trading, they compete with the specialists. Market makers trade principal only, for their own accounts or the accounts of the firm they represent.

Although it is sometimes hard to pinpoint exactly what a "fair and orderly market" looks like, the fact that exchange shares follow an index helps that market function with liquidity and order.

With SPY, for instance, the specialists must keep a strictly orderly market. It is possible to do this because there is plenty of liquidity in the underlying stocks and an abundance of liquidity in the overlying futures contract. In SPY, there are eight full-time market makers on the floor who compete with each other and trade against the specialist. With all this competition, a tight market invariably results.

On the ASE, there is only one specialist per exchange share class. There are, however, unlimited numbers of market makers competing against that specialist. To get an idea of how many market makers can compete on the floor, consider this: There is one specialist on Intel (INTC) options on the ASE, and against this specialist there are about 85 full-time market makers.

Market makers own or lease a membership on the ASE. Their privileges include being able to trade the index shares right on the floor. Their responsibilities include being available, if called upon, to help make a market.

Creating Shares to Fill Market Needs
The second role that index share specialists fulfill is that of "authorized participants" in creating and redeeming index shares. In this role, the spe-

cialist is an ongoing issuer of index shares. Issuing index shares is not an exclusive privilege, nor is it an exclusive responsibility, but as much or more than anyone else, the specialist has an interest keeping an active market. Only specialists trade these shares full-time.

To keep a market active, there have to be ample shares to trade. Shares are created when the need arises. For example, the specialist could create 2 million shares of SPY on Monday and sell them all out by the end of the week. Or he could have SPY shares left, enough to carry him through part or all of the following week. When he runs low, he creates more shares.

Supporting the Lending Market

As mentioned above, index shares can be sold short on a downtick. Remember, it is required to get protection of shares when you short so you can buy back the shares when you want to cover the short. Stock-loan is the operational end of the brokerage process that borrows shares for the future buyback of shorted index shares.

Where does the brokerage firm go to borrow shares? Again, it's to the specialist, whose third role is to create and carry an inventory of index shares and keep shares available for the firms to borrow for their customers.

MARKET MAKERS' TRADING ACTIVITY

There are many differences between market makers and specialists. The market makers are not in charge of maintaining the order book. They can view each product in isolation, since they are not assigned to or limited to trading just one stock or exchange share. And whereas the specialist tries to keep her risk profile neutral to low by hedging her position, the market maker is trying to make money by taking positions, much like any other trader would do.

Market makers will be long or short, depending on their trading view. Sometimes the customer (the investor or trader) is smarter or luckier than the market maker; sometimes the market maker will make the better trade. Being right there on the market floor in the heart of the action, the market maker does, however, have the time and place advantage. The market maker's hope is that by doing enough volume and maintaining low execution costs, at the end of the day he will have made some money.

With the explosion in volume of exchange shares, they have become an important part of the market maker's activity. For instance, as recently as three years ago, if SPY traded a million shares in a day, that would have been a lot. Now, a million shares is a disappointing day. Recently, I brought up the different exchange share classes in my computer and checked the volume. The total for all the exchange share classes came to over 15.0 million shares, and this wasn't a particularly active day—closer to an average day. Conservatively estimated, this is about 10 times the volume of a few years ago.

Although market makers trade against each other, this is not where the majority of the trading is done. Since all the market makers stand virtually in the same place and see much of the same information and trade patterns of an issue, it's hard for one market maker to come to a different conclusion than another market maker. Market makers also compete with brokers and the customers of the brokerage houses.

CREATION AND REDEMPTION OF INDEX SHARES

Each index share class, QQQ, SPY, and so on, creates new shares and redeems outstanding shares in *creation units*. A creation unit size for SPY is 50,000 shares, which runs about $6.0 million. Creation and redemption is done on a continuous basis at the share's NAV. A participating bank or trust company, such as State Street Bank in Boston, is authorized to create and redeem exchange shares. The institution is known as the *trustee*.

As a first step, State Street creates a "basket" of stocks. This basket contains all the stocks in an index, be it QQQ, SPY, or any of the other classes. WEBS are an exception, which we'll get into in the WEBS chapter. Let's say that the class of stocks is SPY, making it the S&P 500 index that has to be replicated. In that basket will be shares of the 500 companies that make up the S&P index, in the same proportion as the stocks exist in the index. As another example, to replicate QQQ requires representing the 100 Nasdaq issues making up that index. So it goes with the other index shares.

One point needs to be very clear: Index shares are not derivatives. The trustee of the creation units receives the actual stocks comprising the index, these stocks having been bought in the open market. These stocks are the pieces of the exchange shares which trade on the ASE.

The production of creation units is a fast-paced affair. First, based on the closing prices of the stocks involved, the trustee calculates the number of shares of each stock needed for a basket. The next trading day, the trustee tells the specialist the exact numbers of shares needed to create a basket, such as 152 IBM shares, 37 Wal-Mart shares, and so on. These shares will weight the basket in exact proportion to the S&P 500 index. The trustee will receive the basket of stocks from the specialist that day. The next morning, when the market opens, the trustee can put out to the specialist a new creation unit. As the value of the S&P 500 stocks moves that day, the price of the new shares of the creation unit will also move.

In creating and redeeming shares, the process is usually very smooth between the specialist and the trustee. A vital consideration arises in the timing, however. The trustee must know a day ahead of time any changes looming for the involved companies. If, for example, IBM is spinning off a division the next day, issuing new shares and diluting the value of outstanding shares, the trustee must know this. When the trustee creates the basket of stocks to form a creation unit, the trustee needs to take the changes in IBM into account so that the right numbers of shares will be included in the basket.

From the standpoint of the investor, the creation process looks like this. To buy index shares, you give your order to a broker or enter it through your online broker. The brokerage firm sends the order to the ASE floor. If the specialist is running low on shares, he may decide to go ahead and order a new creation unit.

The specialist calls State Street Bank, or another trustee, and gives his order. State Street takes the order and processes the transaction. The key to the process is that the transaction between the specialist and the trustee happens *in kind.* The specialist does not deliver $6.0 million in cash. He or she delivers to the trustee the basket of stocks, such as 152 IBM shares, 37 Wal-Mart shares, and so on. The trustee, in turn, delivers to the specialist the index shares, in this case, SPY.

Where did the specialist get the shares? She could have gone out into the market and bought them. Another possibility is that the specialist was carrying some of the shares in inventory, anticipating the need for more shares.

Your purchase of shares is completed within normal settlement dates. Just as you have three days to settle when you purchase a stock, so do you settle your exchange shares in a normal T (for Trade) + 3 (three business days).

The same process is true for the other index shares, except for WEBS. In the case of MDY, for example, the trustee delivers one creation unit consisting of 25,000 index shares. The specialist delivers the 400 stocks making up the index.

After the specialist receives the creation unit, she takes the shares and sells them in whatever amounts the trading floor order flow demands, such as in 500-share, 1200-share, or 300-share pieces.

Sometimes, the specialist can have too many exchange shares on hand and may want to redeem some. The process between the specialist and trustee is now reversed: In the case of SPY, the trustee delivers to the specialist the 500 different stocks comprising the S&P 500 index. The specialist delivers to the trustee 50,000 shares of SPY, which is one creation unit.

It is up to the specialist to judge how many shares of each exchange share class he should keep in inventory to satisfy his trading needs. Ordinarily, the specialist is not at risk by holding creation units. Specialists have various risk-monitoring professionals on staff who determine their risk and minimize it. If the specialist is long SPY, for example, she may hedge with S&P 500 futures. Her goal is to take her net exposure down to zero. Among hedges the specialist can put in place are to short the S&P 500 futures on the Chicago Mercantile Exchange, or to short exchange share options on the ASE.

MORE ON REDEEMING IN KIND

For tax purposes, gains that have accumulated in the index security that is returned to the specialist in a redemption are minimized. This is because the redemption is done in stock from the trustee to the specialist, not in cash. Because the index shares are redeemed in kind, those who continue to hold their shares will be minimally affected by other shareholder redemptions.

THE WEBS EXCEPTION TO THE CREATION
AND REDEMPTION PROCESS

The creation and redemption process outlined above is true for all of the exchange share classes except WEBS. In WEBS creation and redemption, there are normally three institutions involved, whereas one trustee is involved in all the other classes.

The reason is that with WEBS, the WEBS portfolio manager is not creating baskets of stocks to fully replicate an index. WEBS fashion optimized portfolios, and those portfolios are structured to perform closely to the MSCI index of the country that they track. The institutions involved in the WEBS optimized portfolio need the WEBS portfolio manager to advise them regarding which securities to purchase and sell when creating and redeeming WEBS shares.

ARBITRAGING AGAINST RISK

SPY, DIA, and QQQ all trade similarly. The specialists, and sometimes the market makers, protect their long positions by arbitraging with other derivative securities, such as S&P 500 futures, or through the securities that make up the index. For instance, if the Dow Jones Industrial Average is valued at 10,040 and DIA is selling at 100, the specialists and the market makers will readily buy DIA, and to arbitrage, they will short the 30 stocks that make up the Dow Jones index. That locks in their profit. To take the profit, they will later unwind the positions simultaneously.

Sector SPDRs do not have a derivative index to arbitrage against the index shares. Basically, you just add up the value of the underlying shares in the sector SPDRs and compare that to the sector SPDR market price. If the value of the shares in the Energy Sector SPDR, for example, equals 28 a share, and the Energy SPDR is selling for 27, the shares are a buy. The specialist and arbitragers will jump on the index shares, bidding them up or near the 28 level. Both will then hedge their long position by selling short in the market the shares making up the Energy SPDR. Or they could short the exchange share options. An individual can do this, too, or do a partial hedge. For instance, you could short XON as a partial hedge against holding Energy SPDRs.

USING OPTIONS TO TRADE OR INVEST WITH EXCHANGE SHARES

You can trade options on MDY, select SPDRs, and QQQ. These options can all be found on the ASE. You can also trade options on the Dow Jones Industrial Average itself and the Standard & Poor's 500 index. These options are traded on the Chicago Board Options Exchange (CBOE). The Dow Jones and S&P 500 options settle in cash, however, an arrangement that differs from that of the exchange shares. I will get into why cash settlements matter in a later chapter. You cannot trade options on conventional open-end index funds.

OPTIONS ARE USED FOR MYRIAD INVESTMENT OBJECTIVES

Let's say you want income. As an example, suppose you buy 500 shares of QQQ at 100 and sell five 105 calls. This gives the call buyer the right to call the 500 QQQ from you at 105. This is referred to as a *covered call,* covered because you own the stock. One option covers 100 shares of the index security. The call buyer pays you for this right, say two points, each point being $100. The amount paid to you is called a *premium.* So if QQQ doesn't move above 105, you have received the two points for five calls, which amounts to $1000, and you still have 500 QQQ. If QQQ goes lower, at least you have the $1000 premium to cut your loss. If QQQ goes up, say, to 110, your

> Remember, when selling options for income, you are at principal risk. If the stock goes down more than the premium you receive, you have a loss. Even if the amount received when you wrote the option looked attractive as a percentage of the amount you had invested, a loss might ultimately be realized in the trade.

shares will be called from you at 105, giving you a $3500 profit: 2 points $\times$ 500 shares = $1000 for the premium, plus the difference between your purchase of 500 shares at 100 and the stock being called at 105 = $2500. The main thing you are giving up when writing a covered call is the upside potential above 105. Even if QQQ goes to 150, you are still out at 105.

You can also buy the QQQ on margin, thereby increasing your income. Remember, however, that you have to pay interest on the margin money that you borrow to buy shares.

The price at which the buyer can call the index securities from you is called the *strike price,* and there are different strike prices, placed progressively higher, such as 105, 110, 115, and so on. Of course, the amount of premium decreases with the advance of the strike price away from the market price of the security. If QQQ is selling at 106 and the option strike price is 105, the option is considered to be "in the money" by one point. If QQQ is 104, and the option is a 105 strike price, the option is "out of the money" by one point. So the premium to buy QQQ at 105 with the security at 104 is higher than an option with a strike price of 110.

Also, options are perishable. They mature every three months and are then worthless. Option "cycles" are three months apart, such as January, May, September, and January. And cycles are set differently for different stocks. For example, some cycles may be February, June, October, and February. The shorter the length of time left until maturity, the lower the premium the option seller can expect to receive from the option buyer. After all, if you sell a QQQ option at 105 for one month, you can't expect to receive the same as if you sold the buyer a six-month option.

You can also take a side of the market other than selling calls. If you think QQQ will run to 110 from its present 100, but you don't want to put up the money to buy shares, you can buy calls to purchase QQQ at 100. If the shares do run to 110, you can exercise the call and buy the shares at 100. Your cost is increased by the amount of premium that you paid to purchase the call. Or you could also just sell the calls at that point and pocket the profit. If you do get into buying calls in anticipation of a security going higher, you have to realize that what you are doing is speculating. If the security doesn't rise enough above the call price to cover the premium you paid, you've lost money. And the clock is always ticking. Options can and do expire worthless. Usually, the odds of making money are not with the call buyer.

Suppose you own QQQ at 100 and it has run to 110. You are nervous it may dip, but you don't want to sell. You think it may go higher after dipping, or for tax reasons you don't want to sell, or you may have other reasons. One thing that you can do is buy a put. A put gives you the option to put QQQ to the seller at a price, for example, 110. If the shares back down to 103, you can put your shares to the seller at 110. Or, since your put options would be more valuable now, you could keep QQQ and sell the put at a profit. If QQQ doesn't go up or down, but stays at 110, you are just out the premium you paid for the put. Think of it as a form of insurance. If the shares go higher, that's fine. Let your profits run. Again, you are just out the premium cost.

You can also sell or write a call "uncovered," which is what you would be if you sold the option without owning the shares. Another way of saying it is that you are "naked." If the term makes you feel vulnerable, trust me, you are. Say you write an uncovered 105 call of QQQ and receive a premium of 5 points, or $500 per call. You have received a premium for allowing the buyer of the call to call shares from you at 105, so you might have to sell to the buyer shares that you do not own. If QQQ trades up to 112 and the shares are called from you, you will have to go into the open market, purchase them at 112, and take a 7-point loss. You were paid $500 for selling the call, which reduces your loss to $200. Also, in your account you would have had to maintain margin capital, because naked writes can be done only in margin accounts.

If you are of a speculative bent and you think QQQ is not going down—you are just sure of it—you can sell a naked put. Perhaps you sell a put on QQQ for 105. As long as QQQ stays at 105, you are okay. If QQQ goes above 105, you are still okay. The holder of the put won't put QQQ to you, not when he or she can go out in the open market and sell there. It is when QQQ goes down that you will suffer. If QQQ goes to 95, for example, the put holder will put QQQ to you at 105, forcing you to buy the shares at a 10-point loss. Again, when selling naked, you must have margin money in your account so you can buy shares put to you, or to buy stock called from you when you are in a naked call position.

Selling a put naked doesn't always mean that you are speculating. Let's say you want to buy QQQ at 105 but the shares are now 108. Say, too, that 105 puts are paying two points, maturing three months out. So you sell a naked put. If QQQ stays unchanged or goes higher, that's fine. You pocket the $200 and that's the end of it. If QQQ dips and goes to 102, believe me, the buyer of the put *will* put QQQ to you at 105. So you own the shares at 105, the price that you wanted to pay for them originally, plus you received a $200 premium. Your net cost is 103. Although the shares are now worth 102, you are far better off because you are just one point off the market. If you had paid 108, you would be six points off the market.

If you sell a put, the amount required for margin is the premium plus a percentage of the value of the index share. The required percentage varies with different brokerage firms. Naked puts also have the advantage that you do not pay interest on margin money unless and until the index shares are put to you, and when you sell a put, you get the premium right away.

A conservative way to handle the margin requirements of selling puts is to keep enough margin funds in your brokerage account to cover the cost of the shares if the shares are put to you at the strike price. In fact, many brokerage firms require that you do this. This is referred to as a *cash-secured put*.

And there are a multitude of other strategies available, strategies such as buying a call *and* a put, planning to cover one position or the other, depending on the way the market breaks. And depending on your market outlook, you could sell two puts and buy one call, taking a straddle position. There are many other strategies you can use to achieve your goals, depending on whether you are seeking to invest longer term, receive income, or speculate aggressively. The rules and specifications regarding options can be seen in Figure 2-1.

THE HIGHER RISK OF USING OPTIONS ON STOCKS

Index shares have advantages over common stock when you are doing option/equity strategies. Listed index securities, as I have shown, move in an orderly way, which affords more reliability in getting in and out. This is important when you have options on the other side of your trade. There is an advantage of being naked listed index securities options over being naked individual stock options. This is particularly true when the market is especially violent or when unforeseen events occur, as they often do.

Say you are short calls in XYZ Pharmaceuticals. You sold the calls naked because you think the drug industry is overpriced, XYZ has lousy

FIGURE 2-1   Contract Specifications for Index Share Options

Description	Index Share Options are standardized put and call options on underlying Index Shares. Index Shares are securities representing ownership in portfolios of stocks designed to closely track the price performance of individual indexes. Currently, Index Share options are available on Nasdaq-100 Shares, based on the Nasdaq-100 Index; Standard & Poor's MidCap Depositary Receipts, based on the S&P MidCap 400 Index; and nine Select Sector SPDR Funds designed to track specific market sectors: Basic Industries, Consumer Services, Consumer Staples, Cyclical/Transportation, Energy, Financial, Industrial, Technology and Utilities. Like all Exchange-traded options, Select Sector SPDR Fund options are issued, cleared and guaranteed by The Options Clearing Corporation (OCC).
Exercise Style	American. Options may be exercised on any business day prior to the expiration date.
Trading Unit	The minimum trade size is one option contract. The notional value underlying each contract equals 100 multiplied by the Index Share value. One option contract represents 100 underlying Index Shares. "Grand" options, representing 1,000 Index Shares, may also be available.

Conventional Options

Index Shares	Symbol	Grand Symbol	LEAPS Symbols 2000	LEAPS Symbols 2001	Position Limits
MidCap SPDRs	MDY	RDY	LSP	ZMD	31,500
Nasdaq-100 Shares	QQQ	N/A	LQD	ZWQ	13,500
Select Sector SPDR Funds					
Basic Industries Sector	XLB	N/A	LJB	ZJI	13,500
Consumer Services Sector	XLV	N/A	LJC	ZJS	13,500
Consumer Staples Sector	XLP	N/A	LJD	ZJD	13,500
Cyclical/Transportation Sector	XLY	N/A	LJE	ZJE	13,500
Energy Sector	XLE	N/A	LJG	ZJG	13,500
Financial Sector	XLF	N/A	LJH	ZJF	13,500
Industrial Sector	XLI	N/A	LJK	ZJK	13,500
Technology Sector	XLK	N/A	LJL	ZJL	13,500
Utilities Sector	XLU	N/A	LJO	ZJO	13,500

Exercise Price Intervals	Exercise (strike) prices are set at one-point intervals bracketing the current value of underlying Index Shares.
Exercise Price Adjustments	Because of the unpredictable nature of certain distributions associated with Index Shares, such as capital gains distributions, strike prices will be adjusted for such distributions to the nearest 1/8th of a point.
Option Premium Quotations	Stated in points and fractions. One point equals $100. Minimum tick for series trading below 3 is 1/16 ($6.25); for all other series, 1/8 ($12.50).
Expiration Cycle	Up to two consecutive near-term expiration months, plus two additional further-term expiration months in the March cycle are available at any one time. LEAPS® - Long-term Equity AnticiPation Securities® - are also available.
Expiration	The Saturday following the third Friday of the expiration month.
Settlement: Exercises	Settlement based on delivery of underlying Index Shares on the third business day following exercise.
Settlement: Option Trades	Next New York business day.
Minimum Customer Margin for Uncovered Writers	Premium plus 20% of the value of the underlying Index Shares, reduced by any out-of-the-money amount to a minimum of premium plus 10% of the aggregate Index Shares value.
Trading Hours	For Select Sector SPDR Funds: 9:30 a.m. to 4:02 p.m., New York time. For MDY and QQQ: 9:30 a.m. to 4:15 p.m., New York time.
Trading System	Specialist/Registered Options Trader.

earnings, they are bleeding money and everybody on the Street knows it, and their patents are about to expire. But out of the blue—whoops! Monster Pharmaceuticals makes a bid to buy XYZ for twice its market price. Monster wants to market a little-known product that XYZ has been developing. You look at your computer screen and start to sweat. They have stopped trading in XYZ. Indications are that the stock will trade two times higher when it opens. There is nothing you can do.

So you turn off the screen and start poring over your bank accounts to find funds to meet the margin calls that you know will be coming. And you hope that a higher bid for XYZ Pharmaceuticals is not forthcoming.

When you use options on listed exchange shares, you are spreading the risk over a range of stocks. When you pick individual stocks, you usually get much more volatility. Also, exchange shares are tied to an index, and one company's fortunes by itself cannot move an index.

So there is real risk in being naked options on individual stocks. But if you wanted to short the pharmaceutical sector, you can achieve this by using sector SPDRs. In this case, you could write options against the Consumer Staples SPDRs. Your short bet would be spread over 60 stocks, a much safer way to go.

The single-issue risk in stocks is also there if you are naked puts on a stock. For example, say you are bullish on the energy sector, crude oil prices have been down for years, there is a reduced amount of drilling because of the low oil prices, and demand from Asia, a large importer of oil, is down due to a recession. This is not far removed from the recent state of affairs in the oil patch.

Suppose you check up on Offshore Rigs, your favorite drilling company. The stock has gone from 92 to 45. What is your downside? The stock is down about 50 percent from its high. The company has a book value of $52. The p/e multiple, if oil prices stay stable, is 15 times. But if oil prices go up, activity in the oil patch would pick up and the multiple could easily shrink by half. You figure it may take six months for higher oil prices to materialize. So you sell nine-month puts, perfectly willing to have the stock be put to you.

And you are right. Oil prices start to skyrocket, energy looks tight, and the drillers take off. A problem ensues, however. The day that oil prices start to climb, Offshore Rigs makes a number of announcements:

1. The company has to restate earnings for the last two years because of material misstatements in its income statement.

2. There are certain questions regarding the accounting item Goodwill. The question pertains to a company taken over by Offshore Rigs. This could affect the balance sheet negatively.

3. The chief executive officer and chairman of the board have disappeared.

This development may seem farfetched, but it's not. It would not even make the A-list of jaw-dropping bombshells that I've seen.

So, unfortunately, oil takes off and Offshore Rigs drops. And yes, stock is put to you much higher than the present market price. You wish you had never heard of Offshore Rigs.

Instead of selling a naked put on Offshore Rigs, you could sell a naked put on XLE, the Energy Sector SPDR. This would give you representation in the group. Since many companies make up the index shares, if one of the companies in the energy sector blew up, it would not be a total catastrophe. Generally, if you are right on the sector, you will make money, as sector SPDRs usually go with their group.

The other reason you are better off to short the exchange shares than common stock, or to go naked options against exchange shares rather than stock, was covered earlier. Index shares trade in increments of 1/64, a very tight bid and ask, and there is usually real size on either side of the bid/ask. So if you need to buy or sell the equity side of an equity/option equation, you have a better chance with exchange shares.

In a taxable account, when you liquidate securities, you are creating taxable events, regardless of whether they are gains or losses. To be more tax efficient, you could sell index securities as a hedge position against a stock portfolio.

Let's say you have stocks you have held for years, and the stocks have a low tax basis. You are afraid that the prime rate will be raised, making the market tumble about 10 percent or more over the next several months.

If you sell stocks, you will create a capital gains obligation. But if you short one of the exchange shares for a few months, covering when you think the market looks better, you won't create a large capital gains obligation. In fact, if you are right about the market going down, you might create a gain on the short side.

3

INDIVIDUAL AND PROFESSIONAL STRATEGIES FOR USING EXCHANGE SHARES

EQUITIZING CASH FOR INDIVIDUALS AND PROFESSIONALS

Probably the primary use of exchange shares with money managers is to equitize cash in a portfolio. Many money managers do not time the market. Instead, they stay 100 percent exposed to equities at all times. Consequently, exchange shares can be used as a "cash sweep." Any time there are uninvested funds, they are swept into exchange shares. The share class of choice for institutions is mostly SPY because of its liquidity and broad market exposure.

This is something an individual investor can do as well. When you have uninvested cash and want market participation with a minimum of fuss in getting in and out of the market, simply sweep your cash into exchange shares. If you feel it is time to be aggressive in OTC growth issues, sweep into QQQ. If you like the oil sector, sweep into XLE, the Energy Sector SPDR. For the blue-chip, cyclical exposure, sweep into DIA. And so forth.

> The flexibility of exchange shares allows you to get in and out of sectors, groups, and countries quickly, easily, and cheaply. Remember, asset allocation is by far the most important component in investing, more important than market timing or stock selection.

Money managers find that a SPY sweep arrangement gives their trading desks great flexibility. If there were no exchange shares and a manager did not want to use S&P 500 index futures, and there was no cash position, the desk would have to sell a stock to make sure they had funds coming in before making any new buys. Otherwise, the trader would be *forced* to sell a position at any price to raise the cash needed for a new purchase. As you can imagine, if you just have to get out of, say, 500,000 shares of Intel Corp. and there are no buyers, you will experience a lousy trade—or worse.

The manager could tell the traders on the desk to make sure they didn't have cash left in the portfolio. But then the traders would lose their flexibility. What if they saw a block of stock that the manager was very interested in loading up on? The trader couldn't buy. Also, they might have to force stock into the marketplace when they needed to raise cash. When you force stock in, you almost always get a bad price.

Suppose it is 3:50 Eastern time, the market closes at 4:00, and you need to raise cash. If a low bid is the only one that shows up on the floor, you *have* to hold your nose and hit the bid. There is no choice, you need cash. Holding SPY or the other exchange shares negates this problem. You can sell real size at a fair price and settle in three days.

But if a manager is holding SPY to equitize cash, she can tell the traders, "Look, don't worry about the sell side. We can sell off some SPY. Work the buy order, and sell SPY as you need to." This takes the pressure off and gives the trading desk flexibility.

This flexibility can also save the portfolio money, since now the trading desk doesn't have to force trades into the marketplace. Most equity managers, even if they are not mandated to be fully invested, have a propensity to be very close to a hundred percent invested. Money managers feel they are paid to perform. Most think they can pick winners and want to make their bets. That's what makes them great, when they are right, that is.

In general, managers want to make bets where they have value to add, the value being their analytical skills. They want to avoid making bets in the wrong places. And it can be costly to be underinvested. Consider that if a manager holds 2 percent cash, and the market goes up 30 percent, that is 60 basis points to the portfolio that the manager has lost simply because she was long cash. It would have been better for the manager to have bought SPY and participated in the market advance.

Of course, there is always the rationalization that the market could have gone down, and that, therefore, holding SPY would have added to portfolio loss. But then we are getting into the realm of market timing, a technique so difficult—and so inexact—almost invariably requiring the manager's own specific type of discipline and strategy, that it is to be excluded from these examples.

Timing techniques are also employed by individual investors. You may have a timing strategy, developed over the years, that works much of the time. It is hard to teach market timing. There are so many variables that make markets move that each trader must develop a technique for himself. So there are as many timing strategies as there are traders.

There is a choice of which products to use for short-term broad market exposure, SPY or S&P 500 futures, traded on the Chicago Mercantile Exchange.

EQUITIZING CASH: S&P FUTURES COMPARED TO SPY

SPY is pretty simple. It is bought and sold like a stock. With futures, there are many more operational steps involved. Futures require more legal documentation. They have a daily mark-to-the-market requirement. The settlement period for futures is usually next day, not the regular T+3 settlement that you have with SPY.

Marking to the market involves calculating the price of the securities in a portfolio to reflect the portfolio's current market value. Futures are purchased in margin accounts, and the account is calculated daily to ensure the portfolio's compliance with maintenance requirements. If the value of the portfolio goes up, funds can be withdrawn. If the portfolio declines, maintenance funds have to be deposited.

There is an advantage for SPY settling the usual way. If you sell stock and buy SPY to equitize cash, the stock sale will settle the same time as the SPY purchase, and the cash from the sale will cover the buy. But if you sell stock and buy futures, initial margin for the futures must be deposited, usually the next day, depending on the broker's requirements. So some cash must be held for futures. There is also more work required to juggle the cash accounts to settle the sides of a futures/stock trade.

Another problem with a futures contract is that it represents too much money. The futures contract amounts to 250 times the S&P 500 index, and the index is priced at about $1340. This amounts to approximately $335,000 per contract. Of course, purchased on margin, a manager doesn't have to put up that much cash.

Compared to that, SPY, priced, for example, at 134, only costs $134 for one share. Working with this smaller denomination, the manager can more accurately match her exposure with SPY than she can with a futures contract.

For margin use, what many managers do is hold Treasury bills as a cash equivalent. This affords some income in the portfolio's cash portion, but very little. Treasury bills are usually an acceptable instrument for deposit for margin purposes. An individual investor can use Treasury bills also.

Another disadvantage with futures is that once you initiate one side of the futures trade, either buying or selling short, you are pretty much locked into that broker until you close out the position.

When you buy stock or exchange shares *you* own the shares. You can leave them with a broker and still go to another broker to sell them. When trading futures, you are operating on margin and have to satisfy your margin obligations with that specific broker, which locks you in until the trade is completed. With stock, the customer has the flexibility to buy the stock through one broker and sell through another, wherever he thinks he can get the best price and transaction costs. Money managers usually don't hold stocks themselves. Their stock is held by a custodian, usually a bank or trust company.

In setting up a margin account for futures, the customer has to show that she is substantial, that is, she has the means to pay off losses. In addition, there are different levels of accounts, a level for hedgers and one for speculators. Speculators have to show they are able to withstand losses. There are more agreements to sign than when setting up a cash brokerage account. One of the agreements obligates the brokerage firm or customer or both with a daily mark to the market, and the customer agrees to supply additional margin funds if required. In turn, the broker gives assurances that the deposited margin funds will be held in an escrow account. The funds will be used only for the customer's futures contracts, and not for the broker's other obligations. The broker agrees to return funds when and if the margin account becomes overfunded. These contracts are more work for an individual or manager than if they merely purchase SPY.

Every morning, the manager marks his portfolio to the market and does his margin calculations. He then sends funds to the broker if he is underfunded or arranges to receive funds back from the broker if overfunded. Usually, for individual accounts the broker does these calculations. The customer's equity position, hence his margin needs, will change depending if the market goes his way or against him.

SYNTHETIC ACCOUNTS

There are managers who run index programs, mostly for tax-exempt accounts. They index using a *synthetic index*. A synthetic index derives from a synthetic equity. This equity is an instrument made up of derivatives and contains the risk/reward features of an investment in a stock, a basket of stocks, or a weighted basket of stocks equivalent to a stock index. By *derivative* is meant a contract that changes in value with price movements in a related or underlying security, future, or index. In other words, the value of the derivative is "derived" from a related instrument.

The synthetic index approach is a strategy linked to an index, and which uses futures contracts and cash management. All synthetic-account managers do a version of this. Many buy S&P futures, which are very actively traded, and link these futures atop a cash management account.

Managers of these accounts can keep money in a high-grade money market account and maintain a long futures position, which will create index results. Instead of earning a 1.2 percent dividend yield from holding an S&P 500 stock portfolio, the fund will earn a 5 percent rate in the money market fund. The bad news is that the manager has to pay a 3.8 percent annualized premium rate to hold the futures contract.

In traditional indexing, you hold the S&P 500 stocks or SPY, or you can hold one of the other indexes, such as the MidCap 400 stocks or Nasdaq 100. With synthetic indexing, you don't hold any stocks; you get representation in the stock index through futures contracts.

TRANSITIONING AND AVOIDING RISK WITH INDEX SHARES

Another use for SPY and the other exchange shares comes during transitions. Say that one manager is fired and another hired to take her place. Whenever there is a change in managers, some stocks will be sold—often all the stocks—and new ones bought that fit into the new manager's investment strategy. One big concern during the change of managers is maintaining equity exposure while the transition takes place.

A transition strategy that makes sense is to sell the old stocks and at the same time buy SPY or index shares. This keeps cash in the market to participate in any market advance. Of course, SPY is subject to general market risk. But SPY funds are in the bigger stocks, the ones that arguably would fare better in market downturns.

When the new manager is ready to take over, she can simply receive the SPY shares. Then she can make her stock purchases at the pace she prefers and unwind SPY to pay for stock purchases. This is a less frantic, more orderly process than simply giving the new manager portfolios of stock to sell.

Of course, it isn't only SPY that is used for transitions. For a midcap portfolio, for instance, the stocks sold would be replaced by MDY until MDY is handed over to the new manager. Similarly, if a manager had a small-cap portfolio or a portfolio consisting of many OTC stocks, he might want to transition using QQQ.

An individual can do this also. Wondering which midcap stocks to buy, she can buy MDY until she makes up her mind. The same could be said for the other exchange shares. If an individual investor or money manager thinks that now is the time to be in utilities, but doesn't know which issues he wants to be in, the Utilities Sector SPDR is a way to gain participation in the group until he decides. Or an individual might think the OTC market will rebound after a selloff and buy QQQ as an OTC market proxy. Or, to cut down on market risk, against their stock portfolio a manager or individual could short a market sector or index using exchange shares. The trader might be anticipating a market decline and use the short as a hedge position.

An individual can also use exchange shares as a hedge against market declines. If you had big gains in technology stocks but were afraid tech stocks were about to decline, and you do not want to take profits because of the taxes, you might be able to short the Technology SPDR, creating a hedge against your long position. In this instance, you would continue holding your technology stocks, thereby postponing the tax liability. (With this or any investment action, it is advisable to check with your tax advisor about how it might affect your tax circumstances.)

Exchange shares can be used effectively for tax planning purposes by integrating them into your planned holding period. Check with your tax advisor before taking any such action.

Don't forget about options in your investment and trading programs. If you are really concerned about the market tumbling, you can, as a hedge, buy puts on MDY, QQQ, or the sector SPDRs, whichever class most closely resembles your stock portfolio. You would want to use options, however, only if your portfolio resembled the stocks in the optionable exchange share classes. If you have an S&P 500 type portfolio, hedging with options is not possible, since there are no options in SPY.

If your portfolio does relate to an optionable exchange share class, you buy a put, and the market tumbles, you will most likely be protected by the put. Your portfolio will go down with the market, but the value of the put will probably go up. If you are wrong and the market continues up, the value of the put will go to zero, but your portfolio should rise with the general market.

Whether you have just a few stocks or handle millions of dollars in pension assets, strategies with exchange shares do alter the risk/return of the portfolio. Exchange shares are also an easy way to stay in the market without having to research individual issues.

For instance, assume a money manager invests mostly in Nasdaq and other OTC stocks. He is a savvy manager and usually returns about 2 percent better than the Nasdaq 100 index. The manager receives $100.0 million from one of his pension plan customers on the first business day of the quarter. Looking at the market, he concludes prices are really high and just doesn't feel compelled to chase. But if the market continues to run and he doesn't have exposure, he knows he runs the risk of underperforming.

The answer: he buys QQQ. If the stocks in his managed portfolio continue running with the market, then he loses the difference between the return on his stocks and the return on the QQQ. He will be losing about 2 percent by not buying more of his portfolio stocks. If the market does go up and QQQ returns 8 percent the next period, his portfolio stocks would have probably returned 10 percent. But staying out of the market would mean forfeiting an 8 percent advance. If the market declines, this manager hopes that the QQQ and the broad exposure of 100 stocks will provide a downside cushion.

HEDGING STRATEGIES FOR INDIVIDUALS USING EXCHANGE SHARES

Using SPDRs, you too can implement your investment strategies. Just like a money manager, you can cheaply and efficiently buy into or short market sectors and weight your portfolio according to your market view.

For example, if you think the broad market will go up, you can buy SPY. If you think the technology sector will perform well, you can buy XLK along with SPY. If you think energy prices will soften, you can short XLE. If you buy SPY, you hold the energy sector. A short of XLE would leave you net neutral in energy. But then you can short more XLE for a net short position.

If you don't want broad exposure, do not buy SPY. For example, if you feel that interest rates will decline, causing the price of natural resources like oil to drop, then short XLE. If you think lower interest rates will spur more consumer spending, then buy XLK. If you are more sure of your oil scenario, you can overweight the position—buy 500 XLK and short 1000 XLE, for example.

Economic prognoses, and your use of them, can guide your investment decisions using SPDRs. For instance, if it looks like the economy is going into a tailspin, you can short XLB. You could also short XLK. Although technology is a growth area, it is doubtful that in a slowdown people would buy computers when they are putting off the purchase of refrigerators and cars. XLV is vulnerable in a slowdown as well. If times get tough enough, people will even put off going to the movies, buying CDs, and going out to dinner.

To hedge, in this instance, means to take a long and short position simultaneously. The strategy is to guard against a market reversal, mitigating a large loss on either side. If you have an optimistic economic outlook, you could buy XLY, which is tied to economic activity. As a hedge, you could short XLP, which is tied to the general economy, but less so than XLY. If you are mistaken and the economy declines, your shortside XLP will go down, which will result in a profit. But if you are right and the economy goes up, XLP should not go up as much as XLY. Of course, if you think that the economy will soar, you could be aggressive by buying XLK. You could still short XLP as a hedge if you cared to.

Are interest rates headed higher? Is the Federal Reserve about to raise the discount rate? Then short XLU. As interest rates go up, utility and other interest-sensitive stock prices concurrently go down to offer a higher yield. Also, consider shorting the financial stocks, which generally fare poorly in a higher-interest-rate environment. XLE should go higher as inflation rises, reflecting the higher value of this natural resources sector. XLI may fare poorly in such an environment; General Electric dominates that sector and is heavily weighted by its credit business, which could slow. In a general economic slowdown, all of the industrial stocks would likely suffer.

If interest rates are declining, you could put in reverse positions. You could buy XLU. As interest rates decrease, interest-sensitive stocks go up, reflecting the lower yield. You could also buy the financials.

If you think this bull market is playing out and the market will go down, one tactic is to short SPY. For a hedge you could buy XLP, because even in bad economic times people need items like food and drugs. This sector should go down less than the market in general, proxied by SPY. If the market goes up, your long position in XLP should work for you, mitigating your loss in SPY. To be more aggressive, you could short XLK, which contains many high p/e stocks.

If all signs point to the economy continuing on a rapid international expansion, buy XLI, since industrial stocks are so international in scope. Consider shorting XLU, since a higher rate of economic activity may cause interest rates to spike up.

When sifting through the possibilities regarding sector SPDRs, there are no hard-and-fast rules, but all general strategies can easily be put into effect using exchange shares. Hedge positioning is not perfect. Your long position can go down while your short goes up, worsening a trade. But with both a short side and a long side in a trade, a big loss might be avoided. All markets are different. That's what makes them interesting and potentially profitable. In using exchange shares, you are only as limited as your imagination, conviction level, and risk capital.

HEDGING YOUR INCOME WITH EXCHANGE TRADED SHARES
The exchange traded funds are changing the way people think about investments. Among the newly available choices are those of investing or shorting in sectors as a hedge against your income situation.

Suppose, for a moment, that you are employed as an airline pilot. Ordinarily, as an investor you would want to invest for broad market participation, so you would invest in an instrument such as SPY. The problem is that with this investment, you are not hedged against the fact that you work in the transportation industry. As a pilot you have an enormous amount of risk associated with the price of oil. If the price of oil goes up, the airlines might cut back on their number of flights and you might get laid off.

Another example is that if you are a home builder, you have a very high risk of interest rate changes. If interest rates advance, mortgage rates will go up, possibly enough so that people will stop buying homes. Materials, such as lumber, will get more costly, squeezing your profit margin. And your cost of borrowing funds to build homes will increase. These factors can put you out of business.

So what a prudent investor wanting broad market participation would ordinarily buy probably would not square with her "real world" needs, which is a hedge against the financial risk of a decline in income. In other words, your personal economic situation is often at odds with an ideal investment portfolio, which is typically designed without personal circumstances in mind. If you are a pilot, then, you offset the risk of oil prices soaring. If you build homes, you offset interest rates climbing.

So, you're a pilot. To solve this problem, you could short the Transportation Sector SPDR. This would work as a hedge against your losing your job if oil prices went higher. If the price of oil stays down and you keep your pilot job, all well and good. If not, you may lose your job, but at least you will make a profit on the short SPDR position. Another tactic would be to buy the Energy Select SPDR. If oil soars, you hedge your job risk with the long position in the SPDR.

If you're a home builder, you could short the Financial Sector SPDR as a hedge against rising interest rates—and hope that you are wrong on the position. If interest rates go up, the financial sector will probably decline and you will profit from the position, although you will probably suffer in the home-building business. The Utility Sector SPDR would be another good short as a hedge against rising interest rates.

How about hedging in a growth industry? Suppose, for example, you work as a consultant to Internet companies, and your income depends on the continued growth of the technology industry.

To build the ideal portfolio, there some things to consider. You may be bullish on the technology industry, and although it is not a hedge position, you may want to own more technology companies. Perhaps you are prohibited from owning companies such as Microsoft and Cisco because you contract work with them. To solve this problem, you could buy the Technology Sector SPDR to increase your participation in the sector's growth.

Someone else in the same employment situation may be of a different age and different risk category than you are. That person may feel she is overexposed to technology and risk, and prefer to short the Technology Sector SPDR as a hedge against an industry slowdown.

THE COST ADVANTAGE OF EXCHANGE TRADED SHARES

Exchange traded index shares lend themselves perfectly to a hedge position because of their liquidity and sector specificity. There is a large pool of people interested in these instruments as a hedge against losing their jobs. Combined with other traders and investors, the volume trading helps the instruments stay liquid. Institutions, too, might have an interest in hedging.

For instance, an airline might want to short the Transportation SPDR or buy the Energy SPDR as a hedge against its business suffering.

Creating these sector instruments works well for exchange shares. If a conventional fund manager creates a sector fund, ordinarily it does not collect a large amount of assets. If the asset base is small, the fund will have to charge more in fees to make the fund profitable for the management company. Exchange traded shares, because they are an index fund with low costs, can become a successful instrument. Hedge funds, traders, short-sellers, and long-term investors will go into these securities on a trading or short-term basis, whereas a conventional fund is pretty much created for long-term investors.

DIVERSIFYING AND LOWERING EXECUTION COSTS WITH EXCHANGE SHARES FOR HEDGE FUNDS

The transaction costs for trading exchange shares are far less than buying baskets of stocks, especially for institutions such as hedge funds.

A hedge fund is a private investment partnership in which the general partner has made a large personal investment. It is offered to the public by an offering memorandum. Usually, the fund is allowed to take long and short positions, invest in many markets, use derivatives, and employ leverage. Hedge funds also use strategies such as arbitrage and program trading. They can borrow, and they can have a significant impact on the markets.

But execution costs are high for hedge funds, and exchange shares offer savings as well as efficiencies in implementing strategies. For example, if a hedge fund wanted energy sector representation, it would buy a portfolio of energy stocks. For many shares of stock, it would pay at least three cents a share. The reason hedge funds pay that much is because there usually is some expertise required to get a good trade. The broker will have to "massage" the order, perhaps standing on the floor all day looking for buyers or sellers to get the order done.

Instead of buying shares, the hedge fund could buy the Energy Sector SPDR, in effect, an entire portfolio of energy stocks. The fund would thus have representation in the group. Trading would not be a problem, since size is almost never a factor with exchange shares. The fund would not need to pay nearly as much for brokerage, since special handling of the order would not be necessary.

Say that the hedge fund also wanted representation in the consumer staples sector and especially wanted to own tobacco stocks. Among the shares desired is Phillip Morris (MO). The hedge fund would put in an order to buy, say, 50,000 MO at 49 limit. That order could take days to fill, if it got filled at all. So the fund pays three cents a share for the broker to work the order. The fund finally gets filled on MO as well as a basket of consumer stocks. The manager then decides suddenly that the market looks terrible and wants out. Well, he has to sell his large holding of MO and other positions, which may not be easy, especially if other managers are wanting out.

Instead, the hedge fund could buy the Consumer Staples SPDR (XLP). The order would be filled right away, probably around the offer price. And the cost of buying and selling XLP would be much lower because exchange shares are so liquid. A hedge fund should be able to negotiate to trade exchange shares for about a penny or a penny and a half a share, a significant savings.

Of course, this is true for individuals as well. Instead of executing one trade on, say, five or ten different companies to build a portfolio of stocks and paying a commission on each trade, the individual can acquire a ready-made portfolio by buying the sector SPDR and paying just one commission.

It could be argued that a hedge fund could fashion a portfolio that would do better than the sector SPDRs. But it has been estimated that up to 80 percent of success in investing is in selecting the right sector. At the least, by buying exchange shares the fund or individual will be in the right sector cheaply and easily.

But no argument is necessary. The fund or individual can put perhaps 60 to 70 percent in the sector SPDRs and the remaining 40 to 30 percent in individual stock issues. Moreover, in the individual issues, the investor can choose to be as aggressive or conservative as she wants.

EXCHANGE SHARES USED ALONG WITH STOCKS

Exchange shares do not necessarily replace stock investing. They can be used to enhance a portfolio's return and/or lower risk.

If you want to own the Dow Jones stocks but also want to own a few favorites in that index, such as Dupont and Sears, by all means, buy DIA and overweight by purchasing shares of Dupont and Sears. If you want to buy SPY but think energy stocks and technology stocks will run more, then buy SPY and also pick up the Energy SPDR and the Technology SPDR as an overweight. Or if you want to own the S&P 500 but hate the energy and technology stocks, then buy SPY and short the Energy SPDR and Technology SPDRs. Exchange shares do not limit your portfolio. They aid you in fashioning your portfolio.

C H A P T E R

BEHAVIORAL FINANCE

NOISE EVERYWHERE

This feel-good bull market is masking many investment assumptions that stand to be exposed, but they won't be looked at, not while times are good on Wall Street. They may, though, when the market flattens out or goes down. One assumption is that given enough time and sources of information, active managers or individuals can beat the indexes. I showed before that there is ample evidence that the average active manager, over time, does not beat the stock indexes. If this is so, for your core portfolio, why not just buy the index? With the plethora of investment products that the exchange traded shares are offering, and the many new products that will soon be offered, index investing is possible in U.S. markets, sectors of U.S. markets, and countries all around the globe.

The traditional ways of investing can still be used, of course, but adding index products to a portfolio offers broad market exposure and global diversification. The TV market pundits try to find stocks that will go up in value immediately, continue going up, and telegraph when they start to decline. This active approach to investing, whether done by an individual or through a manager, rarely beats the indexes.

Let me illustrate what passes for market advice. Early one Sunday morning I snapped on the TV. Three stock market pundits were attacking each other on whether a stock was going up or down—next week! That's a pretty short time horizon. Since the banter was so good-natured, it was as if it was all a joke, but you had to be on the inside to get it. The repartee was tongue-in-cheek, a posed argument rather than a real one. They appeared as if they were even flaunting the fact that it was staged.

This is noise, gibberish surrounding the market action, investing as entertainment, a way to hold an audience until the next commercial. Shakespeare held his audiences by examining human foibles. These financial people attempt to hold an audience by offering the promise of being able to foresee the next day's market. That's an impossible task.

Any information coming from a TV screen is already known, and has been digested into the market price. It is old news—noise.

Now, I don't mind investing as entertainment. But you can't make money consistently on the basis of noise, and you *can* lose.

Still, even when I go into brokerage offices, the TV screens are constantly aglow, the investment pundits spewing out the latest tip or rumor or hunch. In restaurants and delis dotting the financial districts of New York, Chicago, Houston, San Francisco, and points in between, the never-ending drumbeat of news and noise reverberates from countless TV sets. It is the same in corporate offices. It's like reporting on a high-stakes poker game— which, in some ways, it is.

Who listens to this surfeit of reporting and prognosticating? Who believes this instant-gratification forward reading of what the markets or stocks will do? Many people do. Otherwise, the show would not go on. I, too, get caught up in this frenzy. And when I do, it often costs me money.

So I turn to the academicians, searching for new insights that can not only clarify matters, but find a better way to make a profit.

INVESTORS BEHAVING LIKE PEOPLE

Behavioral finance is gaining adherents as the "efficient market theory" is losing credibility. Basically, the efficient theory espouses the viewpoint that the price of a stock reflects all the available information known about the stock at that time. The assumption is that markets have their own built-in mechanisms to digest all that there is to know about a stock. Behavioral finance sets aside the assumptions of a rational, all-knowing market, and explores the notion that people do not always act, or invest, rationally. The market is always uncertain, there are virtually no investment formulas that will always work, and investment decisions are driven not by rational thought but by psychological factors, most of which are unknown to investors. Furthermore, as in many unconscious psychological biases, these unconscious motives and resulting action are recurring.

TOO MUCH TRADING

Academicians suspect that there is too much trading. They find it difficult to reconcile the amount of trading in equity markets with the trading patterns of rational investors. Of course, some trading must be done, for example, to rebalance portfolios or for tax purposes.

But at issue are such statistics the high turnover rate on the New York Stock Exchange (NYSE), which is running at more than an 80 percent rate. The NYSE publishes a handbook of statistics. In that book they add up total trading volume and divide that by total market capitalization. Recent statistics indicate that for every dollar's worth of stock listed on the NYSE, about $0.80 is traded per year. This is a very high number, and the numbers are even higher on the other exchanges. Nasdaq, for instance, has a turnover rate of more than double that of the NYSE.

Terrance Odean and Brad Barber at the University of California at Davis have done numerous papers on the subject of behavioral finance. Basically, they found that people trade too much and that this overtrading ends in excess losing trades. Also, on average, people hold on to their losing stocks and sell their winners. This is even more surprising considering that there are tax benefits in selling losers and advantages to postponing gains.

Furthermore, Odean's studies concluded that the losers investors held on to significantly underperformed the winners they sold. In other words, if an investor sold a stock and bought another to replace it, a year later, on average, the replacement stock had underperformed the sold stock by about 3 percent. And this is before commissions and the spread in the bid/asked quotes. These expenses make performance even worse.

In a paper entitled "Trading Is Hazardous to Your Wealth," Odean and Barber show that the more actively people trade, the lower their net returns. The data sample consisted of 78,000 households. The study showed that the investors who traded most actively underperformed the least active investors by about 6 percent a year.

OVERCONFIDENCE AND OVERTRADING

Behavioral finance studies deviation from rationality in investment behavior. A propensity for overconfidence among investors, especially men, is one such departure. When investors are overconfident, they almost invariably trade too much.

Rational investors make trades when it is necessary to do so. Besides selling off stocks that subsequently go higher and buying stocks that later decline, the overconfident investor often harbors unrealistic expectations regarding his returns. The noise factor mentioned above is a permanent contributor to this overconfidence. The cable financial talk shows, the Internet chat rooms, the day-trading and stock-tip services: It all generates unnecessary activity that works to the detriment of the investor. Grossman and Steglitz (1980) have explored the relationship between reliance on newsletters, financial magazines, and the like and investment behavior. Add to this scenario the findings from another study by Odean (1980). Overconfident investors hold riskier portfolios than rational investors. In sum, the overconfident investor takes larger risks, trades more, and expends more time and effort for a lower return performance.

THE GENDER FACTOR

Odean and Barber also published a study called "Boys Will Be Boys," in which they revealed that men, in particular, trade too much because of overconfidence. "Boys Will Be Boys" used account data from over 35,000 households and analyzed returns and activity over a six-year period. The data documented that men trade 45 percent more than women and earn risk-adjusted returns that are 1.4 percent less than the returns earned by women. Even more telling are the returns of single people. Single men trade 67 percent more and earn risk-adjusted returns of 2.3 percent less than the returns of single women.

The real paradox here is that in spite of men's tendency toward overconfidence and overtrading, which results in lower returns, there is a preponderance of women who still believe that finances are "men's work."

Additional studies (Lundeberg, Fox, and Puncochar, 1994; Deaux and Ferris, 1997; Deaux and Emswiller, 1994; Lenney, 1997; Deyer and Bowden, 1997; and Prince, 1993) indicate that many men believe they are superior to women in certain tasks. Men often include financial matters among these "masculine tasks." All you have to do to confirm this bias is take a look at the financial industry. Although women's participation is growing, there are many more men than women working on Wall Street, particularly in positions involving investment decision-making.

Even in this gender/confidence equation, the noise factor figures as an influence. Men seem to thrive in an environment of ambivalent information feedback. In this same environment, women seem to underestimate their abilities. All the noise tends to fuel a man's confidence and trading frequency more, but to cause skepticism and hesitation for many women.

THE ELEMENT OF CHANCE

It is not just individual investors who walk into this knowledge trap. To see where excessive "knowledge" can lead, witness some of the recent debacles by very large institutional investors. Among recent mishaps was the near collapse in 1998 of Long Term Capital, a multibillion dollar hedge fund. On the board of the fund were some award-winning economists. John Meriwether, the top investment officer, was a seasoned market professional. If knowledge is power, why did Long Term Capital go awry?

You can have a lot of information, but the information might not help. It might not be relevant. You might not know exactly how to process it. There might be too much to process. Many other factors of which we are unaware are at work regarding stocks.

As an example of the knowledge trap, take the case of a lottery spin. You can study and know almost everything about the cage from which the lottery balls are expelled. You can know every spin ever made, and how many times the number 47 and every other number has come up. You can know how much the balls weigh, where they were manufactured, their physical composition, down to the type of ink used to number them. You can know how long the official ball reader has been employed. You can have reams of information. Still, do you know what number is coming up next? No. Nor can you predict very accurately.

PEOPLE, TRADING, AND STOCK PICKERS

Meir Statman, a professor of finance at Santa Clara University in California, makes the point in a January 1999 paper that even though a person may know that the indexes usually beat the average active money manager, he or she may still prefer to invest with an active manager.

The reasons are diverse, but they seem to reflect that perennial mainstay of human nature, hope. Even though the odds are against it, there is always that hope that the investor will pick the right manager and best the indexes. And it *could* happen.

At bottom, though, this is the same brand of hope you'll find at a casino. Go there; watch the throngs of people gambling. It is widely known that the odds are with the house. Yet the smiles on the faces of the players and the heightened air of anticipation belie the notion that the outsider almost never beats the house. Now, investing is not gambling, but part of the lure of investing is to *pick* a winning stock or money manager.

Statman does not say this optimism is a bad thing. It may not always be profitable, but it gives investors and traders a feeling of well-being. But here's the whole crux of it: This particular way of receiving a feeling of well-being can cost you money. An investor is better off financially finding his feeling of well-being in a different endeavor.

THE IMPORTANCE OF INDEX INVESTING

So what's all this noisemaker, casino talk got to do with index investing?

If traders trade too much because they are overconfident and that excess trading leads to lower returns, what should one do?

Well, *most* people should not be actively trading for short-term profits. If you want to trade that way, use only a small amount, certainly not more than you can afford to lose and never miss. Unless you are a professional, with the time, energy, skill, and knowledge to devote every day into the market, you should invest your funds in a well-diversified, low-cost portfolio. It would seem prudent to place *some* funds in an index or indexes, be it a broad index, a country index, or a sector index. The proportion depends on what your objectives are and how much risk you can stand. Then you can use a portion of your assets for stock-picking or finding a money manager to try to beat the indexes.

Exchange shares are the lowest-cost, most effective way to invest. You can create a broad-based U.S. portfolio by buying DIA, SPY, or MidCap SPY. This position can be augmented by overweighting with sector SPDRs and QQQ. Foreign investing can be accomplished by buying a selection of WEBS.

Then, with your extra time, money, energy, and enthusiasm, go do what you enjoy. If you want to make more money, apply yourself to some facet of your career or business. Usually, you will make more money at something you know.

CHAPTER 5

THE ELECTRONIC INDEX INVESTOR AND TRADER

THE NEW WORLD OF ONLINE TRADING

Because of their ease of trading and vast liquidity, exchange shares lend themselves very well to online trading as well as to longer-term investing. And online trading, only recently the province of a trading minority, has quickly metamorphosed into an efficient, inexpensive way to trade, invest, and gather investment research. Let's cover a few basics of trading to better understand how trades can be executed swiftly.

Electronic technology has gotten so good, so efficient, and the market makers and the equipment mesh so well, that the majority of buy and sell orders get done almost seamlessly. But some orders need special handling.

Smaller stocks, such as pink sheet or OTC bulletin-board stocks, do not have much liquidity and continue to be handled by a floor broker. Pink sheets contain a daily listing of stocks that are not carried in the Nasdaq listings in the daily newspapers. Pink sheets provide details to the market makers on the stocks and the stocks' bid/asked prices. The OTC bulletin board is an electronic listing (e-listing) of OTC stocks that do not meet the minimum net worth and other requirements of the Nasdaq stock-listing system. Bulletin board stocks are continuously updated with prices and other information.

TRADING IN ACTIVE MARKETS

An important tip: An investor should know herself, especially in active markets.

Active markets are characterized by wide price moves and huge volume in a stock. Individual stocks generally swing wider than exchange shares because exchange shares are linked to an index. Some exchange shares, such as QQQ, can, however, rival individual issues in volume size. Active markets generally come about because of an imbalance of orders on one side. There may be all sell orders and no buyers around. Factors that could cause active markets in stocks include a news announcement about the company, an analyst's recommendation, or sudden interest in that company's or exchange share's sector. Index shares also experience active markets during general market swings.

These factors can cause volatility so strong that the market in a stock moves faster than the ability of traders to process trades and give out current quotes. There are risks in trading active markets, for both stock and exchange share traders:

1. If you drop in a market order, there can be a big difference between the quote you receive and the price at which your trade is executed. In addition, the size on either the bid or ask can change rapidly. By the time your market order gets to the floor or the market maker, the size of the bid/ask may no longer be there. Size is not so much a problem with index shares, but price still is.

2. Remember, market orders are executed as they pour in. Market makers and specialists are flooded with orders in active markets. Backlogs of orders can pile up. A quote under these conditions cannot be counted on to be a fresh indication of what is happening at the point of trade.

Even though active markets are risky ones in which to drop market orders, if you positively want an execution, you have to use a market order. Even market orders sometimes do not get done, but it is the best way to attempt to get an order off.

Many people are new to investing, but when investing online or through a conventional broker, the fact remains that an investor who understands the fundamentals has a better chance for success. E-trading operates in markets that move so fast that trading strategies must be used to operate most efficiently, things like placing a limit order instead of a market order in an actively moving market.

In active markets it is advisable to set your price rather than leave yourself open to a disappointing and costly trade. You can do this by entering a limit order. The downside of a limit order is that there is no guarantee you will get your order off. And if a stock or exchange share you are holding is going down, it is better to get off a bad sale than no sale at all. When you *absolutely* want out, then you must use a market order.

Also, when you want to change your limit or cancel a market order, it is best to go through your online broker representative, if the firm has one. Changing or canceling an order yourself in a high-volume situation can be difficult.

DIFFERENCES BETWEEN MARKET ORDERS AND LIMIT ORDERS

A market order is what it sounds like. When a stock order gets to the specialist on the floor, or the market maker on OTC, it is executed at the best possible price. Exchange shares are traded by a specialist on the ASE. Since they are filled quickly, it is hard to cancel a market order.

The biggest factor regarding when and at what price a market order is filled is the number of shares available at the displayed quote. If you place a market order to buy more shares than is shown on the offer side, you may get a *partial fill* right then, so you will buy the number of shares offered. Your order stays alive, though, and the rest will be filled at the next prices available, depending on the prices at which the exchange shares of stock are available. Again, exchange shares usually have an advantage over stock, particularly with larger orders, because size is almost always available on each side of the quote.

When you want to name your price, you enter a *limit order*. This ensures that your stock or exchange shares will be executed at a certain price or better. When you buy, you pay your limit price or less. When you sell, you receive your limit price or more. You can miss the market with a limit order, however.

And don't be surprised if you see your limit price on the tape and don't get a fill. When you place a limit, you get in line behind the other limit orders at your price. Usually, the specialist has to receive an offsetting order or orders that satisfy the price of your limit order for you to get your trade done.

OTHER TYPES OF ORDERS

There are two types of stop orders, stop and stop limit.

A *stop order*, or a *stop-loss order*, is an order to buy or sell at the market once the security has traded at or better than the stop price. Stop orders are usually used to secure a gain or to avoid further loss. In OTC stocks, when the inside bid or offer is equal to your stop price, the order becomes a market order. Inside bid or asked quotes are those between dealers trading for their own inventories. This contrasts with the retail market, in which quotes reflect the prices that individual customers pay to dealers.

Stop orders are used most often in *sell stops*. Let's say you purchase 500 QQQ at 90 and want to protect against the shares going down below 80. You enter a sell stop at 80. If QQQ touches 80 or lower, your order becomes a market order. Your stock is sold, and you are left licking your wounds on that trade. When dealing with an OTC stock, the stop is triggered to become a market order when the bid hits the stop price or below.

A *buy stop* is used when you think QQQ, which is now at 80, will retrace to 90. If that happens, the stock will break out and go to 120. You enter a buy stop at 90. If QQQ touches 90 or higher, the order becomes a market order and you will be filled. With an OTC stock, the stop becomes a market order when the ask hits the top price or higher.

A buy stop can be used for protection in a short position. Assume that QQQ ran to 120 and you sold your shares and shorted 500 shares there. You wanted to risk five points on the short side. You could enter a buy stop at 125. If QQQ reached 125, the stock would be bought at the market and cover the short.

Remember, a stop order does not necessarily save you from wide market swings. If a company comes out with a shocking negative announcement, they could stop trading in a stock and open it much lower, which would trigger your stop order as a market order. With index shares, you don't have these kinds of shocks. Although indexes can and do swing widely and the index shares follow them, they trade in a more orderly fashion.

A *stop limit* is an order to buy or sell at a limit once a security has traded through a stop price. Instead of becoming a market order, the order has a limit price.

You may, for example, hold QQQ at 120, but you are getting nervous. If the stock backs off to 115, you want to sell, but you want to receive at least 113 for the shares. You place a sell stop order at 115, with a 113 limit. If the stock trades at 115, then at 112, you are not due a report.

Table 5-1 summarizes the types of orders that can be transacted.

TABLE 5-1   Different Types of Orders

Order Type	Description	Pros and Cons
Market	The best price available at the time of trade.	The order will get done, probably; but the execution price is uncertain.
Short Sale	Selling stock or exchange shares you do not own; you must get protection from the brokerage firm prior to placing the order.	This order enables you to take advantage of a falling market or stock; the upside risk is unlimited, however. It must be done in a margin account.
Stop Order	Once a security has traded at a stop price, the order becomes a market order.	Serves as protection for a security position; because it becomes a market order, the execution price is uncertain.
Limit	An order to buy or sell with a limit as to price.	You can control the execution price, but there is no guarantee of an execution.
Stop Limit	A stop order that also contains a limit of the execution price.	The execution price minimum is already determined, but the trade may not get done.

ADDITIONAL QUALIFICATIONS ON ORDERS

There are two time conditions on orders, day orders and good-til-canceled (GTC) orders.

A *day order* is good for the present trading day and expires if not executed. If unspecified, an order is considered a day order. A *GTC order* is good until the customer cancels it.

An *all-or-none (AON) order* specifies that the number of shares you buy or sell must trade together or the trade not be done. In listed stocks and index shares, you can only place an AON with a limit.

Placing an AON order might force the specialist to fill you in advance of other orders, especially if he wants to trade on the other side of your order. It may also mean that you won't get filled at all. Moreover, the specialist cannot hold your order in his book. The orders without conditions get filled first.

An *immediate-or-cancel (IOC) order* is used when you want the broker to fill as much of the order as possible at once and cancel the portion of the order she cannot fill. The specialist does not enter the order in her book. She executes as many shares as possible and sends an immediate response. The order must have a limit, and it is done in listed shares only.

A *minimum order* is used when you want the specialist to execute a set number of shares at a limit price with a condition. The first fill must contain a minimum number of shares. For example, if you place an order to buy 2000 QQQ at 90 with a minimum of 1000, the first fill must be 1000 shares. After that first trade, the fills can be of any size. You could also specify that trades be done in certain amounts—lots of 500 shares, for instance.

A minimum order is used when you want to make sure you get enough stock when attempting a trade. Again, you may not get a fill if the stock doesn't reach your price. The order is not held in the specialist's book.

A *fill-or-kill (FOK) order* is the same as the IOC order except that the order must be filled in full or canceled. It allows no partial fill. If the specialist cannot complete the order, it will be canceled at once.

A market order to execute at the closing price or as near to it as possible is a *market-on-close order*. This type of order can be entered on listed or Nasdaq stocks. To be executed, this order must be received at least 20 minutes before the close. A market-on-close makes sense if you have tried to execute a limit order with no success and want to get off a trade before the market closes. Another time to use this order is when you think the price will be best at the end of the trading day.

A *not-held order* is mostly used for larger orders, say 10,000 shares or more. The not-held is employed when you don't want to move the market and when the price you receive is more important than getting the trade done quickly, or at all. On a not-held order you are giving the floor broker discretion in how to complete the order. The discretion has to do with price and size and whether the order is to be completed. Depending on market conditions, you may not get a fill with a not-held order. With exchange shares you would seldom need to employ a not-held order. Their vast liquidity means size is rarely a factor in that market.

Table 5-2 illustrates the conditions you can place on orders, depending on the outcome desired with a particular trade.

TABLE 5-2   Conditions You Can Place on Orders

Order Qualifiers	Pros and Cons
Fill or Kill	The trade is completed or killed. The trade has no standing in the specialist's book, however, and may not get done.
All or None	The complete order will get done or cancelled; there is no certainty of an execution.
Immediate or Cancel	Sets the price, and a portion of the order can execute; no certainty of an execution.
Minimums	Sets a minimum size that the order can trade in; no certainty of an execution.
Not Held	Gives the broker an opportunity to get a better price; no guarantee the trade will get done.
Market on Close	Guaranteed *when* the execution will be done—near the market close; execution price is uncertain.

MORE TRADING NUANCES

Market openings are not normal market conditions. The specialist and market makers must set an opening price based on all the orders accumulated since the prior day's close. One-third of a day's trading can occur at the market open. A limit order, therefore, might be advisable on the opening because the execution price can differ from the prior day's quotes.

Sometimes, it takes a while to receive a report, especially with orders that have conditions. The specialist and market maker stays busy filling orders, updating quotes, and reporting trades. She may get so busy filling orders, she doesn't have time to reflect the fill back to the broker.

MISCONCEPTIONS ABOUT ONLINE TRADING

When you click on the mouse, even if it seems as if you have a direct connection to the market, in fact, you do not. When you click on the order key, the order is relayed to your broker, who then sends it for execution to the marketplace. With exchange shares the order goes from your broker to the

> Remember, you do not send your order to the floor. You send it to your broker, who relays it to the floor or the market maker. Brokers always stand between you and the point of execution.

specialist on the ASE floor. Although systems usually run smoothly, it is not guaranteed they will. Orders can back up, systems can go down, lines can fail, you name it.

Also, when you cancel an order online, the order is not really cancelled until it gets to the market. When you receive an electronic confirmation of a cancel request, this only means your cancel request was received by your broker, not that the order was actually canceled.

WHERE THE ORDER GOES

A click of the mouse, and your order is sent, but to where?

The order leaves your terminal and goes to the broker. The broker relays orders for exchange shares and listed stocks in one of two ways, electronically over lines that feed into the exchange and then route them to the specialist's post, or to a floor broker who then walks the order to the trading post. Bigger orders or complex orders are usually handled by floor brokers.

The actual trading is done by the specialist. The specialist displays limit orders on an electronic work station at his post. The work stations keep track of the orders, sorting them by time and price priority.

The chart represented in Figure 5-1 shows order flows for stock and exchange shares.

GETTING STARTED ONLINE

The investing world has changed dramatically over the last few years. It seems the pace of change picks up almost monthly. To do a good job for herself, an investor needs to be informed about the various types of brokerage firms and the services they provide.

DISCOUNT AND FULL-SERVICE BROKERS

Discount and full-service brokers are rapidly converging. All brokers are offering an increasing number of variations on the discounting and full-service themes.

A discount broker executes trades at lower prices than a full service firm. Most of these firms offer online or conventional "talk to a broker"

FIGURE 5-1   Order Flow for Exchange Shares

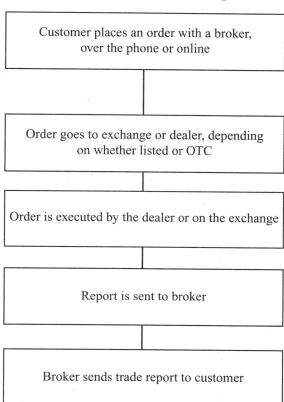

trading. For a listing of discount brokers, turn to Appendix B, The Electronic Index Investor and Trader Research Source.

A full-service broker provides a wide range of services to clients. These services include advice on stocks, bonds, exchange shares, mutual funds, and other investments. Although late to the online game, the full-service firms are starting to allow customers to use their online facilities. They have to. It is estimated that online trading now comprises about 25 percent of all trading.

With so many brokers out there eager to handle your trades, there's no reason not to be with one you are comfortable with. And unless you are a savvy computer user and a bit of a market savant, you should not pick a broker based on execution cost only. Cheapest may not be best for you. Transaction costs have dropped so low over the past few years than even many of the higher online transaction fees are not that big a factor. A successful trade makes execution costs insignificant.

Often, you get what you pay for, and there is a reason some brokers charge so little. They don't offer much in the way of service, and service can be vital when navigating the market on the Internet.

To get started, you open up an account with an e-broker and sit down in front of your computer. You click on the broker's home page. At this site you will find research, stock quotes, market updates, and other information. Then you type in your account number and give your password. It is simple. The home page instructions will walk you through it. Most brokers have built-in safeguards that question your commands so that you don't make a mistake due to unfamiliarity with the broker's systems.

Usually, you can customize your operation. You can select to have the screen default and go directly to trading after you log in. The home page will show available highlights and special features. You can go directly into your account, which shows positions, trade history, trades canceled, checks written, and funds deposited and withdrawn.

No matter where you are in the broker's system, there is usually a "quick quote" option, which is a current quote on stocks or exchange shares.

To place a trade, you click on the trade icon and are routed to the trading screen. You click on a symbol, buy or sell or short, quantity, and any conditions, then send. At this point, most brokers will have some advice appear, as well as the amount of the trade, the bid or offer price, and the commission. Then you click on "place order"—or cancel, if you change your mind—and the order is sent. Shortly after clicking "place order," you can click on status. In an active market you can usually get an execution back within 30 seconds.

DIFFERENT TYPES OF BROKERS

Although it is convenient to label a person a certain financial type, this labeling is always only an approximation. People's financial dealings represent an amalgam of objectives and a range of financial interests and goals. Not only this, people change over time. The investor of today can become the most active trader of tomorrow. Not all of this is due to age. Although financial experts invariably assume that as people age, they get more conservative, in the real world things are just not so predictable. The conservative investor 30 years old can, and sometimes does, become the hippest trader on the planet at 75. So I've broken investors/traders down into four categories, knowing that one can move from one group into another swiftly and easily and also can straddle the categories. After each category is the type of broker that makes a good match.

If you are a long-term investor and don't care so much about trading, you'll want a broker that you think is substantial and will be there in the future. Also, an investor wants access to products other than just exchange shares and stocks. You may want help with mutual funds, options, Treasuries, corporate bonds, tax-free municipal bonds, limited partnerships, and other products. If you're investing for the long-term, execution costs are not as important.

Following are some specific brokers who fit in with long-term objectives:

Fidelity Investments, www.fidelity.com, (800-544-7272): This firm offers an abundance of products and tools for fashioning a portfolio. The company has recently spent a lot of money upgrading its Web site to make sure there is very little downtime on the site.

Charles Schwab, www.schwab.com, (800-435-4000): Management of Schwab is committed to educating and helping individual investors. The firm is cutting-edge in anticipating and filling customer needs.

Waterhouse, www.waterhouse.com, (800-934-4410): *Money* magazine and *Smart Money* magazine rated Waterhouse one of the fastest in execution time. Estimated execution time is 2.8 seconds per transaction. They offer three ways of trading: over the Internet, through a live broker, or with their automated telephone system.

The second investor category includes those who are looking for investment opportunities in either trading or longer-term investments. This is sort of a mixed-bag category, and where most people fit. This group likes to tinker with their investments, stay up on trends, do some trading. They don't want to spend hours each day in front of the computer.

The following brokers are a good match for this category:

DLJ Direct, www.dljdirect.com, (800-825-5723): This company offers access to IPOs, and free DLJ research for accounts of $100,000 and over. No minimum balance is required. Their "Tradetalk" service allows touch-tone automated trading service, quotes, and market updates.

Fidelity Investments, www.fidelity.com, (800-544-7272): Fidelity offers IPOs and a wide range of financial products. Its selection of in-house mutual funds is among the largest. Research and company profiles can be found at the site.

Charles Schwab, www.schwab.com, (800-435-4000): Schwab has special services for customers with accounts over $100,000 and a support team and services to customers with accounts $500,000 and up. Their many branches allow them to help customers with special needs.

The active investor class is the fastest-growing one, unquestionably aided by the Internet. With the explosion of online research and trading, this new class of investors has emerged. Those who once would have spoken to their brokers a few times a week now spend a few hours a day in front of the screen trading and looking for ideas.

Trading from your own terminal with the speed and ease the online brokers offer makes trading kind of fun, especially when you are making money. Figure 5-2 shows market share for the leading online brokers.

The following firms are good brokers for active investors:

Datek, www.datek.com, (888-463-2835): This site offers real-time quotes. They feature the Datek streamer, in which you can load up to 40 stocks, which stocks are updated every few seconds.

Suretrade, www.suretrade.com, (401-642-6900): This broker is a division of Quick & Reilly, which is owned by Fleet Bank. Fleet is merging with BankBoston to make the eighth largest bank in the nation. There are no minimum deposits required and no fees on any special types of accounts, such as IRA accounts.

Discover, www.discoverbrokerage.com, (800-347-2683): Tied in to Morgan Stanley research, Discover research is free for accounts with over $100,000 in assets. In recent years, Discover has been rated number one in *Barron's* twice.

The fourth class of market participant is the active trader. Active traders are not interested in long-term investing. Their objective is to make money, to get in and out of positions as quickly and profitably as possible.

In a broker, this group wants good trading capability and low execution costs. But traders also need stability. They don't want to change firms once they get busy trading. If a firm fails or merges or runs short of capital, its ability to service traders could be disrupted. Traders find interruptions time-consuming and costly.

Among others, these brokers fit the bill:

Datek, www.datek.com, (888-463-2835): Datek offers reliable trading and quick execution reporting. They charge $9.99 for a limit order of up to 5000 shares.

E*Trade, www.trade.com, (800-786-2575): This firm has been operating since 1981 and has over a million customers. For listed orders up to 5000 shares, the commission is $14.95. Over 5000 shares the charge is $14.95 plus $0.01 per share. The company has its own electronic network for executing orders.

Web Street, www.webstreet.com, (800-932-8723): At their "trading pit" you can view market news, your portfolio, quotes, and also place trades. The site features a Nasdaq "level 2" screen where you can check market makers' bids, asked, and sizes.

Sites to learn more about online brokers

www.fool.com: The Motley Fool brokerage center

www.keynote.com: Keynote Systems' online brokerage index

www.gomez.com: Gomez Advisors' Internet broker ratings

www.xolia.com: Online investment assistance

FIGURE 5-2   The Biggest Online Brokers

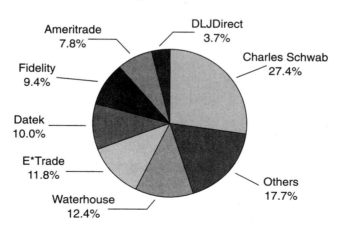

Source: Courtesy of *Business Week*

RESEARCH AND OTHER SERVICES

Probably the best source of research and other financial information is on the Internet. The online brokers supply much of this material. News stories and general market news are found on the online broker's page. You can search for corporate or market developments, even if they happened many months back, and find them online.

Also, traders can pull up charts on stocks and exchange shares. You can find charts going back six months, twelve months, two years, even decades. If you want to change the time frame and draw your own charts, you can design charts as short as one month, two days, one day. You can chart by the hour, by the minute—virtually whatever time frame you want.

So there is plenty of support out there. You just have to find the broker that fits. And just what are your needs? Only you can make that determination. To do that, you have to know something about your financial goals and the type of investor or trader you are.

II

THE DIFFERENT CLASSES OF EXCHANGE SHARES

6

THE SELECT
SECTOR SPDRs

THE IMPORTANCE OF SECTOR SELECTION

Exchange shares are the most useful instruments available to participate in the various sectors of the market. With exchange shares you can choose the group of stocks that offers the most potential for appreciation (to be bought) or decline (to be shorted). The nine sectors of the market can be bought or sold or shorted during market hours. You can also buy or sell, or sell naked, options in the different sectors.

There are many scholarly studies indicating that the predominant factor in making a profit in a portfolio is not market timing or stock selection but investment policy. One such study based on data from 91 large U.S. pension plans over the 1974–1983 period indicated that investment policy explained, on average, 94.6 percent of the variation in total plan return.* A follow-up study of 82 large pension plans over 1977–1987 indicated that,

---

*Brinson, Hood, and Beebower, *Financial Analysts Journal*, July–August 1986.

on average, 91.5 percent of the variation in quarterly total plan returns was due to investment policy.

These studies show that how you allocate your assets is the important factor: stocks or bonds, bonds or cash, energy stocks or utility stocks, basic industries stocks or technology stocks, Japanese stocks or Thailand stocks or Swedish stocks, whatever. Weighting is important, too, the percentage of the total portfolio placed in each sector.

Figure 6-1 illustrates the importance of asset allocation.

With Select Sector SPDRs, the stock selection work has been done for you. The sectors are carved up using the stocks in the S&P 500, probably the most representative group of stocks available. All you have to do is select the sectors that you want to buy or sell or short. If you are right on the sector, chances are you will have a profitable trade.

THE EVOLUTION OF SELECT SECTOR SPDRs

Standard & Poor's has had the S&P 500 index divided into different sectors for years, but it wasn't until Merrill Lynch (ML) came into the picture and devised a way to allow the public to buy and sell the sectors through Select Sector SPDRs that the concept of sector investing became widespread.

Several years ago, WEBS were the only traded exchange shares. Then SPY and MDY were added. The ML strategists determined that they wanted to be part of the exchange share activity and pondered how they could fit in. The strategists created a model equity portfolio. In the model portfolio ML maintained sectors that loosely followed S&P's sector breakdown and contained many of the S&P 500 stocks.

Usually, the words *sector* and *industry* are used interchangeably, but at ML industry groups roll up to equal a sector. For instance, multinational

FIGURE 6-1 The Importance of Asset Allocation

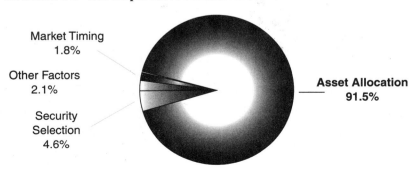

Market Timing 1.8%

Other Factors 2.1%

Security Selection 4.6%

Asset Allocation 91.5%

banks, regional banks, savings and loans, brokerage firms, insurance companies, and REITs are the industry groups that comprise the financial sector.

The portfolio that ML developed was consistent with their sector weighting strategy. They picked the stocks that fit into their categories to complete a sector, such as the consumer staples sector, the energy sector, and so on. The ML strategists overweighted or underweighted the sectors to build the ML model portfolio. The strategist might say, for instance, "I like financials, and I don't like technology stocks so much, so I'll cut my exposure from 30 percent financials and 40 percent technology stocks, normal weighting, to 50 percent financials and 20 percent technology."

This model portfolio was designed for the institutional investor. The model assumed an investment horizon of 12 months, the length of time with which most institutions are concerned. About three years ago, ML decided that in addition to this portfolio, they wanted portfolios for the individual investor. These portfolios would have a three- to five-year investment horizon and would fit a growth or an income objective.

The growth portfolio focuses more on areas such as technology and consumer staples and is less inclined to buy utilities and other income sectors. The reverse is true for the income investor. For example, a 75-year-old person who wanted an equity exposure but also desired an income type of portfolio would buy the financial, energy, and utilities sectors and avoid the technology and consumer staples sectors. Other sectors could be added to further weight the portfolio, depending on the investor's objectives. This system is still essentially being followed.

Once Merrill Lynch had the strategy, they used it in an exchange share format. They put together a new model portfolio using only S&P 500 stocks. They took the S&P 500 index, broke it into sectors, and created Select Sector SPDRs. They then weighted the sectors into portfolios to achieve different objectives, according to each customer's investment profile and goals. Using SPDRs, they ended up with a growth model portfolio, an income model, and a capital appreciation model, customizing portfolios by using different weightings of the Select SPDRs.

INDIVIDUAL- AND INSTITUTIONAL-BUILT PORTFOLIOS

With the development of Sector SPDRs, individuals and institutions can customize their own portfolio. The Sector SPDRs offer a twofold strategy possibility:

1.   If you want to customize the S&P 500 by weighting the different sectors, you can.

2.   If you want a pure sector play, you can accomplish this. If you want technology exposure, for instance, you can purchase the 82 stocks in the S&P 500 by buying the Technology Select SPDR.

THE TYPES OF STOCKS IN THE SELECT SECTOR SPDRs

A listing of the stocks in all the Select Sector SPDRs can be found in Appendix A. The listing includes forward earnings, major sources of revenues, multiples for the industrials, and dividends for the utilities. The reason for showing price-earnings multiples for the industrials is because the types of stocks in the Select Sectors lend themselves to analysis in terms of the price as a multiple of earnings. Except for the Technology Select Sector, the sorts of stocks in the Select Sectors are not explosive growth performers. The P/E multiple can be used to gauge an over or undervaluation. Many of these companies are selling at higher than historical P/E multiples. This is not a bad thing in itself, but raises a caution flag. Investors should question whether future earnings prospects justify this high appraisal.

The Basic Industries Select Sector SPDR (XLB)

The companies in the Basic Industries Select Sector SPDR are just as they sound, basic. They represent the basic industries in the economy: steel, paper, chemicals, gold, and the like. These types of companies are cyclical. They are basic material companies that will move up and down with general economic activity. The group is heavily weighted by chemicals, which makes the group sensitive to the fortunes of chemical stocks: E.I. du Pont de Nemours (DD), 18.93 percent of the group weighting; Monsanto Co. (MTC), 9.43 percent; and Dow Chemical Co. (DOW), 6.38 percent.

The Consumer Services Select Sector SPDR (XLV)

These companies deliver services to the public. The service sector of the economy has grown substantially over the last several years, making it one of the most dynamic sectors of the economy. Normally, the companies in this sector have decent growth rates. The bigger stocks in the group focus on entertainment, but there is also prominent representation from restaurant, cable television, newspaper, and health care companies. Companies with the largest percentage weight in the sector are as follows: Time Warner, Inc., 12.36 percent; Walt Disney Corp., 9.98 percent; McDonalds Corp., 8.41 percent.

The Consumer Staples Select Sector SPDR (XLP)

Companies in this sector are rather impervious to general economic conditions. The sector is replete with beverage, cigarette, cosmetic, drug, and other such companies. These are products that people use every day, and they will continue to purchase them, almost no matter what the economy does. Smokers will light up a cigarette. People will stop and share a soda. Women will use lipstick. If someone gets a headache, she will take an aspirin. The sector is weighted heavily by Merck and Company, Inc., 7.88 percent; Coca-Cola, 7.38 percent; and Pfizer, Inc., 7.29 percent.

The Cyclical/Transport Select Sector SPDR (XLY)

Companies in XLY are very tied to general market activity. If the economy is strong, the companies in the sector will benefit. If the economy is weak, the companies fare poorly. Many of them are retailers, and the type of retailing represented ranges from department stores to specialty apparel. In good economic times, when consumers have money to spend, they will go out and buy durable goods and major items. Included in the sector are companies dealing in basic consumer products, such as autos, washing machines, and auto parts. Dominating the sector are Wal-Mart Stores, 22.03 percent; Home Depot, Inc., 11.49 percent; and Ford Motor Co., 8.53 percent.

The Energy Select Sector SPDR (XLE)

The price of oil and gas affects the companies of the XLE sector more than any other factor. Included in the SPDR are domestic and international oil companies, drillers, refiners, and natural gas explorers and distributors. The companies with the largest percentage representation in the sector are Exxon Corporation, 24.13 percent; Royal Dutch Petroleum, 16.41 percent; and Mobil Corporation, 10.91 percent.

The Financial Select Sector SPDR (XLF)

The biggest driver here is interest rates. These companies have leveraged balance sheets, which makes interest rate changes affect their performance. When rates decline, the companies pay less for the money they borrow, and the financial stocks tend to outperform. When rates head higher, the opposite happens and financials tend to underperform. This SPDR contains everything from multinational banks to brokerage firms and insurance companies. The sector is led by American International Group, Inc., at 7.63 percent of the sector weighting; Citigroup, Inc., 7.19 percent; BankAmerica Corporation, 6.65 percent; and Federal National Mortgage Association, 4.90 percent.

The Industrial Select Sector SPDR (XLI)

This group is made up of major companies that are the industrial component of the S&P 500 index. The largest piece of this sector is General Electric (GE), with a 22.8 percent weighting. Having GE in the sector is slightly misleading because its capital service business is its largest revenue source. GE still qualifies, however, due to its industrial divisions. The other companies in the sector are in construction, waste management services, and electrical equipment. General economic activity is a key component to this sector's prospects. The sector is dominated by the following companies and their percentage weighting to the sector: General Electric, 22.80 percent; Tyco International, 9.40 percent; Minnesota Mining and Manufacturing, 5.62 percent; and Emerson Electric, 5.41 percent.

The Technology Select Sector SPDR (XLK)

XLK is a pure play on the S&P 500 technology stocks. What is missing in this SPDR are some of the newer, volatile OTC issues. But the SPDR has recently added American OnLine, Inc. (AOL), the only pure Internet company listed in the S&P 500. Although technology is viewed as a pure growth area, don't be mistaken. There is a very large cyclical component to the technology segment. When economic activity slows, people stop spending on new computers as well as other items. The larger company weights in this sector are Microsoft, 14.07 percent; Intel Corp., 8.04 percent; IBM, 7.01 percent; and Cisco, 5.96 percent.

The Utilities Select Sector SPDR (XLU)

This sector is comprised of companies that supply electric and gas utilities to consumers. Also included are telephone utilities, which is a group experiencing rapid change. The traditional local phone company is becoming more of a technology company. XLU pays the largest dividend of all the sectors, about 3 percent annualized. In Appendix A you'll find annualized dividends rather than price-earnings multiples, since utilities are usually viewed as a bond substitute or an income investment. The heavier company weights in the sector are SBC Communications, Inc., 14.57 percent; Bell-South Corp., 13.55 percent; and Bell Atlantic Corp., 11.43 percent.

OPTION STRATEGIES USING SELECT SECTOR SPDRs

Depending on the demand and activity in the option market, good returns might be had by purchasing a sector SPDR and writing a covered call against it. Table 6-1 illustrates a sale of one January 2000 call and a simultaneous purchase of XLK. In this example prices were given as of January 26, 1999. The results are given for doing the trade on a margin or cash basis.*

---

*All of the examples in this book disregard taxes and transaction costs; for these kinds of issues, I suggest you consult with your tax advisor.

TABLE 6-1

	Cash	Margin
Buy 100 Shares of XLK at $36.25	$3625	$3625
No Commission	0	0
Total Purchase Price	3625	3625
50% Federal Call Equals Debit Balance		1813
Write 1 January 38 Call (expiring 2000)		
at $5.125	$513	$513
No Commission	0	0
Net Proceeds of Options Sale	513	513
Net Dollar Amount Invested	$3113	$1300

Table 6-2 illustrates the result if XLK is called away. The option seller does not share in profit above 38. The seller has to deliver the shares.

TABLE 6-2

	Cash	Margin
Sell 100 Shares of XLK at $38.00	$3800	$3800
Less Debit Balance		($1813)
Less Interest on Debit Balance @ 8.00% for 359 Days		($108)
No Commission	$0	$0
Equals Net Proceeds of Option Exercise	$3800	$1879
Dollar Outlay	($3113)	($1300)
Subtotal	$688	$579
No Dividends	$0	$0
Net Profit	$688	$579
Percent Return (Net Profit/Dollar Investment)	22.09%	44.57%

Table 6-3 shows what happens if XLK stays at 36.25 a share or moves lower. The writer will retain XLK.

TABLE 6-3

	Cash	Margin
Proceeds of Option Sale	$513	$513
No Commission	$0	$0
Net Proceeds of Option Sale	$513	$513
No Dividends	$0	$0
Subtotal	$513	$513
Interest on Debit Balance		($108)
Net Profit	$513	$404
Percent Return (Net Profit/Dollar Investment)	16.47%	31.11%

Table 6-4 shows the breakeven point. Below this point, the writer will be in a loss position.

TABLE 6-4

	Cash	Margin
Gross Purchase Price of XLK	$3625	$3625
Less Gross Premium	($513)	($513)
No Stock Commission	$0	$0
No Option Commission	$0	$0
Plus Interest		$108
No Dividends	$0	$0
Break-even per Share	$31.13	$32.21

"MARRIED PUTS" USING SELECT SECTOR SPDRs

Another tactic that can be used with sector SPDRs, as well as the other exchange shares, is using a married put. A married put is the simultaneous purchase of exchange shares and a put.

As covered earlier in the book, a put is an option contract that allows the buyer to sell a number of exchange shares at a price, called a strike price, on or before its expiration date. Buying shares and puts simultaneously limits the buyer's loss. The goal is for the shares to appreciate more than the price of the put, plus or minus the "in" or "out" of the money as related to the strike price, less any value when the buyer closes out the position, less the amount of dividends received.

This strategy is important. You can hedge a long position and limit its risk. The put establishes a minimum selling price for the shares during the life of the put, while the long side maintains its unlimited profit potential.

The out of the money or in the money factor could be significant. As an example, if you purchase XLE and an XLE put at 35, and the put strike price is 40, you are in the money by five points. If the strike price is 30, you are out of the money by five points. You receive the dividends while holding the exchange shares; therefore, add any dividends to your profit side.

The thought may occur to you that buying shares and marrying a put to the shares equals a call. Actually it does. You could accomplish this same position by buying a call. But then you would not have the physical security to hold. If you buy XLE at 35 and marry a put to it, for example, and XLE dips to 30 at the put expiration date, you can still hold XLE. Then you can decide to buy another put or just hold the shares. If instead of buying XLE you purchased an XLE call, and if XLE did not appreciate, you would have zero to show for your investment at the call expiration date.

Here's an example of how a married put would work.

Suppose you purchase 500 shares of XLK at 40. Simultaneously, you purchase five put options with a strike price at 40, through nine months. You pay three points per option, the total price being $1500. For $1500 you are now protected against loss, much like buying home insurance. If after eight months or so, XLK is at 35, you simply put your shares to the seller at 40, or keep XLK and sell the five puts. They are worth five points now, plus any time premium. So you can sell the puts for about $2500, deduct the $1500 you paid, and realize a $1000 loss. The loss would have been $2500 without owning the put. The point, however, is that the most you can lose during the put life is $1500, even if XLK goes to $2.00 a share.

Using a married put, you can limit your loss to the cost of the premium paid while maintaining the unlimited upside potential of the exchange shares. Using this strategy makes it possible to go for big gains while limiting risk.

TAKING LOSSES, AVOIDING "WASH SALES," AND
SUBSTITUTING WITH EXCHANGE SHARES

If you have a portfolio with many losses, have decided to take the losses, but still want representation in the group, exchange shares can be useful. For instance, say that you have a portfolio of energy stocks. The price of oil is down, but you expect it to rebound. You want to take the losses, but you don't want out of the energy sector.

When you take a loss, under U.S. tax laws, transactions are deemed *wash sales* if essentially identical securities are bought within 30 days before or after a sale. The losses on wash sales are added to the newly bought securities, and the taken loss is not immediately deductible for tax purposes.

What you can do is double up and then sell after 30 days. For example, suppose you own 500 shares of Exxon, with a five-point loss. You can purchase an additional 500 shares of Exxon, wait 31 days, then sell the 500 original shares. Or you can take a chance and not buy more shares. Simply sell the 500 Exxon and wait 31 days before rebuying Exxon.

Another option is to replace the Exxon shares with XLE. You would get broad oil group representation through the SPDR and not be limited to one stock. Whether or not the wash sale provision is still relevant to your portfolio and its replacement would depend on how similar the shares you are selling are to the shares bought as a replacement. Check with your tax advisor for advice on your portfolio.

7

DIA

THE DOW JONES INDUSTRIAL AVERAGE DURABILITY

Even though the argument is often put forward that an index benchmark is better than an average benchmark, and that indexes with more stocks are better than the Dow Jones Industrial Average (Dow), with only 30, the fact remains that the Dow has been around longer than any market barometer and has as much or more credibility than the other benchmarks.

The main reason the Dow is still prominent is simple: It works. The Dow tells the general direction of the stock market, and it has done this since 1896. As far as the market going up or down, the Dow correlates very well with the S&P 500 index. It matches that index 95 percent of the time. Also, people understand the concept of the Dow. They are comfortable with the use of an average, and with adding up prices and dividing by something. This is true even though the Dow's divisor has changed. Because of stock splits, stock substitutions, spinoffs, and other factors, the divisor was changed in 1928, and Dow Jones continues to upgrade the divisor to keep the average current.

The other market measures are capitalization-weighted, so a point move in a company is magnified by the size of the company. A big company makes more of an impact on the index than a small company. That is not so with the Dow, since it is a price-weighted measure. A point move in a small company has the same impact as a move in a big company. It is debatable which measure is more meaningful.

The Dow Jones is popular with individual investors. The bull market we're experiencing currently has been fueled by money from individuals, whether it is money from 401 (k) plans or profit-sharing plans or from company options or investment funds generated by the present economic prosperity. It's safe to say that very few money managers foresaw the size of the demand coming from the individual sector over the last several years. That brings us to another reason for the popularity of the Dow. Ordinary people relate to the portfolio. The stocks are those of giant, household-name companies that individual investors know. Furthermore, people can relate to just 30 stocks. They typically have about 20 or so in their portfolios, so they relate better to a low number of stocks. Dealing with 500 stocks or 2000 stocks can be confusing.

Besides, when you buy DIA, although it is true that you are buying only 30 stocks, those 30 stocks represent about 20 percent of the $10.0 trillion market capitalization of all U.S. stocks.

Table 7-1 lists the 30 stocks in the Dow Jones Industrial Average. For a fundamental sketch of each stock, see the stock listings in Appendix A.

TABLE 7-1 The DJIA Companies—30 in All

Company Name	Symbol	Price	Weighting (%)
AlliedSignal Inc.	(ALD)	56.2500	2.591
Alcoa Inc.	(AA)	60.7500	2.798
American Express Co.	(AXP)	147.2500	6.783
AT&T Corp.	(T)	46.9375	2.162
Boeing Co.	(BA)	42.9375	1.977
Caterpillar Inc.	(CAT)	56.9375	2.622
Citigroup Inc.	(C)	53.5625	2.467
Coca-Cola Co.	(KO)	57.5625	2.651
DuPont Co.	(DD)	62.1875	2.864
Eastman Kodak Co.	(EK)	69.8125	3.215
Exxon Corp.	(XON)	73.5625	3.388
General Electric Co.	(GE)	131.8750	6.074

TABLE 7-1 (*Continued*)

Company Name	Symbol	Price	Weighting (%)
General Motors Corp.	(GM)	67.750	3.120
Home Depot,Inc.	(HD)	75.8750	3.495
Hewlett-Packard Co.	(HWP)	72.2500	3.325
International Business Machines Corp.	(IBM)	93.6250	4.312
Intel Corp.	(INTC)	79.6875	3.670
International Paper Co.	(IP)	52.3750	2.412
J.P. Morgan & Co.	(JPM)	130.4375	6.008
Johnson & Johnson	(JNJ)	104.8125	4.828
McDonald's Corp.	(MCD)	42.4375	1.954
Merck & Co.	(MRK)	80.3750	3.702
Microsoft Corp.	(MSFT)	92.8750	4.278
Minnesota Mining & Manufacturing Co.	(MMM)	95.0000	4.376
Philip Morris Cos.	(MO)	23.9375	1.102
Procter & Gamble Co.	(PG)	106.5000	4.905
SBC Communications Inc.	(SBC)	50.3125	2.317
United Technologies Corp.	(UTX)	59.8750	2.758
Wal-Mart Stores Inc.	(WMT)	56.0000	2.579
Walt Disney Co.	(DIS)	27.0000	1.243

THE DOW JONES INDUSTRIAL AVERAGE PERFORMANCE

Figures 7-1 and 7-2 illustrate the performance of the Dow over a period of time.

In Figure 7-1, notice how steep the climb is that started in 1986. Do conditions now represent a blowoff phase or the continuation of an upward climb? Chartists have their opinion. The problem is, chartists could read the future either way. Perhaps time will tell.

Figure 7-2 shows that most of this century's market advance has come during the last 40 years or so. The first 60 years were pretty dull for the averages. It is interesting to note that during this long-term climb in the Dow, companies have gone out of business, people have been born and died, industry sectors have risen and fallen, buggy companies are gone, huge land trusts are not around, and locomotive manufacturers are history. Yet the Dow Jones Average has climbed relentlessly, paused, declined, and climbed some more.

FIGURE 7-1   Dow Jones Industrial Average, 1968–1999

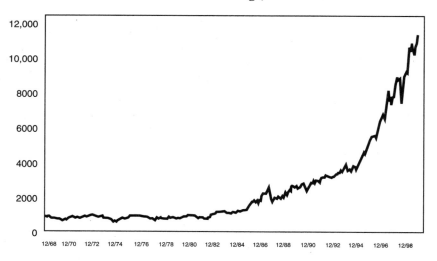

FIGURE 7-2   Dow Jones Industrial Average, 1996–1999

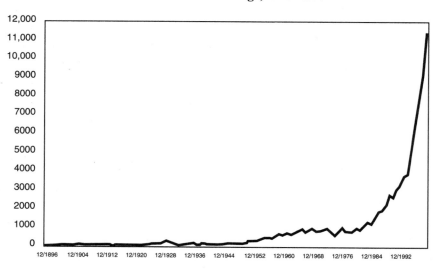

> A very good reason to buy index shares for the long term is that although individual companies come and go, worldwide business activity continues to spur new highs in the broader averages and indexes.

VALUE VERSUS GROWTH STOCKS IN THE DOW

Growth stocks are the stocks of companies that are growing faster than average, and for which this growth level is expected to continue. Investors will pay a higher multiple of earnings to own growth stocks. *Value stocks* are stocks of companies that have high intrinsic value, such as a high book value, a high rate of sales to price, a high cash position, or some other undervalued feature. Many people consider Dow stocks to be value stocks rather than growth issues. This is not necessarily true. For instance, Alcoa (AA) was considered a value stock early in 1999, when it was selling at about 30. Six months later, the stock was selling in the 45 area, a gain of 50 percent. Because it appreciated so much in value, does this mean it was a growth stock at 30? If it was a value stock at that price, is it still a value stock? A value or growth designation is highly subjective. Price is such a strong influence on classification. Probably, too much is made of stock "style"; what is important is appreciation, no matter what style.

One thing is certain about the stocks in the Dow. Many are of a cyclical nature. Stocks such as DD, GM, and IP are older, more established companies, the types of companies that have always been included in the Dow. Cyclical companies tend to go up and down with the general economy. Add to this that the people at Dow Jones want to change the composition of the average as little as possible. They feel that low turnover allows the average to offer a steady measurement of certain stocks during many market fluctuations. And Dow Jones feels that this stability is what makes investors trust the Dow Jones Average. Other benchmarks experience more turnover. For instance, the S&P 500 turns over about one stock per month in its portfolio.

Another characteristic of the Dow is that it is a big-stock index. It is not a weathervane for smaller stocks, but its direction is not totally irrelevant for them. Anything that happens in the world's economies will ultimately affect the Dow Jones stocks, and this, in turn, will affect the other market benchmarks. If the Dow is going up, there is a general feeling of prosperity, and the consequent investor euphoria will eventually spill over to the smaller stocks.

No benchmark is perfect for all investors all of the time, but the Dow has withstood the test of time. It's probably the closest thing we have to a "gauge for all seasons."

MARRYING A "LEAPS" TO DIA

A strategy to protect against the downside risk of owning DIA while at the same time participating in its upside potential is to marry a LEAPS based on the Dow Jones Industrial Average to DIA. You buy them simultaneously. LEAPS stands for long-term equity anticipation securities. These are options that are traded on an exchange and are issued with an original life of two years or more. Both calls and puts are available in LEAPS. When the remaining life of LEAPS falls into the range of other options, they become ordinary options. LEAPS based on the Dow Jones Industrial Average are traded on the CBOE. LEAPS and other options based on the S&P 500 index are also traded there.

Marrying a LEAPS to DIA allows you to go for a long-term move in the Dow while limiting your risk. Usually, the cost for this protection is relatively low. You can also sell LEAPS and take in income.

Here is an example, the prices as of mid-June 1999.

You buy 100 shares of DIA at 109⅜. You also buy one Dow Jones Industrial Average LEAPS put, strike price 110, maturing December 2001 at 13¾. Remember, while you hold DIA, you receive any dividends paid, which reduces your cost. The dividends received on 100 DIA until December 2001, two and a half years, amounts to approximately $282.50. So the total risk—the price of DIA, plus the price of the put, minus the dividends to be received—is $1.030.

On the amount of money invested, the total amount risked, as a percentage, is about 9 percent. Over two and a half years (from mid-June 1999 until December 2001), you are risking not an annualized 9 percent, but a total 9 percent. And your upside potential is unlimited. Once DIA trades at 111³/₈, your costs are recaptured and you are in a breakeven posture. If over the next two and a half years DIA goes up over 111³/₈, the trade is profitable.

As an investment posture, this trade makes a lot of sense. It is a reasonable bet that DIA will do something big, either up or down, over the next two and a half years. For example, during the last two and a half years, DIA has gone up substantially. It has climbed by more than 40 percent in the last 12 months. History is an uncertain guide in investment matters, but if DIA continues to go up, you participate. If DIA goes down big, you are protected. That's a reasonable posture to take.

OUT-OF-THE-MONEY PUTS—LIKE BUYING DISCOUNT TERM LIFE INSURANCE

Often, options that are out of the money have a smaller time premium to the strike price than in-the-money options. For instance, with XLK at 50, a call with a strike price at 48 often will have a larger premium than a call with a strike price of 52. I am not referring to the intrinsic value of the call here—certainly, the call at 48 has a two-point value—but the value of the call due to the time remaining, and also the not-intrinsic, "where you think the shares will go" premium. Also, with XLK at 50, a put with a strike price of 52 will often have a larger premium than a put with a strike at 48.

There are times when marrying an out-of-the-money put to DIA or another exchange share makes sense.

> Using out-of-the-money puts—either as married puts or puts bought for speculation—often provides more leverage and profit potential than in-the-money puts.

Let's say DIA is selling at 110 and you want to buy it for the long term, but you think the market looks risky over the next six months. Check the prices of the out-of-the-money puts and LEAPS. Out-of-the-money options sometimes get little attention, and bargains can develop. Dow Jones Industrial Average options trade at strike price intervals of one point, so there are many investment possibilities.

If you think you have a 50 percent potential gain in a position over a 12- to 18-month period, it is probably worth paying 5 to 8 percent to protect your downside. Ordinarily, if you can keep the expense down under 5 percent, it makes sense to do the trade. But there are no fixed rules. How much gain and risk do you think the position entails, and what are you willing to pay to offset that risk? Every trade really is unique unto itself.

Premiums and index price change constantly. For a current listing of available LEAPS, visit the Web page of the Chicago Board Options Exchange at www.cboe.com. As of this writing, trading in Dow Jones Industrial Average options usually ceases on the business day preceding the exercise valuation day of the expiration month. Ordinarily, valuation is done on the third Friday of the month, so trading would cease on the third Thursday of the month of expiration.

CASH SETTLEMENTS—CLOSING OUT A DOW JONES INDUSTRIAL AVERAGE LEAPS PUT MARRIED TO DIA

Let's suppose that you did marry a LEAPS to DIA and now it is time to settle the trade. This is a cash settled transaction rather than a security versus cash transaction. In a cash transaction, you do not put DIA to the put seller and receive cash. You sell the LEAPS put in the open market and receive cash to take your profit.

Say you purchase 100 shares of DIA at 110 and buy one December 2001 LEAPS, strike price 110, at 10. If, for example, DIA goes down to 80, your put will be worth 30, plus any time premium. So you have lost 30 points on DIA and made 20 points net on the put. When you settle, you sell the put on the options market and sell or keep DIA.

For example, suppose you buy DIA and decide you want to hold it long term, but you think the market is going nowhere for a few months. You decide to take in premium income by selling calls on the Dow Jones Industrial Average. When you go to your broker to sell calls on the CBOE, your broker will probably require a margin deposit. Most firms will not count DIA holdings as a cover in a Dow call. If you get a delivery notice against your call, you have to deliver cash, and what you are holding is DIA.

A reasonable argument to your broker is that DIA will go up as the average goes up. Your broker will take the position that if the Dow Jones Average is called from you, you will have to sell DIA to raise cash. The broker's concern is that there is a lag between the time you receive the notice and sell your DIA, and that DIA may dip, leaving you short of cash to satisfy the call.

The same cash settlement applies if you purchase a Dow Jones Average call on the CBOE. Upon maturity date, if the Dow has gone up, you cannot call DIA. You can only sell the call and receive your profit in cash.

8

C H A P T E R

SPY AND MDY

USES OF SPY

Buying, selling, or shorting SPY is a way to take advantage of the first listed exchange shares. It took years of work for the ASE to structure exchange shares, and more years to receive approval from the SEC to trade them. SPY is a very important development in the investing world. If broad-based diversification is desired by an individual or institution, SPY gives it in an easy, tradeable format. SPY is an advanced methodology because it incorporates all of the features of conventional index funds and at the same time provides flexibility that conventional funds do not. SPY paved the way for other exchange share classes, both current and planned, such as country indexes and sector country indexes.

The original SPY was structured as a depositary receipt. A depositary receipt represents shares that are held in the vault of a bank or trust company, and it entitles the holder to all the dividends of the underlying stock. The purpose is to provide investors with the broad-based indexed market participation, and also to offer trading advantages beyond what they could get with an open-end index fund. SPY can be contrasted with such funds as Vanguard or Fidelity or Schwab S&P 500 index or broad-based funds.

Once the SPY concept was formalized into a product, it took the SEC about two years to approve it for trading. The delay had to do with a regulation in the Investment Company Act of 1940. This regulation specified that if the shares were labeled a mutual fund, a prospectus had to be delivered to each individual who purchased shares. Since a person might buy shares and sell them a few minutes later, there was no practical way to send a prospectus every time a person bought SPY.

The prospectus problem reflected problems in the Investment Company Act of 1940, commonly referred to as the "40 Act." The 40 Act requires investment companies to register with and be regulated by the SEC. It spells out the rules investment companies must follow in reporting to the SEC, promoting products, pricing securities that will be sold to the public, and allocating a fund's portfolio.

A depositary receipt does not require a prospectus, so SPY was launched that way. Subsequent decisions by the SEC allowed the ASE to structure SPY into a unit trust. This negated the need for the delivery of a prospectus on each purchase.

When it traded as a depositary receipt, the purchasers of the original SPY experienced nothing different from the usual security trading procedure. Back-office people did have to execute some additional paperwork and tracking. The biggest difference between the present SPY and the old depositary-receipt SPY is that the SEC has issued rules making it easier for the exchange share sponsors to develop, register, and maintain the shares.

The pioneering SPY opened the market to a new class of asset mechanisms. The development of SPY was as momentous an occasion as the introduction, in the early 1980s, of options and futures on broad market indexes. When SPY was first introduced, some market commentators thought a basket index was no different than a commodity, like pork bellies. You could also trade futures and options against SPY, which made SPY even more commoditylike. The reality is that exchange shares are much tamer than commodities, even though they can be bought on margin and shorted on downticks. Unlike commodities, there is no leverage in the shares, since they are fully backed by the underlying stocks in the indexes.

SPY was the pioneer and started a revolution. Now stock exchanges, both domestic and international, are moving to list exchange traded shares over a wide range of additional asset classes, categories, and subcategories. New products allow money managers and individuals to determine in a much more sophisticated way how they want to allocate assets to the various segments of the market.

SPY—PROXY FOR THE STOCK MARKET

An intriguing characteristic of SPY and the workings of that index is that it immediately captures everything the market is saying about which industries are growing and which companies in those industries are gaining favor.

In 1980, for instance, energy stocks were soaring, and the S&P 500 had a very high weighting in energy stocks. Energy stocks have since receded in importance and today represent a far smaller proportion of the index, under 10 percent. In contrast, technology, which had a 9 percent weighting in the index in 1980, has grown in importance. Today, technology has about a 21 percent share in the S&P index.

Another example of the changing weighting of the S&P is that without incurring any capital gains, the S&P switched Exxon from the number-one weighting in the index in the 1980s to number-eight weighting today. At the same time, they elevated General Electric and Microsoft to the top index weightings. Microsoft's sector of the economy was still small. A new age started for technology in the 1980s, and Microsoft grew and entered the S&P in 1994. Microsoft continued to expand until it now constitutes about 9 percent of the S&P 500 index. And the technology sector stocks now constitute about 21 percent of the S&P index.Similarly, the finance sector accounted for only about 10 percent of the index in 1980. Financial stocks now constitute about a 16 percent of the S&P 500 index weighting.

So the S&P index, without selling any stocks and incurring the concomitant capital gains, reweighted itself to capture the U.S. economy's earnings momentum. This reweighting is done very simply. If Microsoft stock advances four points, for instance, that appreciation is multiplied by the number of outstanding Microsoft shares. This multiplies into a higher weighting in the S&P 500 index.

The S&P 500 Committee guides the index by adding those companies that will lead the way for the economy in the future. The committee stays aware of industries in which the index is underrepresented relative to the overall U.S. economy, as well as which industries should be pared.

In the early 1990s, for instance, the committee ascertained that the index was underrepresented in the financial sector. It moved very aggressively to add more financial companies. It also became apparent that technology was exploding, was becoming the growth engine of the U.S. economy. The committee moved aggressively to beef up the technology segment of MDY and SPY.

The committee and its analysts review 56 peer groups of companies on a constant basis. It also tracks 124 industries, publishes detailed research studies on 52 broad industry categories, and does an enormous amount of monitoring of 11 economic sectors.

So it is virtually impossible that a company would gain a large market share of any industry unnoticed and untracked by the committee. S&P may choose to not put a company into an index for some reason, but the committee would surely know about that company.

LIQUIDITY—A KEY TO THE INDEX COMPANIES

Liquidity is important for SPY and MDY stocks. For instance, Berkshire Hathaway (BRK.A) is a major, dominant company, but it is not in the S&P index and will probably never be. The reason is that Warren Buffett, the chief executive officer, has put together a $100 billion-plus company. S&P knows the company, its business, and its performance.

The reason BRK.A is not in the index is that the Buffett family owns such a large proportion of the outstanding shares that BRK.A could not possibly trade in the index without upsetting the price of the shares and causing havoc in the price of the derivatives that are traded against the indexes.

The price of BRK.A would be disrupted and trade abnormally higher or lower due to its lack of liquidity. The stock is listed on the NYSE and trades so little that there usually is no action until a half-hour or so after the market opens. If BRK.A. were in the S&P, traders could move the stock up or down on very little volume, which would cause swings in the price of the S&P index. Specialists and traders would take positions in SPY and MDY and at times hedge using BRK.A stock. Traders would attempt to buy or short shares of Berkshire against the specialists and other traders. In short, including BRK.A in the S&P 500 would cause an ongoing nightmare.

Much ado is made of a stock being added to or dropped from the indexes. Traders, investors, and arbitragers all focus closely on any addition to or deletion from the index. It is really not that important an event. The committee can get any stock it wants into the indexes. All that is involved

---

Large stocks with little float do not belong in the S&P 500 index. They just don't trade enough. For this reason, you will never see Warren Buffett's Berkshire Hathaway in the index.

is transferring approximately 7 percent of the outstanding shares into the indexes. This should not have a lasting effect on the share price.

The 7 percent of the stock will be bought by various sources after a stock addition. The conventional index funds, such as Vanguard or Fidelity, will buy shares of the newly listed company. The portfolio managers who structure the exchange shares, such as State Street Trust Company, will buy shares. And other portfolio managers, such as Barclays Global Investors, will also buy shares. So, roughly 7 percent of the outstanding shares of a newly added company will end up with the owners of the indexes, including exchange share holders.

This leaves 93 percent of the shares still floating, a very liquid situation.

But in the Berkshire Hathaway matter, the Buffett family owns about 45 percent of the company. One of the partners, Charles Munger, owns a large amount, too. Other large blocks are with family friends and will not trade. S&P could garner the 7 percent that it needs to add BRK.A to the index, but after that, the lack of liquidity would make it impossible to predict the ability to trade in the stock.

For instance, if BRK.A did not trade all morning, which often happens, and one of the institutions wanted to lay off risk by purchasing shares and could not, the institution would have a problem. By laying off risk, I mean buying the underlying shares in the index against a hedge position. Perhaps the institution shorted SPY and needs to buy the underlying index stocks as a hedge.

S&P does not want stocks that are not liquid. S&P is in the business of providing "investable indexes," that is, indexes that are extremely liquid. Organizations, such as conventional index funds or exchange traded shares, do mimic the S&P 500 or MidCap 400 indexes and receive the same investment results as the index. If S&P adds a stock to one of their indexes, it is a given that the stock can be traded easily, and no market turmoil will result from buying and selling that stock in institutional-level proportions.

THE S&P INDEX STOCK SELECTION PROCESS

The S&P Index Committee is always measuring to make certain that their indexes reflect what is current in the U.S. economy and are an accurate reflection of the composition of the U.S. markets. The committee screens a database of about 10,000 companies, scrutinizing the market capitalizations of the stocks that comprise the different sectors and ascertaining the relative importance of the different industries.

And the committee constantly plans ahead. For instance, if the committee spots a company in the technology industry or some other growth sector of the small-cap group, and it appears as if the company will reach $700 million to $800 million in market capitalization in the near future, the committee may consider the company a candidate to join the S&P MidCap 400 index. Once the company grows to $1.0 billion in size, and as soon as there is an opening, it could be added to the MidCap index.

The committee meets monthly and employs a staff that works on a full-time basis. Ordinarily, SPY stocks are replaced by companies from MDY. Companies in MDY are preapproved for a move into SPY, so once a company in SPY is removed, S&P already knows its replacement. If a change is forced upon SPY by an unexpected event, the S&P Index Committee huddles in a special meeting and picks a replacement. The need for an emergency replacement is rare, however.

The committee rarely deletes a company on its own initiative. It merely responds to the marketplace. When it ascertains that an industry in the index is no longer a growth industry, it will start deleting companies in that industry from the index. Or if the committee decides a company is no longer representative of its sector, the company is deleted.

The index staff always has enough S&P 500 and 400 candidate companies identified. The staff constantly monitors corporate actions in the financial and industrial areas. If there is a merger or a takeover bid involving one of the SPY or MDY candidate companies that takes it out of contention to be moved up, the index staff knows it immediately.

The market valuation of the S&P 500 or MDY 400 stocks can also decline. There are stocks in the S&P 500 index that have fallen below $500 million in market cap. These are called "fallen angels," companies that have fallen on hard times for one reason or another and whose prices have fallen with their lower earnings.

But a stock will not be deleted just because of a short-term decline. The committee deletes a company from the indexes if it goes bankrupt or merges or shrinks to the point that it no longer is a good representative of its market segment.

GLOBAL REALIGNMENT

There is about a 20 percent technology weighting in the U.S. economy. Whether you are weighting large-cap indexes or MDY or small-cap indexes, the weighting is about 20 percent. The Wilshire 4500 stock index, the Wilshire 5000 index, and the Russell indexes all show technology at about that same weighting. The markets have made their decision and spoken about the relative importance of the different sectors. This sector weighting even spreads beyond the United States to sectors in economies around the globe.

For instance, when a global perspective is taken, the U.S. healthcare industry stands out. The healthcare industry is much larger in the United States than in any other country in the world. A cursory perusal of the European and Asian indexes shows clearly that healthcare is only about half as large in those regions as in the United States. The reason for this is because most of the major global pharmaceutical companies are located in the United States. Since the companies are domiciled here, major advertising and marketing efforts are made in the United States. Consequently, public knowledge and acceptance and use of pharmaceuticals are much higher in the United States.

But pharmaceutical use will grow and spread from the United States to the rest of the world. Because of this global growth, S&P created a healthcare sector as one of its global economic sectors. S&P believes this sector will grow explosively over the next 25 years.

And world economies will continue changing. For example, the transportation sector, so important early in this century, has shrunk to less than 1 percent of the U.S. economy. The S&P Index Committee is preparing to drop transportation as a major economic sector for its global indexes. The committee has discovered that this shrinkage of the transportation sector is also occurring globally.

Change is a constant S&P must deal with, both domestically and internationally. And although the committee resists changes in the indexes, realizing that one of the advantages of indexing is its low turnover rate, which results in lower transaction costs, both the U.S. economy and the world economy are dynamic, undergoing constant change. Since 1964, there have been 740 changes in the S&P 500 index, all things considered a remarkably high figure. In only about 36 years, 740 companies have disappeared out of the premier blue-chip list of the S&P 500, a turnover of about 150 percent.

This statistic confirms that over long periods of time, very few companies and very few CEOs are capable of keeping pace indefinitely with the swift-moving brand of capitalism that has characterized the late twentieth and early twenty-first centuries. Generally speaking, companies are going to go out of business or be taken over by other companies. Something is going to happen to dismantle almost every business, even if the enterprise keeps performing.

One interpretation of this phenomenon of disappearing companies is that high earnings margins are just about impossible to maintain. High margins attract lower margin companies to buy out the high margin companies, or if they cannot buy them out, the lower margin companies will compete with the high margin ones. Either way, margins are driven lower. This is the essence of the present dynamism in global economics.

LEADERS OF THE S&P 500, AND RISKS IN THE INDEX

If you want to know the S&P 500 market leaders, simply peruse the top several stocks in each of the sector SPDRs in Appendix A. A few top companies comprise a large portion of each sector. A total of 41 stocks constitute about 50 percent of the index, a very concentrated weighting for an index. The second 50 percent of the index is made up of the remaining 459 stocks!

The S&P index allows investors to own the top companies in the U.S. economy. In the top 41 stocks are such names as Coca-Cola, Microsoft, PepsiCo, AT&T, General Electric, Exxon, IBM, Cisco, Intel, and many more. Also, every top drug company is represented in the index.

This heavy concentration, although in good companies, is not without risk, however. Although the index is comprised of 500 names, you are not necessarily getting that broad an exposure. Those 41 companies comprising about half of the S&P index are money-making machines, and they control large operating margins. Coca-Cola, for instance, has a return on total capital of 51 percent. Microsoft reports operating margins of 25 percent.

The question is: How long will it be until competitors shrink the margins of even these behemoths? It is true that no other company can come along and replace Coca-Cola. Nevertheless, the history of high margin companies is that these margins are vulnerable. At one time all 740 companies that have been replaced in the index were high margined companies, too.

In times of market declines, this sobering thought could lead you to consider shorting SPY as a proxy for higher margined stocks.

Because the S&P 500 is so concentrated, the top 41 companies comprising about 50 percent of the index, sector weighting is very important. For maximum gains potential, you should consider buying a select SPDR or two instead of or in addition to SPY.

FIGURE 8-1   S&P 500 Index Values

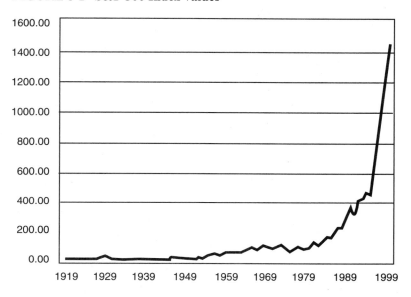

Courtesy of Standard & Poor's

THE EVOLUTION OF MIDCAP

The term *MidCap* was created by the Index Committee in the early 1990s. The S&P MidCap 400 index was launched in 1991. At that time the median market cap for the MidCap companies was about $650 million. Today, the median market cap is close to $3.0 billion.

MidCap stocks represent a unique asset class in the sense that they represent companies that have graduated from the riskiness of the small-cap arena. MDY stocks have achieved a high enough level of market capitalization, financing capability, and managerial maturity that they can weather the economic cycles of their industries.

The Index Committee attempts to keep turnover at both indexes at a minimum. However, when an MDY company grows to between $7 and $10 billion market capitalization, the committee will usually take it out of the index, when possible, and move it up into SPY. The company would have to stay at $7 to $10 billion for a period of time, though. The committee would not just move a company up into the S&P 500 index on the basis of a quick runup.

TABLE 8-1 Standard & Poor's MidCap 400—Market Value Rankings as of December 31, 1999

Mkt Value Rank	Ticker	Company	Shares	Price	(Mil $) Market Value	% of 400	Cumulative %	CUSIP	Industry Group
1	VRTS	Veritas Software	259.175	143.125	37094.422	4.02	4.02	923436109	Computers (Software & Services)
2	SEBL	Siebel Systems, Inc.	192.762	84.000	16192.008	1.76	5.78	826170102	Computers (Software & Services)
3	MXIM	Maxim Integrated Prod	273.358	47.187	12899.081	1.40	7.18	57772K101	Electronics (Semiconductors)
4	BGEN	Biogen, Inc.	150.242	84.500	12695.449	1.38	8.56	090597105	Biotechnology
5	INTU	Intuit, Inc.	195.323	59.937	11707.172	1.27	9.83	461202103	Computers (Software & Services)
6	MEDI	MedImmune Inc.	67.419	165.875	11183.127	1.21	11.04	584699102	Biotechnology
7	LLTC	Linear Technology Corp.	154.312	71.562	11042.953	1.20	12.24	535678106	Electronics (Semiconductors)
8	UVN	Univision Communications	101.935	102.187	10416.483	1.13	13.37	914906102	Broadcasting (Television, Radio & Cab'
9	ALTR	Altera Corp.	199.475	49.562	9886.480	1.07	14.44	021441100	Electronics (Semiconductors)
10	HDI	Harley-Davidson	151.320	64.062	9693.938	1.05	15.49	412822108	Leisure Time (Products)
11	VTSS	Vitesse Semiconductor	153.470	52.437	8047.583	0.87	16.37	928497106	Electronics (Semiconductors)
12	BRW	BroadWing Inc.	216.251	36.875	7974.256	0.87	17.23	111620100	Telephone
13	TDS	Telephone & Data Systems	61.756	126.000	7781.256	0.84	18.08	879433100	Telephone
14	CHIR	Chiron Corp.	181.650	42.375	7697.419	0.84	18.91	170040109	Biotechnology
15	SYK	Stryker Corp.	96.980	69.625	6752.233	0.73	19.64	863667101	Health Care (Medical Products & Supp
16	MI	Marshall & Ilsley Corp.	106.507	62.812	6689.971	0.73	20.37	571834100	Banks (Regional)
17	TIF	Tiffany & Co.	72.124	89.250	6437.067	0.70	21.07	886547108	Retail (Specialty)
18	JBL	Jabil Circuit	87.674	73.000	6400.202	0.69	21.76	466313103	Manufacturing (Specialized)
19	EGRP	E*Trade Group	244.434	26.125	6385.838	0.69	22.45	269246104	Investment Banking/Brokerage
20	ATML	Atmel Corp.	201.604	29.562	5959.918	0.65	23.10	049513104	Electronics (Semiconductors)
21	SCI	SCI Systems Inc.	72.095	82.187	5925.308	0.64	23.74	783890106	Electrical Equipment
22	CTAS	Cintas Corporation	111.091	53.125	5901.709	0.64	24.38	172908105	Services (Commercial & Consumer)
23	LGTO	Legato Systems Inc.	84.981	68.812	5847.755	0.63	25.02	524651106	Computers (Software & Services)
24	CDN	Cadence Design Systems	243.507	24.000	5844.168	0.63	25.65	127387108	Computers (Software & Services)
25	QLGC	QLogic Corp.	36.547	159.875	5842.952	0.63	26.29	747277101	Electronics (Semiconductors)
26	SANM	Sanmina Corp.	58.333	99.875	5826.008	0.63	26.92	800907107	Electrical Equipment
27	CKFR	Checkfree Holdings	54.779	104.500	5724.406	0.62	27.54	162816102	Services (Data Processing)
28	CDO	Comdisco, Inc.	153.140	37.250	5704.465	0.62	28.16	200336105	Services (Computer Systems)
29	SBL	Symbol Technologies	88.481	63.562	5624.074	0.61	28.77	871508107	Electrical Equipment
30	MLNM	Millennium Pharmaceuticals	44.391	122.000	5415.702	0.59	29.36	599902103	Biotechnology
31	ERTS	Electronic Arts	63.206	84.000	5309.304	0.58	29.93	285512109	Computers (Software & Services)

TABLE 8-1 (Continued)

#	Ticker	Company							Sector
32	CEFT	Concord EFS Inc.	205.660	25.750	5295.745	0.57	30.51	206197105	Services (Data Processing)
33	WPO	Washington Post	9.378	555.875	5212.996	0.57	31.07	939640108	Publishing (Newspapers)
34	FRX	Forest Laboratories	83.568	61.437	5134.209	0.56	31.63	345838106	Health Care (Drugs-Major Pharmaceuticals)
35	APCC	American Power Conversion ...	192.595	26.375	5079.693	0.55	32.18	029066107	Electrical Equipment
36	ZION	Zions Bancorp	85.503	59.187	5060.709	0.55	32.73	989701107	Banks (Regional)
37	HBCCA	Hispanic Broadcasting 'A'	54.349	92.218	5011.997	0.54	33.27	43357B104	Broadcasting (Television, Radio & Cable)
38	FSCO	First Security Corp. (Utah)	195.756	25.531	4997.895	0.54	33.81	336294103	Banks (Regional)
39	DST	DST Systems Inc.	63.408	76.312	4838.823	0.52	34.34	233326107	Services (Data Processing)
40	NVLS	Novellus Systems Inc.	39.106	122.531	4791.707	0.52	34.86	670008101	Equipment (Semiconductor)
41	SNPS	Synopsys Inc.	70.845	66.750	4728.904	0.51	35.37	871607707	Computers (Software & Services)
42	FISV	Fiserv Inc.	122.626	38.312	4698.109	0.51	35.88	337738108	Services (Data Processing)
43	CVG	Convergys Corp.	152.712	30.750	4695.894	0.51	36.39	212485106	Services (Commercial & Consumer)
44	SBUX	Starbucks Corp.	182.189	24.250	4418.083	0.48	36.87	855244109	Restaurants
45	WFT	Weatherford Int'l. Inc.	108.088	39.937	4316.765	0.47	37.34	947074100	Oil & Gas (Drilling & Equipment)
46	NE	Noble Drilling Corp.	131.439	32.750	4304.627	0.47	37.81	655042109	Oil & Gas (Drilling & Equipment)
47	NBR	Nabors Industries	138.774	30.937	4293.321	0.47	38.27	629568106	Oil & Gas (Drilling & Equipment)
48	RATL	Rational Software	87.333	49.125	4290.234	0.47	38.74	75409P202	Computers (Software & Services)
49	WON	Westwood One, Inc.	55.462	76.000	4215.112	0.46	39.19	961815107	Broadcasting (Television, Radio & Cable)
50	CF	Charter One Financial	212.171	19.125	4057.770	0.44	39.64	160903100	Savings & Loan Companies
51	CPN	Calpine Corp.	62.895	64.000	4025.280	0.44	40.07	131347706	Power Producers (Independent)
52	MTP	Montana Power	110.201	36.062	3974.124	0.43	40.50	612085100	Electric Companies
53	PPE	Park Place Entertainment	304.879	12.500	3810.988	0.41	40.92	700690100	Gaming, Lottery & Parimutuel Companies
54	GENZ	Genzyme Corp.	84.130	45.000	3785.850	0.41	41.33	372917704	Biotechnology
55	TSN	Tyson Foods	229.585	16.250	3730.756	0.40	41.73	902494103	Foods
56	FTN	First Tennessee National	130.374	28.500	3715.659	0.40	42.13	337162101	Banks (Regional)
57	NETA	Network Associates Inc.	139.216	26.687	3715.327	0.40	42.54	64093B106	Computers (Software & Services)
58	NCR	NCR Corp.	96.562	37.875	3657.286	0.40	42.93	62886E108	Computers (Hardware)
59	ABK	Ambac Financial Group	69.920	52.187	3648.950	0.40	43.33	023139108	Financial (Diversified)
60	CY	Cypress Semiconductor	109.290	32.375	3538.264	0.38	43.71	232806109	Electronics (Semiconductors)
61	MCHP	Microchip Technology	50.935	68.437	3485.864	0.38	44.09	595017104	Electronics (Semiconductors)
62	RLR	ReliaStar Fin'l Corp.	88.751	39.187	3477.930	0.38	44.47	75952U103	Insurance (Life/Health)
63	SYMC	Symantec Corp.	58.143	58.625	3408.633	0.37	44.84	871503108	Computers (Software & Services)
64	CDWC	CDW Computer Centers	43.214	78.625	3397.701	0.37	45.21	125129106	Retail (Computers & Electronics)
65	HMA	Health Management Assoc.	253.357	13.375	3388.650	0.37	45.58	421933102	Health Care (Hospital Management)
66	VISX	VISX Inc.	64.313	51.750	3328.198	0.36	45.94	92844S105	Health Care (Medical Products & Supplies)
67	JNY	Jones Apparel Group	122.505	27.125	3322.948	0.36	46.30	480074103	Textiles (Apparel)
68	WAT	Waters Corporation	62.190	53.000	3296.070	0.36	46.66	941848103	Electronics (Instrumentation)
69	SEPR	Sepracor Inc.	33.135	99.187	3286.578	0.36	47.01	817315104	Health Care (Drugs-Generic & Other)
70	MYL	Mylan Laboratories	129.230	25.187	3254.981	0.35	47.36	628530107	Health Care (Drugs-Generic & Other)
71	ASD	American Standard Cos.	70.733	45.875	3244.876	0.35	47.72	029712106	Manufacturing (Diversified)

TABLE 8-1 (Continued)

Mkt Value Rank	Ticker	Company	Shares	Price	(Mil $) Market Value	% of 400	Cumu- lative %	CUSIP	Industry Group
72	ESV	ENSCO Int'l	137.308	22.875	3140.921	0.34	48.06	26874Q100	Oil & Gas (Drilling & Equipment)
73	RDA	Readers Digest Assoc.	106.470	29.250	3114.248	0.34	48.40	755267101	Publishing
74	KSE	KeySpan Corp.	133.866	23.187	3104.018	0.34	48.73	49337W100	Natural Gas
75	NES	New England Electric System	59.117	51.750	3059.305	0.33	49.06	644001109	Electric Companies
76	SDS	SunGard Data Systems	128.237	23.750	3045.629	0.33	49.39	867363103	Services (Computer Systems)
77	AFC	Allmerica Financial	54.256	55.625	3017.990	0.33	49.72	019754100	Insurance (Property-Casualty)
78	SE	Sterling Commerce Inc.	88.319	34.062	3008.366	0.33	50.05	859205106	Computers (Software & Services)
79	DLTR	Dollar Tree Stores	62.025	48.437	3004.336	0.33	50.37	256747106	Retail (Discounters)
80	AYE	Allegheny Energy Inc.	110.436	26.937	2974.870	0.32	50.70	017361106	Electric Companies
81	BJS	BJ Services	70.847	41.812	2962.290	0.32	51.02	055482103	Oil & Gas (Drilling & Equipment)
82	AGE	Edwards (A.G.), Inc.	92.092	32.062	2952.700	0.32	51.34	281760108	Investment Banking/Brokerage
83	HRL	Hormel Foods Corp.	72.458	40.625	2943.606	0.32	51.66	440452100	Foods
84	HRD	Hannaford Bros.	42.252	69.312	2928.592	0.32	51.98	410550107	Retail (Food Chains)
85	GLM	Global Marine	174.419	16.625	2899.716	0.31	52.29	379352404	Oil & Gas (Drilling & Equipment)
86	CDP	Consolidated Papers	90.762	31.812	2887.366	0.31	52.60	209759109	Paper & Forest Products
87	MAN	Manpower Inc.	75.856	37.625	2854.082	0.31	52.91	56418H100	Services (Employment)
88	DVN	Devon Energy Corp.(New)	85.793	32.875	2820.445	0.31	53.22	25179M103	Oil & Gas (Exploration & Production)
89	FDO	Family Dollar Stores	172.884	16.312	2820.170	0.31	53.53	307000109	Retail (Discounters)
90	BOW	Bowater Inc.	51.667	54.312	2806.164	0.30	53.83	102183100	Paper & Forest Products
91	SCG	SCANA Corp.	103.573	26.875	2783.524	0.30	54.13	805898103	Electric Companies
92	ANF	Abercrombie & Fitch Co.	103.033	26.687	2749.693	0.30	54.43	002896207	Retail (Specialty-Apparel)
93	DPL	DPL Incorporated	158.630	17.312	2746.282	0.30	54.73	233293109	Electric Companies
94	UNIT	Unitrin, Inc.	72.343	37.625	2721.905	0.30	55.02	913275103	Insurance (Property-Casualty)
95	POM	Potomac Electric Power	118.531	22.937	2718.805	0.29	55.32	737679100	Electric Companies
96	IVX	IVAX Corp.	105.521	25.750	2717.166	0.29	55.61	465823102	Health Care (Diversified)
97	NU	Northeast Utilities	131.566	20.562	2705.326	0.29	55.91	664397106	Electric Companies
98	BJ	BJ's Wholesale Club	73.658	36.500	2688.517	0.29	56.20	05548J106	Retail (General Merchandise)
99	VSH	Vishay Intertechnology	84.657	31.625	2677.278	0.29	56.49	928298108	Electrical Equipment
100	ISCA	International Speedway	53.125	50.375	2676.172	0.29	56.78	460335201	Leisure Time (Products)
101	SSW	Sterling Software Inc.	84.247	31.500	2653.781	0.29	57.07	859547101	Computers (Software & Services)
102	VVI	Viad Corp.	94.970	27.875	2647.289	0.29	57.35	92552R109	Services (Commercial & Consumer)
103	IDTI	Integrated Devices Tech	91.057	29.000	2640.653	0.29	57.64	458118106	Electronics (Semiconductors)
104	DQE	DQE, Inc.	75.313	34.625	2607.713	0.28	57.92	23329J104	Electric Companies

TABLE 8-1 (*Continued*)

#	Ticker	Company						
105	MUR	Murphy Oil	44.974	57.375	2580.383	0.28	626717102	Oil & Gas (Exploration & Production)
106	WSM	Williams-Sonoma Inc.	56.011	46.000	2576.506	0.28	969904101	Retail (Specialty)
107	GPT	Greenpoint Financial Corp.	107.829	23.812	2567.678	0.28	395384100	Savings & Loan Companies
108	RHI	Robert Half Int'l	89.706	28.562	2562.228	0.28	770323103	Services (Employment)
109	DL	Dial Corp.	105.376	24.312	2561.954	0.28	25247D101	Household Products (Non-Durables)
110	SYB	Sybron Int'l.	103.764	24.687	2561.674	0.28	87114F106	Health Care (Medical Products & Supplies)
111	AVT	Avnet, Inc	41.945	60.500	2537.673	0.28	053807103	Electronics (Component Distributors)
112	CBSS	Compass Bancshares	113.658	22.312	2535.994	0.28	20449H109	Banks (Regional)
113	SPW	SPX Corp.	31.182	80.812	2519.895	0.27	784635104	Electrical Equipment
114	DSS	Quantum Corp.-DSSG Stock	164.767	15.125	2492.101	0.27	747906204	Computers (Peripherals)
115	ESRX	Express Scripts 'A'	38.521	64.000	2465.344	0.27	302182100	Health Care (Managed Care)
116	NCBC	National Commerce Bancorp	108.238	22.687	2455.650	0.27	635449101	Banks (Regional)
117	NST	NSTAR	60.142	40.500	2435.751	0.26	67019E107	Electric Companies
118	ARW	Arrow Electronics	95.990	25.375	2435.746	0.26	042735100	Electronics (Component Distributors)
119	SII	Smith International	48.914	49.687	2430.414	0.26	832110100	Oil & Gas (Drilling & Equipment)
120	ILN	Illinova Corp.	69.939	34.750	2430.380	0.26	452317100	Electric Companies
121	CCN	Chris-Craft Industries	33.635	72.125	2425.924	0.26	170520100	Broadcasting (Television, Radio & Cable)
122	TE	TECO Energy	129.448	18.562	2402.879	0.26	872375100	Electric Companies
123	NEG	Energy East	114.407	20.812	2381.096	0.26	29266M109	Electric Companies
124	GILD	Gilead Sciences	43.926	54.125	2377.495	0.26	375558103	Biotechnology
125	USG	USG Corp.	49.441	47.125	2329.907	0.26	903293405	Building Materials
126	NIS	NOVA Corp.	73.625	31.562	2323.789	0.25	669784100	Services (Data Processing)
127	SON	Sonoco Products	101.969	22.750	2319.795	0.25	835495102	Containers & Packaging (Paper)
128	PHSY	PacifiCare Health Sys	43.571	53.000	2309.263	0.25	695112102	Health Care (Managed Care)
129	IFMX	Informix Corp.	201.346	11.437	2302.895	0.25	456779107	Computers (Software & Services)
130	NFB	North Fork Bancorp.	130.403	17.500	2282.053	0.25	659424105	Banks (Regional)
131	MNMD	MiniMed Inc.	31.105	73.250	2278.441	0.25	60365K108	Health Care (Medical Products & Supplies)
132	KEA	Keane Inc.	71.680	31.750	2275.840	0.25	486665102	Services (Computer Systems)
133	LIT	Litton Industries	45.570	49.875	2272.804	0.25	538021106	Electronics (Defense)
134	KMI	Kinder Morgan, Inc.	112.560	20.187	2272.305	0.25	49455P101	Natural Gas
135	ACS	Affiliated Computer Svcs.	49.343	46.000	2269.778	0.25	008190100	Computers (Software & Services)
136	WEC	Wisconsin Energy	117.878	19.250	2269.152	0.25	976657106	Electric Companies
137	LGE	LG&E Energy	129.677	17.437	2261.243	0.25	501917108	Electric Companies
138	PKS	Premier Parks	78.249	28.875	2259.440	0.25	740540208	Leisure Time (Products)
139	BLC	Belo (A.H.) Corp.	118.440	19.062	2257.763	0.24	080555105	Publishing (Newspapers)
140	SKS	Saks Incorporated	144.811	15.562	2253.621	0.24	79377W108	Retail (Department Stores)
141	NI	NiSource Inc.	125.056	17.875	2235.376	0.24	65473P105	Electric Companies
142	MRBK	Mercantile Bankshares	68.929	31.937	2201.420	0.24	587405101	Banks (Regional)

117

TABLE 8-1 (Continued)

Mkt Value Rank	Ticker	Company	Shares	Price	(Mil $) Market Value	% of 400	Cumulative %	CUSIP	Industry Group
143	ASBC	Associated Banc-Corp	63.977	34.250	2191.212	0.24	68.00	045487105	Banks (Regional)
144	PMA	PMI Group	44.670	48.812	2180.454	0.24	68.24	69344M101	Consumer Finance
145	FNV	FINOVA Group Inc.	61.227	35.500	2173.559	0.24	68.47	317928109	Financial (Diversified)
146	LNT	Alliant Energy	78.737	27.500	2165.268	0.23	68.71	018802108	Electric Companies
147	LEA	Lear Corporation	67.100	32.000	2147.200	0.23	68.94	521865105	Auto Parts & Equipment
148	FVB	First Virginia Banks	49.689	43.000	2136.627	0.23	69.17	337477103	Banks (Regional)
149	HRS	Harris Corp.	79.569	26.687	2123.498	0.23	69.40	413875105	Communications Equipment
150	MKC	McCormick & Co.	70.791	29.750	2106.032	0.23	69.63	579780206	Foods
151	AEOS	American Eagle Outfitters	46.658	45.000	2099.610	0.23	69.86	02553E106	Retail (Specialty-Apparel)
152	PLCM	Polycom Inc.	32.829	63.687	2090.797	0.23	70.09	73172K104	Communications Equipment
153	HB	Hillenbrand Industries	65.467	31.687	2074.486	0.23	70.31	431573104	Manufacturing (Diversified)
154	LM	Legg Mason	57.186	36.250	2072.993	0.22	70.54	524901105	Investment Banking/Brokerage
155	FMER	FirstMerit Corp.	89.802	23.000	2065.446	0.22	70.76	337915102	Banks (Regional)
156	SHX	Shaw Industries	133.785	15.437	2065.306	0.22	70.99	820286102	Textiles (Home Furnishings)
157	TCB	TCF Financial	82.950	24.875	2063.381	0.22	71.21	872275102	Banks (Regional)
158	ACXM	Acxiom Corp.	85.927	24.000	2062.248	0.22	71.43	005125109	Services (Advertising/Marketing)
159	AWK	American Water Works	96.915	21.250	2059.444	0.22	71.66	030411102	Water Utilities
160	PL	Protective Life Corp.	64.502	31.812	2051.970	0.22	71.88	743674103	Insurance (Life/Health)
161	TGP	The Timber Co.	82.858	24.625	2040.378	0.22	72.10	373298702	Paper & Forest Products
162	MCN	MCN Energy Group Inc.	39.476	51.437	2034.306	0.22	72.32	55267J100	Natural Gas
163	ADTN	Adtran Inc.	59.868	33.687	2030.547	0.22	72.54	00738A106	Communications Equipment
164	MEC	MidAm Energy Hldgs. (New)	55.621	36.000	2016.803	0.22	72.76	59562V107	Power Producers (Independent)
165	TDW	Tidewater Inc.	78.365	25.312	2002.356	0.22	72.98	886423102	Oil & Gas (Drilling & Equipment)
166	ICN	ICN Pharmaceuticals	86.658	22.687	1983.614	0.22	73.19	448924100	Health Care (Drugs-Generic & Other)
167	UDS	Ultramar Diamond Shamrock	103.057	18.875	1966.053	0.21	73.41	904000106	Oil & Gas (Refining & Marketing)
168	AKS	AK Steel Hldg. Corp.	74.994	25.937	1945.201	0.21	73.62	001547108	Iron & Steel
169	OSSI	Outback Steakhouse	109.630	17.625	1945.157	0.21	73.83	689899102	Restaurants
170	RJR	RJ Reynolds Tobacco Hldgs.	46.710	41.000	1932.229	0.21	74.04	76182K105	Tobacco
171	MLM	Martin Marietta Materials	141.157	13.437	1915.110	0.21	74.25	573284106	Construction (Cement & Aggregates)
172	WH	Whitman Corp.	114.480	16.375	1896.797	0.21	74.45	96647R107	Beverages (Non-Alcoholic)
173	IGL	IMC Global Inc.	54.041	34.687	1874.610	0.20	74.65	449669100	Chemicals
174	LNCR	Lincare Holdings	42.365	43.875	1874.547	0.20	74.86	532791100	Health Care (Specialized Services)
175	SYKE	Sykes Enterprises	—	—	1858.764	0.20	75.06	871237103	Services (Computer Systems)

118

TABLE 8-1 (*Continued*)

#	Ticker	Company						CUSIP	Industry
176	PNR	Pentair Corp.	48.177	38.500	1854.815	0.20	75.26	709631105	Manufacturing (Diversified)
177	SDW	Southdown	35.900	51.625	1853.338	0.20	75.46	841297104	Construction (Cement & Aggregates)
178	STK	Storage Technology	100.179	18.437	1847.050	0.20	75.66	862111200	Computers (Peripherals)
179	MLHR	Miller (Herman)	80.024	23.000	1840.552	0.20	75.86	600544100	Office Equipment & Supplies
180	IGT	International Game Technology	90.107	20.312	1830.298	0.20	76.06	459902102	Gaming, Lottery & Parimutuel Companies
181	MBG	Mandalay Resort Group	90.592	20.125	1823.164	0.20	76.26	562567107	Gaming, Lottery & Parimutuel Companies
182	UCU	UtiliCorp United	92.921	19.437	1806.152	0.20	76.45	918005109	Electric Companies
183	NFG	National Fuel Gas	38.798	46.500	1804.107	0.20	76.65	636180101	Natural Gas
184	HUB.B	Hubbell Inc. (Class B)	64.750	27.250	1764.438	0.19	76.84	443510201	Electrical Equipment
185	BID	Sotheby's Holdings	58.789	30.000	1763.670	0.19	77.03	835898107	Services (Commercial & Consumer)
186	CCB	CCB Financial	40.485	43.562	1763.628	0.19	77.22	124875105	Banks (Regional)
187	REY	Reynolds & Reynolds	77.239	22.500	1737.878	0.19	77.41	761695105	Office Equipment & Supplies
188	ORI	Old Republic Int'l	126.233	13.625	1719.925	0.19	77.60	680223104	Insurance (Property-Casualty)
189	FAST	Fastenal Company	37.939	44.937	1704.884	0.18	77.78	311900104	Retail (Building Supplies)
190	HIB	Hibernia Corp.	160.316	10.625	1703.358	0.18	77.97	428656102	Banks (Regional)
191	UFS	U.S. Foodservice	101.518	16.750	1700.427	0.18	78.15	90331R101	Distributors (Food & Health)
192	SOI	Solutia Inc.	110.143	15.437	1700.333	0.18	78.34	834376105	Chemicals (Specialty)
193	LZ	Lubrizol Corp.	54.610	30.875	1686.084	0.18	78.52	549277104	Chemicals (Specialty)
194	DME	Dime Bancorp Inc.	110.840	15.125	1676.455	0.18	78.70	25429Q102	Savings & Loan Companies
195	CNF	CNF Transportation Inc.	48.376	34.500	1668.972	0.18	78.88	12612W104	Air Freight
196	IBP	IBP, Inc.	92.265	18.000	1660.770	0.18	79.06	449223106	Foods
197	GMT	GATX Corp.	49.156	33.750	1659.015	0.18	79.24	361448103	Railroads
198	ASFC	Astoria Financial	54.384	30.437	1655.313	0.18	79.42	046265104	Savings & Loan Companies
199	PSD	Puget Sound Energy, Inc.	84.561	19.375	1638.369	0.18	79.60	745332106	Electric Companies
200	SVRN	Sovereign Bancorp	219.286	7.453	1634.367	0.18	79.78	845905108	Savings & Loan Companies
201	ROST	Ross Stores	90.470	17.937	1622.806	0.18	79.95	778296103	Retail (Discounters)
202	DBD	Diebold, Inc.	68.953	23.500	1620.396	0.18	80.13	253651103	Manufacturing (Specialized)
203	MHK	Mohawk Industries	60.625	26.375	1598.984	0.17	80.30	608190104	Textiles (Home Furnishings)
204	FLO	Flowers Industries	100.308	15.937	1598.659	0.17	80.48	343496105	Foods
205	CNW	CK Witco Corp.	118.936	13.375	1590.769	0.17	80.65	12562C108	Chemicals (Specialty)
206	CATP	Cambridge Technology Partners	60.408	26.250	1585.710	0.17	80.82	132524109	Services (Computer Systems)
207	PFGI	Provident Financial Group Inc.	44.031	35.875	1579.612	0.17	80.99	743866105	Banks (Regional)
208	WL	Wilmington Trust Corp.	32.565	48.250	1571.261	0.17	81.16	971807102	Banks (Regional)
209	EAT	Brinker International	65.420	24.000	1570.080	0.17	81.33	109641100	Restaurants
210	CIV	Conectiv	93.008	16.812	1563.697	0.17	81.50	206829103	Electric Companies
211	DF	Dean Foods	39.130	39.750	1555.418	0.17	81.67	242361103	Foods
212	APOL	Apollo Group	77.261	20.062	1550.049	0.17	81.84	037604105	Services (Commercial & Consumer)
213	AFG	American Financial Grp Hldg..	58.407	26.375	1540.485	0.17	82.01	025932104	Insurance (Property-Casualty)
214	BOH	Pacific Century Financial Corp.	80.243	18.687	1499.541	0.16	82.17	694058108	Banks (Regional)

TABLE 8-1 (*Continued*)

Mkt Value Rank	Ticker	Company	Shares	Price	(Mil $) Market Value	% of 400	Cumulative %	CUSIP	Industry Group
215	LYO	Lyondell Chemical Co.	117.594	12.750	1499.324	0.16	82.33	552078107	Chemicals
216	CYN	City National Corp.	45.404	32.937	1495.494	0.16	82.50	178566105	Banks (Regional)
217	HHS	Harte-Hanks, Inc.	68.666	21.750	1493.486	0.16	82.66	416196103	Services (Advertising/Marketing)
218	FMO	Federal-Mogul	73.827	20.125	1485.768	0.16	82.82	313549107	Auto Parts & Equipment
219	OGE	OGE Energy Corp.	77.801	19.000	1478.219	0.16	82.98	670837103	Electric Companies
220	BEC	Beckman Coulter Inc.	29.052	50.875	1478.021	0.16	83.14	075811109	Health Care (Medical Products & Supplies)
221	SFS	Santa Fe Snyder Corp.	184.415	8.000	1475.320	0.16	83.30	80218K105	Oil & Gas (Exploration & Production)
222	IPL	IPALCO Enterprises	85.728	17.062	1462.734	0.16	83.46	462613100	Electric Companies
223	PSS	Payless ShoeSource Inc. Hldg.	31.064	47.000	1460.008	0.16	83.62	704379106	Retail (Specialty)
224	BKS	Barnes & Noble	69.403	20.625	1431.437	0.16	83.77	067774109	Retail (Specialty)
225	ART	ACNielsen	57.912	24.625	1426.083	0.15	83.93	004833109	Services (Advertising/Marketing)
226	LEE	Lee Enterprises	44.398	31.937	1417.961	0.15	84.08	523768109	Publishing (Newspapers)
227	TECD	Tech Data Corp.	52.021	27.125	1411.070	0.15	84.23	878237106	Retail (Computers & Electronics)
228	MEG.A	Media General	26.599	52.000	1383.148	0.15	84.38	584404107	Publishing (Newspapers)
229	NMG.A	Neiman-Marcus Group 'A'	49.017	27.937	1369.412	0.15	84.53	640204202	Retail (Department Stores)
230	MPS	Modis Professional Svc.	96.041	14.250	1368.584	0.15	84.68	607830106	Services (Employment)
231	KLT	Kansas City Power & Light	61.898	22.062	1365.625	0.15	84.83	485134100	Electric Companies
232	SRP	Sierra Pacific Resources (New)	78.414	17.312	1357.542	0.15	84.98	826428104	Electric Companies
233	CBT	Cabot Corp.	66.112	20.375	1347.032	0.15	85.12	127055101	Chemicals
234	ELY	Callaway Golf Co.	76.073	17.687	1345.541	0.15	85.27	131193104	Leisure Time (Products)
235	MRA	Meritor Automotive Inc.	69.118	19.375	1339.161	0.15	85.41	59000G100	Auto Parts & Equipment
236	RYN	Rayonier Inc.	27.464	48.312	1326.855	0.14	85.56	754907103	Paper & Forest Products
237	SRM	Sensormatic Electronics	76.082	17.437	1326.680	0.14	85.70	817265101	Electrical Equipment
238	LANC	Lancaster Colony	40.025	33.125	1325.828	0.14	85.84	513847103	Consumer (Jewelry, Novelties & Gifts)
239	HNI	HON Industries	60.355	21.937	1324.038	0.14	85.99	438092108	Office Equipment & Supplies
240	FHCC	First Health Group Inc.	49.065	26.875	1318.622	0.14	86.13	320960107	Health Care (Managed Care)
241	HTN	Houghton Mifflin	31.096	42.187	1311.863	0.14	86.27	441560109	Publishing
242	DV	DeVRY Inc.	69.442	18.625	1293.357	0.14	86.41	251893103	Services (Commercial & Consumer)
243	OEI	Ocean Energy Inc.(New)	166.873	7.750	1293.266	0.14	86.55	67481E106	Oil & Gas (Exploration & Production)
244	CMH	Clayton Homes	139.398	9.187	1285.680	0.14	86.69	184190106	Homebuilding
245	WGL	Washington Gas Light	46.473	27.500	1278.008	0.14	86.83	938837101	Natural Gas
246	HSC	Harsco Corp.	40.141	31.750	1274.477	0.14	86.97	415864107	Manufacturing (Diversified)
247	IBC	Interstate Bakeries	70.125	18.125	1271.016	0.14	87.11	46072H108	Foods

120

TABLE 8-1 (Continued)

#	Ticker	Company							Category
248	BGP	Borders Group	78.098	16.062	1254.449	0.14	87.24	09709107	Retail (Specialty)
249	XRAY	Dentsply Int'l	52.800	23.625	1247.246	0.14	87.38	249030107	Health Care (Medical Products & Supplies)
250	MPL	Minnesota Power Inc.	73.461	16.937	1244.246	0.13	87.51	604110106	Electric Companies
251	STR	Questar Corp.	82.441	15.000	1236.615	0.13	87.65	748356102	Natural Gas
252	SZA	Suiza Foods Corp.	31.201	39.625	1236.340	0.13	87.78	865077101	Foods
253	IMN	Imation Corp.	36.453	33.562	1223.454	0.13	87.92	45245A107	Photography/Imaging
254	NBL	Noble Affiliates	57.046	21.437	1222.924	0.13	88.05	654894104	Oil & Gas (Exploration & Production)
255	IT.B	Gartner Group	87.990	13.812	1215.362	0.13	88.18	366651206	Services (Computer Systems)
256	FHS	Foundation Health Sys Inc.	122.255	9.937	1214.909	0.13	88.31	350404109	Health Care (Managed Care)
257	CDD	Cordant Technologies	36.715	33.000	1211.595	0.13	88.44	218412104	Aerospace/Defense
258	BTH	Blyth Industries	48.489	24.562	1191.011	0.13	88.57	09643P108	Consumer (Jewelry, Novelties & Gifts)
259	TFX	Teleflex	37.971	31.312	1188.967	0.13	88.70	879369106	Manufacturing (Specialized)
260	TGH	Trigon Healthcare Inc.	39.266	29.500	1158.347	0.13	88.83	89618L100	Health Care (Managed Care)
261	CLE	Claire's Stores	51.170	22.375	1144.929	0.12	88.95	179584107	Retail (Specialty)
262	SWFT	Swift Transportation	64.334	17.625	1133.887	0.12	89.07	870756103	Truckers
263	TRN	Trinity Industries	39.458	28.437	1122.087	0.12	89.20	896522109	Manufacturing (Diversified)
264	BBC	Bergen Brunswig	134.207	8.312	1115.596	0.12	89.32	083739102	Distributors (Food & Health)
265	VLO	Valero Energy	55.754	19.875	1108.111	0.12	89.44	91913Y100	Oil & Gas (Refining & Marketing)
266	DCI	Donaldson Co.	46.032	24.062	1107.645	0.12	89.56	257651109	Manufacturing (Specialized)
267	RPM	RPM Inc.	108.020	10.187	1100.454	0.12	89.68	749685503	Chemicals (Specialty)
268	OCR	Omnicare, Inc.	91.296	12.000	1095.552	0.12	89.80	681904108	Health Care (Specialized Services)
269	BWA	Borg-Warner Automotive	27.040	40.500	1095.120	0.12	89.91	099724106	Auto Parts & Equipment
270	FBN	Furniture Brands Int'l	49.363	22.000	1085.986	0.12	90.03	360921100	Household Furn. & Appliances
271	CSL	Carlisle Companies	30.129	36.000	1084.644	0.12	90.15	142339100	Manufacturing (Diversified)
272	HC	Hanover Compressor Hldg. Co.	28.724	37.750	1084.331	0.12	90.27	410768105	Oil & Gas (Drilling & Equipment)
273	HP	Helmerich & Payne	49.497	21.812	1079.653	0.12	90.39	423452101	Oil & Gas (Drilling & Equipment)
274	ABF	Airborne Freight	48.642	22.000	1070.124	0.12	90.50	009266107	Air Freight
275	YRK	York International	38.971	27.437	1069.267	0.12	90.62	986670107	Manufacturing (Specialized)
276	WBST	Webster Financial Corp.	45.296	23.562	1067.287	0.12	90.73	947890109	Savings & Loan Companies
277	CQ	COMSAT Corp.	53.033	19.875	1054.031	0.11	90.85	205641D107	Telecommunications (Cellular/Wireless)
278	WABC	Westamerica Bancorp	37.605	27.937	1050.590	0.11	90.96	957090103	Banks (Regional)
279	RE	Everest Reinsurance Hldgs.	46.958	22.312	1047.678	0.11	91.08	299808105	Insurance (Property-Casualty)
280	LE	Lands' End	30.149	34.750	1036.756	0.11	91.19	515086106	Retail (Home Shopping)
281	CHD	Church & Dwight	38.848	26.687	1034.285	0.11	91.30	171340102	Household Products (Non-Durables)
282	OXHP	Oxford Health Plans	81.520	12.687	1028.581	0.11	91.41	691471106	Health Care (Managed Care)
283	SCHL	Scholastic Corp.	16.540	62.187	1025.891	0.11	91.53	807066105	Publishing
284	KSTN	Keystone Financial	48.707	21.062	1024.414	0.11	91.64	493482103	Banks (Regional)
285	UFC	Universal Foods	50.278	20.375	1014.769	0.11	91.75	913538104	Foods
286	KMT	Kennametal Inc.	30.179	33.625	1014.769	0.11	91.86	489170100	Metal Fabricators

TABLE 8-1 *(Continued)*

Mkt Value Rank	Ticker	Company	Shares	Price	(Mil $) Market Value	% of 400	Cumulative %	CUSIP	Industry Group
287	IDA	IDACORP Inc. Hldg. Co.	37.612	26.812	1008.472	0.11	91.97	451107106	Electric Companies
288	HSB	HSB Group Inc.	29.115	33.812	984.451	0.11	92.07	40428N109	Insurance (Property-Casualty)
289	ALEX	Alexander & Baldwin	43.124	22.812	983.766	0.11	92.18	014482103	Shipping
290	CYT	Cytec Industries	42.224	23.125	976.430	0.11	92.29	232820100	Chemicals (Specialty)
291	ATG	AGL Resources Ltd.	56.912	17.000	967.504	0.10	92.39	001204106	Natural Gas
292	OCAS	Ohio Casualty	60.083	16.062	965.083	0.10	92.50	677240103	Insurance (Property-Casualty)
293	GGC	Georgia Gulf	30.967	30.437	942.558	0.10	92.60	373200203	Chemicals
294	TECUA	Tecumseh Products Co.	19.955	47.187	941.627	0.10	92.70	878895200	Machinery (Diversified)
295	WXS	Westpoint Stevens	53.390	17.500	934.325	0.10	92.80	961238102	Textiles (Home Furnishings)
296	AHG	Apria Healthcare Group	52.042	17.937	933.503	0.10	92.90	037933108	Health Care (Specialized Services)
297	HE	Hawaiian Electric Industries	32.213	28.875	930.150	0.10	93.00	419870100	Electric Companies
298	ALK	Alaska Air Group	26.403	35.125	927.405	0.10	93.10	011659109	Airlines
299	OLS	Olsten Corp.	81.308	11.312	919.797	0.10	93.20	681385100	Services (Employment)
300	DEX	Dexter Corp.	23.042	39.750	915.920	0.10	93.30	252165105	Chemicals (Specialty)
301	TSAI	Transaction Systems Architects	32.551	28.000	911.428	0.10	93.40	893416107	Computers (Software & Services)
302	PMS	Policy Management Systems	35.572	25.562	909.309	0.10	93.50	731108106	Services (Computer Systems)
303	DOL	Dole Foods	55.835	16.250	907.319	0.10	93.60	256605106	Foods
304	NNS	Newport News Shipbuilding	32.972	27.500	906.730	0.10	93.70	652228107	Aerospace/Defense
305	KELYA	Kelly Services	35.892	25.125	901.787	0.10	93.80	488152208	Services (Employment)
306	PZB	Pittston Brink's Group	40.861	22.000	898.942	0.10	93.89	725701106	Services (Commercial & Consumer)
307	ALB	Albemarle Corp.	46.748	19.187	896.977	0.10	93.99	012653101	Chemicals (Specialty)
308	PXD	Pioneer Natural Resources	100.306	8.937	896.485	0.10	94.09	723787107	Oil & Gas (Exploration & Production)
309	CTP	CMP Group Inc. Hldg. Co.	32.443	27.562	894.210	0.10	94.19	125887109	Electric Companies
310	OLN	Olin Corp.	45.051	19.812	892.573	0.10	94.28	680665205	Chemicals (Diversified)
311	ITG	Investment Technology (New)	31.021	28.750	891.854	0.10	94.38	46145F105	Services (Computer Systems)
312	CRUS	Cirrus Logic	65.576	13.312	872.981	0.09	94.47	172755100	Electronics (Semiconductors)
313	MTX	Minerals Technologies	21.150	40.062	847.322	0.09	94.57	603158106	Chemicals (Specialty)
314	MENT	Mentor Graphics	64.200	13.187	846.638	0.09	94.66	587200106	Computers (Software & Services)
315	JEC	Jacobs Engineering Group	25.924	32.500	842.530	0.09	94.75	469814107	Engineering & Construction
316	KDN	Kaydon Corp.	30.787	26.812	825.476	0.09	94.84	486587108	Machinery (Diversified)
317	IV	Mark IV Industries	46.568	17.687	823.672	0.09	94.93	570387100	Auto Parts & Equipment
318	CAR	Carter-Wallace	44.982	17.937	806.865	0.09	95.01	146285101	Personal Care
319	HMN	Horace Mann Educators	41.028	19.625	805.175	0.09	95.10	440327104	Insurance (Property-Casualty)

TABLE 8-1 (*Continued*)

#	Ticker	Company						CUSIP	Industry
320	UCR	UCAR International	45.088	17.812	803.130	0.09	95.19	90262K109	Iron & Steel
321	AG	AGCO Corp.	59.546	13.437	800.149	0.09	95.28	001084102	Machinery (Diversified)
322	NDSN	Nordson Corporation	16.464	48.250	794.388	0.09	95.36	655663102	Manufacturing (Specialized)
323	PZL	Pennzoil-Quaker State (New)	77.973	10.187	794.350	0.09	95.45	709323109	Oil & Gas (Refining & Marketing)
324	PZZA	Papa John's Int'l.	30.444	26.062	793.447	0.09	95.53	698813102	Restaurants
325	FULL	Fuller (H.B.) Co.	14.037	55.937	785.195	0.09	95.62	359694106	Chemicals (Specialty)
326	FOE	Ferro Corp.	35.288	22.000	776.336	0.08	95.70	315405100	Chemicals (Specialty)
327	GTK	GTECH Holdings Corp.	34.865	22.000	767.030	0.08	95.79	400518106	Gaming, Lottery & Parimutuel Companies
328	NCOG	NCO Group Inc.	25.374	30.125	764.392	0.08	95.87	628858102	Services (Commercial & Consumer)
329	FSS	Federal Signal	46.100	16.062	740.481	0.08	95.95	313855108	Manufacturing (Specialized)
330	MODI	Modine Mfg.	29.515	25.000	737.875	0.08	96.03	607828100	Auto Parts & Equipment
331	LFB	Longview Fibre	51.677	14.250	736.397	0.08	96.11	543213102	Paper & Forest Products
332	ARV	Arvin Industries	25.829	28.375	732.898	0.08	96.19	043339100	Auto Parts & Equipment
333	UFI	Unifi, Inc.	59.205	12.312	728.962	0.08	96.27	904677101	Textiles (Specialty)
334	CNL	Cleco Corp. Hldg. Co.	22.509	32.062	721.695	0.08	96.35	12561W105	Electric Companies
335	RDK	Ruddick Corp.	46.438	15.500	719.789	0.08	96.43	781258108	Retail (Food Chains)
336	SUP	Superior Industries	26.651	26.812	714.580	0.08	96.50	868168105	Auto Parts & Equipment
337	UVV	Universal Corp.	30.982	22.812	706.777	0.08	96.58	913456109	Agricultural Products
338	WCS	Wallace Computer Services	41.916	16.625	696.854	0.08	96.66	932270101	Office Equipment & Supplies
339	STE	STERIS Corp.	67.498	10.312	696.073	0.08	96.73	859152100	Health Care (Medical Products & Supplies)
340	WCLX	Wisconsin Central Trans.	51.250	13.437	688.672	0.08	96.81	976592105	Railroads
341	WAC	Warnaco Group	55.635	12.312	685.006	0.07	96.88	934390105	Textiles (Apparel)
342	PSSI	PSS World Medical Inc.	70.922	9.437	669.326	0.07	96.95	69366A100	Distributors (Food & Health)
343	ARG	Airgas Inc.	70.210	9.500	666.995	0.07	97.02	009363102	Chemicals
344	VRC	Varco Int'l	65.273	10.187	664.969	0.07	97.10	922126107	Oil & Gas (Drilling & Equipment)
345	PNM	Public Service of New Mexico	40.774	16.250	662.578	0.07	97.17	744499104	Electric Companies
346	SLVN	Sylvan Learning Systems	50.955	13.000	662.415	0.07	97.24	871399101	Services (Commercial & Consumer)
347	MWHS	Micro Warehouse, Inc.	35.781	18.500	661.949	0.07	97.31	59501B105	Retail (Home Shopping)
348	QHGI	Quorom Health Group	70.658	9.312	658.003	0.07	97.38	749084109	Health Care (Hospital Management)
349	PCP	Precision Castparts	24.510	26.250	643.388	0.07	97.45	740189105	Aerospace/Defense
350	FLS	Flowserve Corp.	37.324	17.000	634.508	0.07	97.52	34354P105	Manufacturing (Specialized)
351	WLM	Wellman, Inc.	33.933	18.625	632.002	0.07	97.59	949702104	Textiles (Specialty)
352	CVD	Covance Inc.	58.381	10.812	631.245	0.07	97.66	222816100	Health Care (Specialized Services)
353	OMX	OfficeMax Inc.	113.337	5.500	623.354	0.07	97.73	67622M108	Retail (Specialty)
354	GLT	P.H. Glatfelter Co.	42.225	14.562	614.902	0.07	97.79	377316104	Paper & Forest Products
355	AME	Ametek, Inc.	32.174	19.062	613.317	0.07	97.86	031100100	Manufacturing (Diversified)
356	BOBE	Bob Evans Farms	39.475	15.437	609.395	0.07	97.93	096761101	Restaurants
357	CRS	Carpenter Technology	21.930	27.437	601.704	0.07	97.99	144285103	Iron & Steel

123

TABLE 8-1 (*Continued*)

Mkt Value Rank	Ticker	Company	Shares	Price	(Mil $) Market Value	% of 400	Cumulative %	CUSIP	Industry Group
358	WMO	Wausau-Mosinee Paper	51.417	11.687	600.936	0.07	98.06	943315101	Paper & Forest Products
359	BN	Banta Corp.	26.591	22.562	599.959	0.07	98.12	066821109	Specialty Printing
360	OG	Ogden Corp.	49.466	11.937	590.500	0.06	98.19	676346109	Services (Commercial & Consumer)
361	PRGO	Perrigo Co.	73.346	8.000	586.768	0.06	98.25	714290103	Personal Care
362	CBRL	CBRL Group, Inc.	58.628	9.703	568.875	0.06	98.31	12489V106	Restaurants
363	SJM.A	Smucker (J.M.)	29.009	19.500	565.676	0.06	98.37	832696108	Foods
364	SQA.A	Sequa Corp.	10.370	53.937	559.332	0.06	98.43	817320104	Aerospace/Defense
365	BDG	Bandag Inc.	21.912	25.000	547.800	0.06	98.49	059815100	Auto Parts & Equipment
366	TRL	Total Renal Care Hldgs.	81.189	6.687	542.951	0.06	98.55	89151A107	Health Care (Specialized Services)
367	SR	Standard Register Co.	27.853	19.375	539.652	0.06	98.61	853887107	Office Equipment & Supplies
368	MAH	Hanna (M.A.)	48.900	10.937	534.844	0.06	98.67	410522206	Chemicals (Specialty)
369	CSK	Chesapeake Corp.	17.516	30.500	534.238	0.06	98.73	165159104	Paper & Forest Products
370	IEI	Indiana Energy	29.788	17.750	528.737	0.06	98.78	454707100	Natural Gas
371	STEI	Stewart Enterprises, Inc.	108.600	4.750	515.850	0.06	98.84	860370105	Services (Commercial & Consumer)
372	SHLM	Schulman (A.), Inc.	31.132	16.312	507.841	0.06	98.89	808194104	Chemicals (Specialty)
373	OSG	Overseas Shipholding Group	33.672	14.812	498.767	0.05	98.95	690368105	Shipping
374	GVA	Granite Construction	27.026	18.437	498.292	0.05	99.00	387328107	Engineering & Construction
375	JBHT	Hunt(J.B.) Transport Serv Inc.	35.637	13.843	493.350	0.05	99.06	445658107	Truckers
376	RT	Ryerson Tull, Inc. (New)	24.774	19.437	481.545	0.05	99.11	78375P107	Metal Fabricators
377	CPU	CompUSA Inc.	92.712	5.125	475.149	0.05	99.16	204932107	Retail (Computers & Electronics)
378	BKH	Black Hills	21.350	22.187	473.703	0.05	99.21	092113109	Electric Companies
379	AIN	Albany International	30.409	15.500	471.340	0.05	99.26	012348108	Manufacturing (Specialized)
380	DRYR	Dreyer's Grand Ice Cream	27.706	17.000	471.002	0.05	99.31	261878102	Foods
381	SDRC	Structural Dynamics Research	35.726	12.750	455.507	0.05	99.36	863555108	Computers (Software & Services)
382	NCI	Navigant Consulting	41.642	10.875	452.857	0.05	99.41	63935N107	Services (Commercial & Consumer)
383	ROL	Rollins, Inc.	30.076	15.000	451.140	0.05	99.46	775711104	Services (Commercial & Consumer)
384	BEV	Beverly Enterprises (New)	102.496	4.375	448.420	0.05	99.51	087851309	Health Care (Long Term Care)
385	BOCB	Buffets Inc.	42.059	10.000	420.590	0.05	99.56	11982208	Restaurants
386	AIND	Arnold Ind.	24.628	14.062	346.331	0.04	99.59	042595108	Truckers
387	CLF	Cleveland-Cliffs	11.053	31.125	344.025	0.04	99.63	185896107	Iron & Steel

TABLE 8-1 (*Continued*)

388	ACN	Acuson Corp.	26.722	12.562	335.695	0.04	99.67	005113105	Health Care (Medical Products & Supplies)
389	SSSS	Stewart & Stevenson Services	27.992	11.843	331.530	0.04	99.70	860342104	Manufacturing (Diversified)
390	EY	Ethyl Corp.	83.465	3.937	328.643	0.04	99.74	297659104	Chemicals (Specialty)
391	MXM	MAXXAM Inc.	7.001	42.875	300.168	0.03	99.77	577913106	Aluminum
392	LNCE	Lance, Inc.	29.958	10.000	299.580	0.03	99.80	514606102	Foods
393	STAR	Lone Star Steakhouse	33.093	8.921	295.252	0.03	99.84	542307103	Restaurants
394	VL	Vlasic Foods Int'l	45.502	5.687	258.793	0.03	99.86	928559103	Foods
395	IMC	International Multifoods	18.739	13.250	248.292	0.03	99.89	460043102	Foods
396	NCH	NCH Corp.	5.408	44.562	240.994	0.03	99.92	628850109	Services (Commercial & Consumer)
397	BUR	Burlington Industries	52.913	4.000	211.652	0.02	99.94	121693105	Textiles (Specialty)
398	OS	Oregon Steel Mills	25.777	7.937	204.605	0.02	99.96	686079104	Iron & Steel
399	MAG	MagneTek, Inc.	24.101	7.687	185.276	0.02	99.98	559424106	Electrical Equipment
400	HMY	Heilig-Meyers Co.	59.874	2.750	164.654	0.02	100.00	422893107	Retail (Specialty)

Due to mergers, acquisitions, and takeovers, the Index Committee had to move approximately 48 companies into the S&P 500 index in 1998. That is a large number of companies, a rate of four per month! The S&P 500 has the potential of capturing all the market gain by moving companies up from MDY to SPY after the companies have demonstrated solid growth. MDY continues to be a good breeding ground for SPY candidates.

MDY contains many companies, especially in the banking and utility sectors, that will never grow to be major companies. The committee discovered that many banks and utilities are constrained from growth. So it limits the number of banks and utilities that it allows into the index. MDY will contain only a geographic representation of utilities and country banks. It will not have an equal weighting of these sectors with more growth-oriented sectors like technology.

Table 8-1, shown on pages 114–125, lists the stocks in MDY.

THE MIDCAP VALUATION
The MidCap index and the S&P small-cap index are the most undervalued indexes. MDY has a P/E multiple of about 22 times. The P/E on SPY is about 28 times. And yet MDY had faster earnings growth than SPY for 1999. Also, forward earnings estimates on a five-year basis are higher for MDY than SPY.

FIGURE 8-2   S&P MidCap 400 Index Value

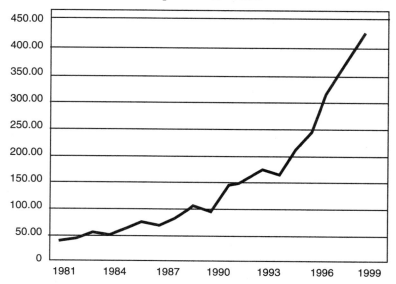

So, buying into MDY is a bet that it will perform better than SPY, a prudent posture, given that MDY has a lower valuation and a higher growth outlook than SPY. An aggressive investor could buy MDY and short SPY if she really felt that the dichotomy between large-cap and midcap stocks would widen.

But the earnings composition of the two indexes is very different, necessitating a call on whether you think earnings elsewhere than the United States will advance or decline. MDY companies, unlike SPY companies, are not heavily weighted in foreign earnings. About 40 percent of the earnings of the companies comprising SPY come from offshore. Less than 20 percent of MDY's earnings comes from foreign countries.

C H A P T E R   9

QQQ

THE DEVELOPMENT OF QQQ

The Nasdaq 100 index has been in existence since 1985. At that time the Nasdaq was attempting to develop a brand name for the exchange. The exchange wanted some sort of index that would attract investors to the premier stocks at the exchange.

In 1997 the strategic planning team at the Nasdaq stock exchange worked on strategies for participating in the burgeoning international stocks area and Internet-related trading opportunities. One of the outgrowths of this analysis was the consensus that crating an exchange traded share class of securities on the Nasdaq 100 index would be a great step in helping to heighten the brand recognition of the Nasdaq name. This led Nasdaq to create QQQ.

QQQ has a different relationship with the exchange it is traded on than any of the other securities that are traded on an exchange. DIA is listed on the American Stock Exchange (AMEX). SPY is listed on the AMEX. But

QQQ is created by Nasdaq/AMEX and traded at the AMEX. AMEX is a stock market that licensed its index and listed it as well. So Nasdaq/AMEX has different objectives with QQQ than just seeing how big they can make the fund or how much revenue they can generate from volume. The many possible public relations benefits are as important as the other factors.

So the original idea for Nasdaq was to use QQQ to promote its name; QQQ also gave investors another way to invest in Nasdaq stocks, thereby attracting more money to the Nasdaq stock market.

The planning team finalized its plan for QQQ in 1998. The intent was to have QQQ be the first exchange traded shares to not trade on the AMEX. The AMEX was a competitor then of Nasdaq. The planning team had compiled market data through testing and determined QQQ would do very well.

Just before Nasdaq was ready to start trading QQQ, negotiations to merge started between the AMEX and Nasdaq. This put a hold on the QQQ release. Plans to trade were dropped until after the merger was completed, which occurred on November 2, 1998. The Nasdaq/AMEX then decided not to launch QQQ between Thanksgiving and Christmas, usually a slow market time. The AMEX rebalanced the Nasdaq 100 index in December and launched QQQ on March 10, 1999.

The launch was successful. QQQ set a record for number of shares traded on the first day of a new exchange share product: 2.6 million. The assets continued pouring in, swelling QQQ's assets to $1.0 billion within five weeks. And the success continued. QQQ grew to over $2.0 billion in less than four months, another record. QQQ's volume has been averaging 5.5 million shares a day. It is the second most heavily traded security on the AMEX. Some days, it is the most actively traded. This has enhanced the Nasdaq 100 index's visibility and made it one of the most closely watched indexes for market direction.

STOCKS IN QQQ

The list of underlying stocks in the Nasdaq 100 index has evolved gradually into today's official designation, which is "the 100 biggest domestic and international nonfinancial stocks on the Nasdaq exchange." Inclusion in the list is simple: size. Market capitalization is calculated by multiplying the market price by the number of outstanding shares.

Figure 9-1 shows the industry weightings of QQQ.

Besides size, there are some other requirements for being in QQQ. The company has to have been "seasoned" on the Nasdaq or another recognized exchange, generally for at least two years. Nasdaq is not going to put into the index a company that has just gone public, even if it does meet the size

FIGURE 9-1   Nasdaq 100 Industry Weightings by Market Value

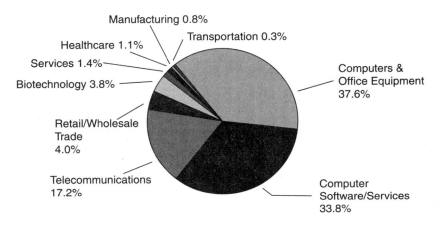

Manufacturing 0.8%

Transportation 0.3%

Healthcare 1.1%

Services 1.4%

Biotechnology 3.8%

Computers &
Office Equipment
37.6%

Retail/Wholesale
Trade
4.0%

Telecommunications
17.2%

Computer
Software/Services
33.8%

Source: NASD. As of July 31, 1999.

criteria. The company has to be a nonfinancial company, since Nasdaq has a separate Financial 100 index. The index does allow non-U.S. companies. For example, Ericsson Telephone and Reuters Group are included. In other indexes, such as the S&P 500 index, foreign companies are generally excluded. In addition, the security must have an average daily trading volume of 100,000 shares per day.

The stocks comprising QQQ are listed in Table 9-1.

TABLE 9-1   The Stocks of QQQ

Company Name	Symbol	% of Index (Adjusted)
3Com Corporation	COMS	0.43
Adaptec, Inc.	ADPT	0.25
ADC Telecommunications, Inc.	ADCTI	0.69
Adelphia Communications Corporation	ADLAC	0.44
Adobe Systems Incorporated	ADBE	0.37
Altera Corporation	ALTR	0.98
Amazon.com, Inc.	AMZN	0.73

TABLE 9-1 (*Continued*)

Company Name	Symbol	% of Index (Adjusted)
American Power Conversion Corporation	APCC	0.34
Amgen Inc.	AMGN	1.7
Apollo Group, Inc.	APOL	0.08
Apple Computer, Inc.	AAPL	1.27
Applied Materials, Inc.	AMAT	1.36
Applied Micro Circuits Corporation	AMCC	0.47
At Home Corporation	ATHM	0.58
Atmel Corporation	ATML	0.26
Bed Bath & Beyond Inc.	BBBY	0.28
Biogen, Inc.	BGEN	0.85
Biomet, Inc.	BMET	0.33
BMC Software, Inc.	BMCS	0.43
BroadVision, Inc.	BVSN	0.62
Chiron Corporation	CHIR	0.59
CIENA Corporation	CIEN	0.59
Cintas Corporation	CTAS	0.34
Cisco Systems, Inc.	CSCO	6.61
Citrix Systems, Inc.	CTXS	0.78
CMGI, Inc.	CMGI	1.78
CNET, Inc.	CNET	0.25
Comcast Corporation	CMCSK	0.93
Compuware Corporation	CPWR	0.28
Comverse Technology, Inc.	CMVT	0.6
Concord EFS, Inc.	CEFT	0.25
Conexant Systems, Inc.	CNXT	0.83
Costco Wholesale Corporation	COST	0.58
Dell Computer Corporation	DELL	2.05
Dollar Tree Stores, Inc.	DLTR	0.13
eBay Inc.	EBAY	0.74
EchoStar Communications Corporation	DISH	0.53
Electronic Arts Inc.	ERTS	0.24

TABLE 9-1 (*Continued*)

Company Name	Symbol	% of Index (Adjusted)
Fiserv, Inc.	FISV	0.28
Gemstar International Group, Limited	GMST	0.84
Genzyme General	GENZ	0.27
Global Crossing Ltd.	GBLX	2.22
Herman Miller, Inc.	MLHR	0.06
i2 Technologies, Inc.	ITWO	1.06
Immunex Corporation	IMNX	1.37
Intel Corporation	INTC	5.58
Intuit Inc.	INTU	0.95
JDS Uniphase Corporation	JDSU	3.34
KLA-Tencor Corporation	KLAC	0.68
Legato Systems, Inc.	LGTO	0.13
Level 3 Communications, Inc.	LVLT	1.16
Linear Technology Corporation	LLTC	0.93
LM Ericsson Telephone Company	ERICY	0.82
Lycos, Inc.	LCOS	0.47
Maxim Integrated Products, Inc.	MXIM	1.07
MCI WORLDCOM, Inc.	WCOM	2.21
McLeodUSA Incorporated	MCLD	0.49
MedImmune, Inc.	MEDI	0.59
Metromedia Fiber Network, Inc.	MFNX	0.73
Microchip Technology Incorporated	MCHP	0.14
Microsoft Corporation	MSFT	9.4
Molex Incorporated	MOLX	0.21
Network Appliance, Inc.	NTAP	0.89
Network Associates, Inc.	NETA	0.2
Network Solutions, Inc.	NSOL	0.46
Nextel Communications, Inc.	NXTL	2.78
NEXTLINK Communications, Inc.	NXLK	0.37
Northwest Airlines Corporation	NWAC	0.07
Novell, Inc.	NOVL	0.72

TABLE 9-1 (*Continued*)

Company Name	Symbol	% of Index (Adjusted)
NTL Incorporated	NTLI	0.71
Oracle Corporation	ORCL	3.51
PACCAR Inc.	PCAR	0.18
PacifiCare Health Systems, Inc.	PHSY	0.1
PanAmSat Corporation	SPOT	0.59
Parametric Technology Corporation	PMTC	0.4
Paychex, Inc.	PAYX	0.54
PeopleSoft, Inc.	PSFT	0.48
PMC - Sierra, Inc.	PMCS	0.65
QLogic Corporation	QLGC	0.33
QUALCOMM Incorporated	QCOM	6.53
Quintiles Transnational Corp.	QTRN	0.2
RealNetworks, Inc.	RNWK	0.53
RF Micro Devices, Inc.	RFMD	0.37
Sanmina Corporation	SANM	0.34
SDL, Inc.	SDLI	0.47
Siebel Systems, Inc.	SEBL	0.91
Sigma-Aldrich Corporation	SIAL	0.18
Smurfit-Stone Container Corporation	SSCC	0.22
Staples, Inc.	SPLS	0.37
Starbucks Corporation	SBUX	0.31
Sun Microsystems, Inc.	SUNW	2.65
Synopsys, Inc.	SNPS	0.22
Tellabs, Inc.	TLAB	0.8
USA Networks, Inc.	USAI	0.41
VERITAS Software Corporation	VRTS	2.04
VISX, Incorporated	VISX	0.11
Vitesse Semiconductor Corporation	VTSS	0.43
VoiceStream Wireless Corporation	VSTR	0.67
Xilinx, Inc.	XLNX	0.99
Yahoo! Inc.	YHOO	2.22

STOCK REPLACEMENT

Every year, at the end of November, to coordinate with the upcoming December "triple witching" day, Nasdaq calculates an annual ranking to ensure that the index does in fact represent the top 100 companies. At that time, if necessary, Nasdaq will drop some companies and add others. Triple-witching occurs on the day when stock options, index options, and index futures all expire. This occurs at market close on the third Friday of March, June, September, and December. The triple-witching occurrence often leads to volatile trading and large volume.

As with any index, replacements are necessary from time to time. For instance, when a QQQ company is merged out of existence, the Nasdaq architects calculate when the company will cease existence and plan its replacement. Nasdaq keeps the replacement stock confidential until about three days before the substitution is done. They don't want people pretrading an issue in the knowledge that it will shortly become part of an index.

INDEX COMPOSITION

Because of the present makeup of the underlying securities, the index is now heavily weighted toward technology. This stands to reason since technology stocks have appreciated mightily in this giant bull market.

FIGURE 9-2   Nasdaq 100 versus S&P 500 and DJ Industrial

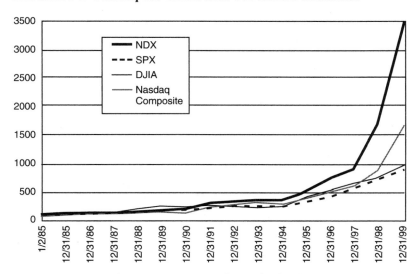

Source: FactSet Research Systems, Inc. Data as of December 31, 1999.

The big names in the Nasdaq 100 are Microsoft, Cisco, Intel, Dell, and MCI Worldwide. Obviously, these issues drive the index. All are technology stocks. Taken together, they account for about 38 percent of the capitalization of the index.

One of the reasons for the popularity of QQQ is that the index represents the Nasdaq Stock Exchange, and to most people this exchange means growth. Another reason is that the exchange traded share structure works so well and is perfectly suited for both investors and traders. In addition, whereas some of the other indexes, the S&P 500 index and the Dow Jones Industrial Average, for example, afford a variety of ways for people to invest in them, there are not many ways outside of QQQ to invest in the stocks on the Nasdaq. QQQ solves the problem of investing or trading in Nasdaq. You don't have to decide which stock to buy or sell short. You just buy or short QQQ and participate in the performance of an entire basket of stocks.

10

CHAPTER

WEBS

CONSIDERING FOREIGN INVESTING

Let me tell you something about my background, and how I traveled to the global investment village we now live in and discovered WEBS.

Almost 35 years ago, I got my brokerage license and went to work for Merrill Lynch. After a number of years Merrill separated institutional and individual clients, making it necessary for me to decide which kind of accounts I wanted to maintain. I wanted both, so I moved over to Lehman Brothers. Years later, after becoming a Lehman Brothers vice president, I accepted a job building and managing an office for SG Cowen & Co., the boutique investment banking firm. The office grew, and I was made a partner. After several years, I went out on my own to manage money and write for *The San Francisco Examiner*, Delta Airlines' *Sky* magazine, and other publications.

I started writing this book partly because of my stock market experience. For the first 20 years I was involved in the markets, they generally went down. Now, stocks have gone up since about 1982. I am getting a little gun-shy. And I keep staring the chart shown here as Table 10-1.

TABLE 10-1 Annual Market Performance and Ranking for 17 MSCI Indexes and S&P 500—periods ending 12/31. In U.S. Dollars—(Reivestment of Net Dividends, except for Mexico (Free) and S&P 500)*

Ranking	1998	1997	1996	1995	1994	1993	1992
1.	Belgium 67.75%	Mexico (Free) 53.92%	Spain 40.05%	Switzerland 44.12%	Japan 21.44%	Hong Kong 116.70%	Hong Kong 32.29%
2.	Italy 52.52%	Switzerland 44.25%	Sweden 37.21%	S&P 500 37.58%	Sweden 18.34%	Malaysia (Free) 110.00%	Mexico (Free) 24.98%
3.	Spain 49.90%	Italy 35.48%	Hong Kong 33.08%	Sweden 33.36%	Netherlands 11.70%	Singapore (Free) 73.41%	Malaysia (Free) 17.76%
4.	France 41.54%	S&P 500 33.36%	Canada 28.54%	Spain 29.83%	Italy 11.56%	Mexico (Free) 49.35%	Switzerland 17.23%
5.	Germany 29.43%	Spain 25.41%	Netherlands 27.51%	Netherlands 27.71%	Belgium 8.24%	Switzerland 45.79%	S&P 500 7.62%
6.	S&P 500 26.81%	Germany 24.57%	United Kingdom 27.42%	Belgium 25.88%	Singapore (Free) 5.81%	Sweden 36.99%	Singapore (Free) 4.49%
7.	Switzerland 23.53%	Netherlands 23.77%	Malaysia (Free) 25.89%	Hong Kong 22.57%	Australia 5.40%	Germany 35.64%	France 2.81%
8.	Netherlands 23.23%	United Kingdom 22.62%	S&P 500 22.96%	United Kingdom 21.27%	Germany 4.66%	Netherlands 35.28%	Netherlands 2.30%
9.	United Kingdom 17.80%	Belgium 13.55%	France 21.20%	Canada 18.31%	Switzerland 3.54%	Australia 35.17%	Belgium -1.47%
10.	Sweden 13.96%	Sweden 12.92%	Mexico (Free) 18.70%	Germany 16.41%	S&P 500 1.32%	Spain 29.78%	United Kingdom -3.65%
11.	Australia 6.07%	Canada 12.80%	Australia 16.49%	France 14.12%	United Kingdom -1.63%	Italy 28.53%	Germany -10.27%
12.	Japan 5.05%	France 11.94%	Germany 13.58%	Singapore (Free) 12.19%	Canada -3.04%	Austria 28.09%	Austria -10.65%
13.	Austria 0.35%	Austria 1.57%	Italy 12.59%	Australia 11.19%	Spain -4.80%	Japan 25.48%	Australia -10.82%
14.	Hong Kong -2.92%	Australia -10.44%	Belgium 12.03%	Malaysia (Free) 5.16%	France -5.18%	United Kingdom 24.44%	Canada -12.15%
15.	Singapore (Free) -3.59%	Hong Kong -23.29%	Austria 4.51%	Italy 1.05%	Austria -6.28%	Belgium 23.51%	Sweden -14.41%
16.	Canada -6.14%	Japan -23.67%	Switzerland 2.28%	Japan 0.69%	Malaysia (Free) -19.94%	France 20.91%	Japan -21.45%
17.	Malaysia (Free) -29.49%	Singapore (Free) -40.46%	Singapore (Free) 0.33%	Austria -4.72%	Hong Kong -28.90%	Canada 17.58%	Spain -21.87%
18.	Mexico (Free) -33.53%	Malaysia (Free) -68.11%	Japan -15.50%	Mexico (Free) -20.37%	Mexico (Free) -40.55%	S&P 500 10.08%	Italy -22.22%

MSCI: Morgan Stanley Capital International

*Assumes reinvestment of net dividends except for the Mexico (Free) and the S&P 500 Indices. Net dividends means dividends after reduction for taxes withheld at source. The Mexico (Free) and S&P 500 Indices reflect gross dividends since Mexican and U.S. companies do not withhold tax from U.S. investors. U.S. Market represented by the S&P 500 Index. The dividend withholding rate used by MSCI is that relevant for residents of Luxembourg, and such rate is higher than the rate applicable to U.S. residents in the case of the following WEBS Index Series: Australia (30% vs. 15%), Austria (15% vs. 11%) and Germany (15% vs. 10%).

Past performance is no guarantee of future results, nor do index results represent any past or expected future performance of WEBS. It is not possible to invest in an index. Indices are unmanaged, and do not bear expenses, unlike WEBS. Foreign markets may be volatile and performance is subject to market fluctuations, political risks and currency risks.

Annual total return in U.S. $ for each country index is based on the change for the period of 1/1 through 12/31 in the market and currency value of the individual stocks comprising each index, assuming reinvestment of any dividends.

Funds Distributor Inc., Distributor.

For more information on WEBS, including a prospectus which details charges and expenses, please call 800-810-WEBS.

Please read the prospectus carefully before you invest.

Sources: Lipper Analytical Services, Morgan Stanley Capital International, and Standard and Poor's Corporation
MSCIFACT
1/99

Stock markets around the globe really do move independently of each other. Does it make sense to have all of your money here in the United States? Maybe yes, maybe no. But if you decide to diversify globally, which I suggest you do, WEBS have simplified doing just that.

I have traded foreign stocks for years. You just can't appreciate how hard it was to keep up with them before WEBS. There were time differences, currency differences, and problems with getting research, problems getting research in English, and problems getting valid quotes. I spent hours converting currencies only to see my numbers grow cold because of currency market changes. It was really hard. WEBS make it easy.

WEBS, and being able to invest worldwide, fit into my investment philosophy. I am risk averse. I'm constantly reminded that if you lose 30 percent, you have to make over 40 percent just to break even. It hurts more to lose $10,000 than it feels good to make another $10,000. Money put into the stock market is risk capital.

Also, it take enormous time and effort to keep up with the markets. Most investors don't want to get into the day-to-day grind of day-trading or short-term trading. Most people would rather go to the movies, go dancing, take a trip, or go jog or play golf—anything other than the mind-numbing minutiae of guessing market trends, company developments, and investor sentiment. There has been an explosion in market "information," of which most is informative, but it's not useful. The trader and stock market banter, the day-trader's tips and the cable TV savant's latest market or company prognosticating is known in academic circles as "noise." Noise is market information that appears and sounds significant, but it has no lasting implications for market prices. Studies have shown that noise actually costs investors money; the most active market traders make the least money. Most investors would just like to make money and not be bothered with the details.

Everybody has a different risk profile, how much risk they can stand. The more profit sought, the higher the risk that must be taken. It takes some work to assess your risk profile and how much you can stand to lose. I'd often prefer to take a contrarian view. I would rather look to buy stocks when no one else wants them. I prefer to ferret through blown-out stocks and groups and countries to find value that will be recognized over time. Using this strategy, I've bought a number of stocks for myself and/or clients: IBM in the fifties, before it went up four times; Reading and Bates around five, before it went up six times; and recently, Japanese WEBS, which have appreciated about 40 percent.

In this extended U.S. bull market, momentum players have been the real winners. Momentum operators buy stocks that are making new highs, the ones that everyone else is buying, betting that the stocks will make even higher highs. But this bull market can't go on forever (long in the tooth would be an understatement), and when the market turns, these same momentum players will short stocks, the stocks that others are dumping, and follow them to new lows. This, then, is a reasonable time to look to foreign markets for their relative value vis-à-vis the U.S. market.

By almost all valuations, the U.S. markets are high. *The New York Times*, in February 1999, carried an article stating that the ratio of market capitalization to gross national product in the United States was 140 percent. This number is twice as high as it was in Indonesia or Brazil at the time of their market collapses, and the U.S. market has gone higher since that observation.

With WEBS, a quick call to your broker or a mouse-click through your online broker can buy you foreign markets. And as was covered earlier, an index approach to participating in foreign markets takes the stock decision-making quandary out of the equation. WEBS are new. They've been out about three years. They track the indexes of 17 countries around the globe, encompassing both mature and emerging markets. The most prominent stocks of each country are found in WEBS. With them, you can profit by being in the right country, and, of course, you can short WEBS and bet on a declining market in any given country.

THE GROWTH OF NON-U.S. MARKETS
The reason to invest internationally isn't only because of lofty U.S. market valuations. Opportunities are on the increase internationally. The U.S. market is still the largest in the world, but its share of world market capitalization is shrinking. As Figure 10-1 shows, almost 54 percent of the world's stocks are now outside the U.S.

The reason for the shrinking U.S. share of the global market is the rapid growth of companies abroad. The United States has undergone a restructuring in its economy, and now the rest of the world is following suit. Globally, government-run services, such as telephone companies, banks, and airlines, are being *privatized*. Privatization involves the sale of equity ownership in state-owned businesses to private investors. It may be done for government revenue or simply to change a country's financial system. These companies are then being listed on foreign exchanges and competing on a global scale. This development is expected to continue.

FIGURE 10-1 The Surging Expansion of Overseas Markets

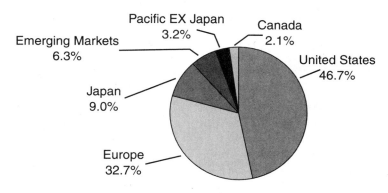

Source: MSCI 8/31/98.

PROFIT POTENTIAL AND RISK IN FOREIGN MARKETS

Figure 10-2 shows that from August 1993 to August 1998, the U.S. market, as measured by the MSCI index, was outperformed by eight foreign equity markets, even though the U.S. market put in one of its strongest performances over that time.

Certainly, that country or countries you invest in will dictate whether you have a profitable trade. It has been estimated that 80 percent of international investment returns comes from the country selected for investment, as opposed to the selection of stocks. Investing by country rather than by stock implies you are investing top-down rather than bottom-up. *Top-down* means that you look first at general economic trends, then find industries and companies that will benefit from these trends. In the bottom-up approach you search for companies that look like outstanding value, no matter what general economic conditions are. The theory here is that good stocks will do well no matter what.

Do not underestimate the risks in going international, however. Markets outside of the United States are often more volatile, especially emerging markets. Sometimes foreign markets suffer from political unrest, currency fluctuations, and changes in economic and social policy. They can get very thin, making it hard to get trades done.

FIGURE 10-2   Five-Year Performance of World Equity Markets

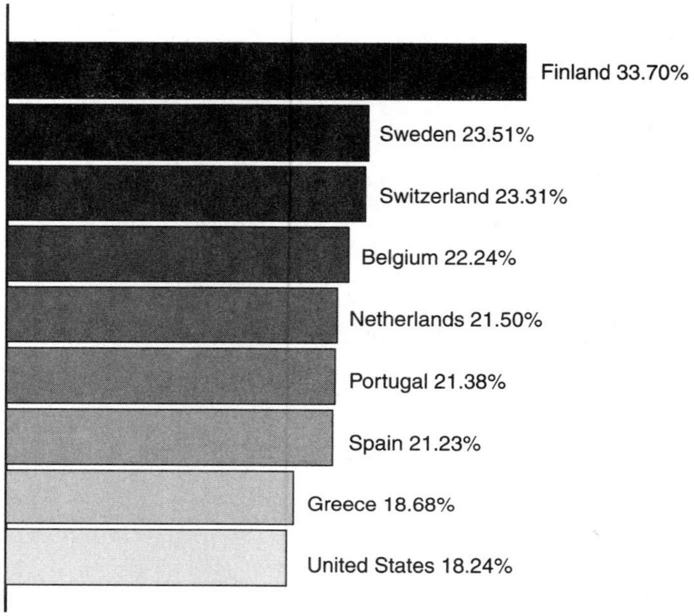

Source: Lipper Analytical Services.

DEVELOPED AND EMERGING MARKETS
In general, developed markets are considered to be the 20 markets that make up the Morgan Stanley Capital International Europe, Asia, Far East index (MSCI EAFE). These markets include Austria, Belgium, Denmark, Finland, France, Germany, Ireland, Italy, Netherlands, Norway, Spain, Sweden, Switzerland, and the United Kingdom in Europe, and Australia, Japan, Hong Kong, Malaysia, New Zealand, and Singapore in Asia. Canada is also a developed market, but not part of EAFE. Emerging markets are those that are less developed, and because of their relative "youth," the risks attendant to investing in them are greater.

MSCI AND THE WORLD MARKETS
In 1969 the Capital Group, a major investment management firm based in Los Angeles, started the Capital International indexes to use as research tools. The Capital Group was a pioneer in the international investing area.

In 1987 the investment banking firm Morgan Stanley purchased rights to use these indexes. Morgan Stanley used them to build client interest in its international capabilities and to develop its international investing activity. Over time, the MSCI indexes became an important business for Morgan Stanley. The people creating the indexes and making the portfolio adjustments were employed by the Capital Group and were based in Geneva, Switzerland. The people marketing the indexes and making the enterprise into a larger business were employed by Morgan Stanley.

In 1998 this structure changed. Morgan Stanley and Capital Group created a separate entity and named it MSCI, Inc. MSCI, Inc. is majority owned by Morgan Stanley, with Capital Group retaining an interest. The approximately 125 employees of the new entity report to MSCI, Inc. About 80 of them are based in Geneva, mostly "back-office" people, and perform the index calculations, index editing, and portfolio maintenance. All of the index portfolio decisions are made by the people in the Geneva office. There is a clear separation between client service and orientation and the back-office people. This keeps a wall between the decision-makers and the clients and cuts down on the possibility of "front-running" or other misuse of inside information. *Front-running* is when an individual takes a stock position based on an event that is not yet public knowledge. When a company is added to an index, for instance, the stock will run up in anticipation of the index managers having to buy the stock to put into the index.

Activity has grown tremendously for MSCI over the past five years. It has expanded its product line to take the company in the direction of more specialized investment strategies. MSCI is growing beyond pure index calculations and into the realm of structured products and exchange listed products. Although MSCI finds its functions becoming more complex, it is still grounded in the concept of trying to capture the performance of the various markets, both equity and fixed-income. People can use the products as passive (meaning indexed) tools or as active management tools.

THE CHANGING INTERNATIONAL BENCHMARKS

The MSCI Europe, Asia, and Far East (EAFE) index is the recognized standard benchmark for U.S.-based asset managers that are managing international portfolios. In the United States the concept of managing developed foreign markets and emerging foreign markets as two separate mandates is disappearing. Managers are concluding that if they manage developed and emerging accounts as separate portfolios and separate mandates and separate decisions, the managers have to decide how much to allocate to the emerging markets and how much to put into the developed markets. Making allocations can be risky. For example, emerging markets collapsed in the summer of 1998 and burned the managers and their clients' portfolios.

As a result, many pension plans and other institutional plan sponsors are adopting an index that MSCI developed called the Morgan Stanley All Country World Index (ACWI). The ACWI is a mix of developed markets and emerging markets. It allows managers to have representation in foreign stocks without having to make allocations between the developed and emerging foreign countries.

HOW WEBS STAY IN COMPLIANCE

WEBS are managed by Barclays Global Investors (BGI). This firm is a leader in quantitative equity management, managing over $600 billion around the globe. Each WEBS series closely tracks the MSCI index for the country the WEBS operate in. The goal of WEBS is to track the index; therefore, the index could decline and WEBS could still be successful in their tracking requirement.

BGI goes through all 17 portfolios each day; it makes sure that they are compliant with SEC regulations and also that the portfolios track the MSCI index. There are two major areas of concern. First, there is a 25 percent single issue rule. The SEC has mandated that no mutual fund can hold any single stock at a weight greater than 25 percent of the portfolio. The rule is to guarantee that when investors invest in a mutual fund, they won't have, say, 80 percent of their money invested in a single stock. Second, there is a 5/50 rule. This rule dictates that all of the stocks with a weight of 5 percent or greater of the fund cannot equal a total weight of more than 50 percent of the total fund portfolio. These rules seem fair. The SEC's intent is that the investor not be misled by purchasing a mutual fund that is heavily concentrated in either a subset of stocks or the same stocks.

The rules require that a quarterly check be made to prove compliance. That's why BGI monitors daily to make sure each portfolio is in compliance. To accomplish this, systems are used. For each of the 17 portfolios, a single check is run daily. This check looks across and verifies which portfolios are out of compliance and why. In addition, there is a series of diagnostics BGI runs periodically that report any "exceptions" to its predetermined portfolio model. If something comes up, then it digs deeper. Perhaps one stock has appreciated to the point that it now comprises 25.4 percent of the portfolio instead of the 25 percent allowed. BGI will then decide either to sell the 0.4 percent of the stock or to wait a day or so to see if market action readjusts the position back to compliance. The portfolio managers want to avoid selling if possible. They are careful about incurring transaction costs to the portfolio. Low turnover keeps costs low and enhances a fund's performance. Coming into a quarter's end, BGI will rebalance to make sure compliance measurements are met.

WEBS TRACK THE MSCI INDEX

WEBS are not set up to mirror the major indexes of each country. For instance, the Japanese WEBS do not track the Nikkei, which is the major Japanese index. Nor do the U.K. WEBS track the FT-30 index, the major U.K. index. As far as tracking the European markets, BGI estimates that overall, WEBS correlate over 90 percent to each country's MSCI indexes. Austria drops down to about an 86 percent correlation. Mexico and Canada WEBS have a very close correlation to those MSCI indexes, about 95 percent. The Far East countries are the ones that have the least correlation to the indexes. Usually, these WEBS correlate about 80 to 85 percent with the indexes.

CONCENTRATION PROBLEMS

In countries where there is a high concentration of one stock in the MSCI index, BGI has a problem tracking the index. For example, Royal Dutch used to comprise 35 percent of the Netherlands MSCI index. Because of the SEC single-issue rule, the Netherlands WEBS could only hold 25 percent of the issue. The managers, therefore, carried a 25 percent weighting of Royal Dutch and watched it closely. If the stock jumped up in price to where it comprised, say, a 30 percent portfolio weighting, they would sell off 5 percent. If it moved up to 25.4 percent of the portfolio, they would probably do nothing until their rebalancing at the end of the quarter. Royal Dutch has since merged, obviating that situation.

So on a daily basis, the managers at BGI are doing two things simultaneously. They are making sure that the WEBS portfolios track the MSCI country indexes as closely as possible, and they are keeping the portfolios compliant with SEC mutual fund rules.

Not all 17 WEBS have concentration problems, but five or six do require quite a bit of massaging on a daily basis. Another five or six occasionally have 25 percent issue problems.

In Belgium, for instance, there is a problem arising from the SEC rule that the stocks that have a 5 percent or greater portfolio weighting can only add up to 50 percent of the portfolio. The Belgium MSCI index has only 16 names in it. It is immediately obvious that there will be a WEBS diversification problem. If you take all of the stocks that weigh 5 percent or greater, they equal 87 percent of the portfolio. Essentially, BGI cannot index Belgium in a conventional way. The "overweight" 37 percent causes BGI to have to reallocate. Automatically, the WEBS manager has to shave off the larger-cap stocks in the MSCI index and replace them with smaller-cap stocks to create a WEBS portfolio.

As an example, TRACTEBEL will be underweighted by 2 percent; UCB by 1 percent; PETROFINA by 2 percent; and so on. Then the manager will reallocate this underweighting to small-cap stocks. This reallocation process is no mean feat, but BGI does it well. BGI predicts its tracking "error" (error being the difference between the stock selection to create a subset in a WEBS reallocation compared to the stocks in the MSCI index) at under 2 percent.

Now, this reallocation to smaller-caps can cost in terms of performance results. Recently, the larger-cap stocks, globally, have been performing better than small-cap stocks. If a country's WEBS are underweighted in large-cap stocks and large-caps perform well, the WEBS will lag that country's MSCI index performance. This underperformance has been known to figure over 10 percent. But by the same token, this dominance of large-caps over small-caps can swiftly change. Small-caps can outperform large-caps, causing WEBS to outperform the MSCI indexes.

In bigger markets with more stock names to choose from, this balancing is not necessary.

CONSTANT MONITORING BY THE WEBS PORTFOLIO MANAGER
BGI has devised software programs to maintain the "baskets" of stock in each WEBS. A basket is a group of stocks that comprise a country WEBS. Throughout the day, the manager does her checks. Her screen shows the number of shares, name of stock, local price, currency rate, the portfolio weight that the stock comprises, the value of the position, and the benchmark weight, which is the MSCI index weight.

The manager is looking at the comparison between the WEBS portfolio weighting in each issue and the index weighting. Through this comparison and compliance with SEC regulations, the WEBS portfolio is constructed and maintained.

This juggling act keeps the portfolio managers under tight constraints. They are not going to go off on a hunch or load up on a stock just because they like it. They have to stay within these mandated guidelines.

Staying with the 25 percent rule, the manager will follow the screen throughout the day to see if an issue rises above that number. As for the 5/50 rule, several times throughout the day, the portfolio manager will take all the stocks that are 5 percent and above and all that stocks that are below 5 percent and run a total.

The 5/50 rule can create problems for WEBS managers in a few countries. For instance, if you add up all the 5 percent names in the Switzerland index, they will amount to 82 percent of the portfolio; and this 82 percent consists of only about 5 names. Tracking this index is vastly different from tracking a big, diverse portfolio such as the United Kingdom or Japan.

Another SEC rule has to do with industry concentration. BGI is limited as to how many stocks in the portfolio can be operating in the same industry. Another software program the manager constantly monitors shows all of the industries that the portfolio is invested in, the industries' weights in the portfolio, the allowable weights for compliance purposes, and the difference between compliance weights and actual weights.

Sometimes, the manager will not carry a name because the issue doesn't trade as actively as BGI would like. The issue may be too hard to buy in the size needed, or once bought, too hard to sell. The manager runs liquidity reports, which give the liquidity factor of a basket. Usually, the manager's objective is that if he has to sell his whole position, it will account for only around 10 percent of the daily volume of the stock. Certainly he wants to be less than 20 percent of the stock's daily volume.

TIME DIFFERENCES

One complication factor arises out of the difference between the close of the index price against the price of the WEBS on the AMEX. This can vary because of time changes. For instance, in San Francisco, Hong Kong is 17 hours ahead. The Hong Kong market opens at 9:30 a.m., when it is 4:30 p.m. the previous day in San Francisco and the U.S. markets have just closed. The Hong Kong markets close at 3:30 p.m., so it is 10:30 a.m. in San Francisco. If the U.S. market rallies, that will often push the WEBS prices higher in anticipation of a higher opening in Far East markets the next day.

European market times are closer to the U.S. market time than the Far Eastern markets. The markets in Mexico and Canada trade at the same times as the United States. Any development or market action in Canada and Mexico will receive immediate reaction on the WEBS of those countries, since they are trading on the ASE.

THE FUNCTION OF THE WEBS SPECIALIST

The time factor difference creates a challenge for the specialist in making an orderly market in WEBS. When U.S markets rally or decline, bidding up or down Far Eastern WEBS, the specialist is really guessing at what price the underlying WEBS securities will open in the Far East.

But they do a good job. One specialist on the floor related to me how in February 1998, there were volatile moves in the Hong Kong markets. They rallied sharply one evening. The next morning, the specialist, anticipating the Hong Kong WEBS would rally further on the ASE, opened the WEBS about 3 percent higher than the closing of the NAV of the prior night's trading in Hong Kong. Buyers continued flooding in throughout the day.

Pondering what he should do, the specialist continued taking the WEBS prices higher. Remember, he was estimating at what price the NAV of the underlying stocks in the WEBS would trade that evening on the Hang Seng, the major Hong Kong exchange. Influenced by the continued buying on the AMEX, the specialist took the Hong Kong WEBS up 10 percent, then 12 percent, until by the end of the day, the Hong Kong WEBS finished up about 17 percent over the previous closing NAV.

On the opening of the Hang Seng Exchange, the WEBS underlying stock traded up about 15 percent, and the Hang Seng that session closed up about 17 percent. This case demonstrates how the specialist, in his role of maintaining an orderly market, can be pretty accurate in predicting a market's moves.

WEBS are an effective tool for U.S. investors and traders to trade during the day in the United States. They also give investors an opportunity to get in and out of a foreign market during the U.S. trading hours, when that foreign market is not open.

ABOUT CURRENCY RISK

Currency risk goes with the purchaser or short seller of the WEBS. The return on virtually all graphs dealing with international investing, including WEBS, is stated in terms of U.S. dollars. For the buyer or short seller, currency risk and reward are connected with the extent that the dollar weakens or strengthens against the WEBS country, translating into a profit or loss in addition to any trading results.

There are actions you can take to protect yourself against currency swings. One of these is to hedge yourself by shorting the currency of the country of the WEBS you bought. You can also buy forward currency of the country of the WEBS you have shorted.

DIVIDENDS

Cash dividends flow through to WEBS holders. Every August, a dividend distribution is made to WEBS shareholders. Some of these dividends are fairly good. The Hong Kong WEBS paid at a rate of 3.73 percent over a recent 12-month period. The Austria WEBS paid at a rate of 7.3 percent, although this was not a true rate, since a large capital gains was included. The Belgium WEBS, also with a large capital gain, paid at a rate of 8.1 percent. Although each market has to be looked at from a risk and reward perspective, these rates are rather high, and could be considered as a bond or other fixed-income substitute.

WEBS EXPENSE RATIOS
As was covered in Chapter 1, expense ratios are already built into the price of the exchange shares. There is no expense other than brokerage fees in buying WEBS. WEBS expense ratios average about 1 percent of the assets under management, a reasonable amount, and about as well as an investor can do when buying foreign securities. Most foreign mutual funds have a ratio of 140 to 150 bp, and there are expense ratios of up to 200 bp in other foreign mutual funds.

DIVERSIFICATION THROUGH FOREIGN MARKETS
One reason to invest abroad is because of the greater growth that is expected there than in the United States. Also, the U.S. market sells at a high valuation. Geographical diversification just makes sense. Take a look at the following charts. Figure 10-3 shows the EAFE countries' returns received each year over the past 20 years.

Figure 10-4 shows these same returns compounded over that same 20 years. These returns disregard commissions, taxes, and other expenses.

FIGURE 10-3   Return of EAFE 1979–1998

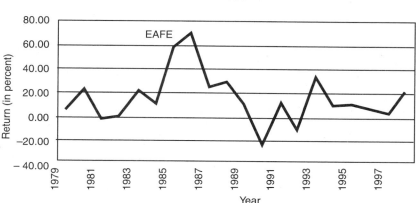

FIGURE 10-4   20-Year Return of EAFE

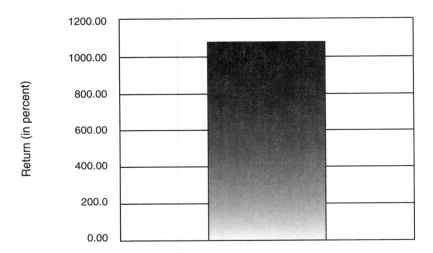

It is possible to fashion an EAFE portfolio for yourself. If you buy all of the 17 WEBS portfolios, you will capture 97 percent of EAFE. In fact, you could attempt to outperform EAFE by overweighting or underweighting WEBS country selections. Or you could select a smaller sampling of countries that constitute EAFE and attempt to gain a return that might exceed the EAFE index.

ANALYZING FOREIGN MARKETS

When developing a specific type of portfolio, a focused country-allocation portfolio, you must have a strategy (top-down) of making country decisions. Typical considerations are whether, for example, to be in Japan or overweighted in the United Kingdom. Or should you have an exposure to Belgium, and if so, how much? So you have to decide which countries are attractive, then achieve exposure by using WEBS.

Also, you can be more aggressive if you wish. If you don't like Japan, for instance, why have any Japan at all in your portfolio? If you like Belgium, why carry only 5 percent or 6 percent in your portfolio? Why not carry 20 percent or 30 percent?

You can fashion any type of portfolio you want, many countries for a more diversified portfolio or fewer for a concentrated, focused, and aggressive portfolio. WEBS allow these strategies perfectly. Using a top-down approach, a simple portfolio structure like WEBS works well. WEBS already have a portfolio that can be used according to the investment that you create. You must predetermine which countries are the best to invest in and which to avoid or sell short, then weight the selected countries properly to be fully invested. This simple way to invest is also low in cost. The only expenses are the brokerage fees. Then periodic monitoring is required.

Many money managers use WEBS for their portfolios. For example, Murray Johnstone International, Ltd., headquartered in Glasgow, Scotland, manages over $7.5 billion worldwide. Murray Johnstone employs WEBS for one of its niche portfolios, using its own top-down research selection process.

Following are some factors to consider when analyzing the economic prospects for a country.

THE ECONOMIC PICTURE

1. *The currency.* With the implementation of the euro, the common currency for 11 European countries, currency swings within Europe will be much less volatile. But is the currency sound in the WEBS countries you invest in? A weak currency can send investors pouring out of a country, causing havoc in its stock and bond markets.

2. *Wages.* Spiraling wages will ultimately force the price of a country's goods and services higher, therefore damaging its international trade performance. Ultimately, this affects the country's stock and bond markets negatively. If wages are steady or headed downward, this could increase a country's trade position.

3. *Economic growth.* A country must have growth industries to continue to grow. There is a global switch under way from low-tech to high-tech industries. National boundaries have dropped in significance as the information age roars ahead. Some countries will be left behind, and others will grow.

4. *Fiscal policy.* Governments can stimulate business activity by increasing purchases and by cutting taxes. This releases funds into the private sector. Government can also reverse this process and slow activity. It is crucial that government have not only the will to spur activity to keep a country economically healthy but also the expertise. There is nothing like political uncertainty to send funds fleeing out of a country.

5. *Current account.* To keep a record of a country's economic transactions with the rest of the world, a current account of imports and exports of goods and services is kept. A current account that shows a

worsening balance of payments might be a warning sign of a deteriorating trade position.

MONETARY POLICY

1. *Inflation.* When the cost of items rises, causing a decrease in the purchasing power of a country's currency, inflation might be raising its ugly head. This can cause serious damage to a country's economic and investment prospects. Moderate inflation can be tolerated, but if inflation is accelerating far above a country's norm, there might be trouble ahead.

2. *Money supply.* If money is tight, causing interest rates to move higher, slowdowns in economic activity may lie ahead. Governments have mechanisms to loosen and tighten the money supply and steer the economy. In times of stress, however, governments may be restricted in their options. For instance, during a period of high inflation and low economic activity, governments cannot raise the money supply, since this would bring on more inflation.

STOCK VALUES

Once you have checked the underlying economic fundamentals of a country, take a look at that country's WEBS stock composition. The stocks can be found in Bloomberg Financial Network or other financial information sources.

If a country has many high-yielding stocks, this may suggest that the growth and earnings of the companies are rather stagnant and that the yield compensates for this. Checking future earnings prospects is vital. It is also important to gauge where in the market cycle a country is. Growing earnings projections in a market that has fallen is the ideal state. Even being a little early—buying a market that has sold off but has bright earnings potential over the longer-term—is close to ideal. Speak to some brokers in the country you are considering buying into and get their market assessment and outlook. Usually, there are brokers in any country available who speak English.

Look at the price/earnings multiples of the stocks underlying a country's WEBS. The best time to buy is when P/Es are low. I'm reminded of the year 1974, when the Dow Jones Industrial Average was in the mid-700s and the P/E of the average was about eight times. Pessimism abounded and everybody had given up on stocks. Today, the P/E is around 25. The thing to do is to ferret out those countries that can advance in P/E in the future.

Also, consider the price-to-book-value ratio (P/BV). This is the ratio of the market price of a stock to its book value. A high P/BV, perhaps three or higher, may represent a growth stock. A stock selling at book value or less may be a bargain, and a value investment. If a country is embarking on a restructuring, such as has happened in the United States over the last 10 years, low P/BV stocks may represent real value.

The price-to-sales ratio (P/S) is another commonly used ratio. P/S is the ratio of the market price of a stock to its sales per share. P/S is a true ratio, since sales are harder to manipulate than, say, earnings per share or book value per share. A company with a large amount of sales per share needs only a small drop in expenses to increase earnings. Value investors appreciate this.

WHEN TO SELL

Out of the 17 WEBS, you will probably want to own only five or six at any one time if you are attempting to beat the EAFE index. Depending on how much time you want to give to your investments, you should monitor—quarterly, semiannually, or annually—the countries in which you are invested. If you own countries that you would not buy, you should consider selling them and replacing them with more attractive countries.

You also could sell when problems appear in a country. Perhaps a country's trade balance is deteriorating or its currency is declining. The stock market in that country may continue performing well, but you want to get out before fundamentals force the markets lower. And if you sell early, you may want to put in a short, with a sell cover limit up about 10 percent.

Markets can also get ahead of themselves. Consider selling after a market has performed well but the valuations have gotten high and ahead of the fundamentals. Often, the pride of owning a country that has done well can affect your judgment. It's sometimes best to leave some profit on the table for the next buyer.

Today, there is an abundance of information about foreign markets, so you can research which markets to be in. You can check newspapers, such as *The Financial Times*. Also, peruse the home page of Morgan Stanley Dean Witter and Standard & Poor's, which will guide you to their foreign markets research.

VALUE AND GROWTH IN WORLDWIDE INVESTING

The best place to search for value is in markets that have underperformed. Currently, Austria has sat still for three years and could be getting ready to move. On the contrary, the United States, selling at its lofty heights, and with currency weakness starting to surface, looks vulnerable. The economy in the United States is about as good as it can get. Although the U.S. markets could go higher, diversification at this time makes sense, at least as a hedge. Diversify into countries that have had down markets and are starting to come out of it, like Singapore, Austria, and Mexico.

IN A NUTSHELL—THE FOREIGN ECONOMIC LANDSCAPE

Australia—WEBS price, $10^3/_4$. The country has very strong economy now, but there is risk from its growing negative trade imbalance. This could cause rising interest rates and a weakening currency. The Australia WEBS have been one of the better performers, up about 12 percent this year. There is no reason to buy the country at this level.

Austria—$9^1/_2$. This economy has been weak, but it is likely to improve soon. Austria is an extraordinary value market. The P/BV is 1.9, meaning that assets are valued very cheaply. Price to cash is 8.3. Cash is high as a percentage of the stocks' market price. The market has been down for the last three years, yet earnings forecasts are for 20 percent gains each year for the next two years. The market is overlooked by investors because of its small size. This market can be bought.

Singapore—$8^1/_4$. This market crashed in 1997 and was soft until September 1998. It was a cheaply valued market at the crash low but has doubled since then, making it less attractive. But the economy is improving significantly. The interest rate outlook is favorable, and money supply is strong, making for a liquid monetary picture. The earnings outlook is favorable, with upgrades taking place. It's an interesting market to buy.

Japan—$14^1/_4$. The WEBS were up about 40 percent in 1999, a good market performer. Japan's economy has stopped deteriorating, but economic data looking forward is mixed. Value is also mixed. P/BV is good, and stock price to cash is also favorable. P/E multiples, however, are very high, and dividends are low. This market is a buy.

Hong Kong—$12^1/_4$. This WEBS is a similar situation to that of Japan. Hong Kong is no longer a value market. Although earnings are improving, the market has run up over 33 percent. Hong Kong is a buy.

Italy—$23^3/_4$. A relatively undervalued market that has not performed very well for three years, lately, it has been strong. The Italian stock market is rather thin, leading sometimes to violent price moves. The government is encouraging more medium-sized companies to list shares to reduce this problem. Buy for the longer term.

Mexico—13^1/$_2$. This WEBS has more than doubled over the last 12 months, reflecting a return of growth to the region. Continued growth in the United States and Brazil remains important for Mexico's economic health. Keeping in mind that investing in emerging market countries, such as Mexico, entails higher risks than developed countries, this country is a buy.

Belgium—18^1/$_8$. This is an attractive market from a value standpoint, although the market has not performed well recently. The dividend yield is about 2.5 percent, and a large capital gain boosted it over 8 percent for the last 12 months. The economy appears fairly healthy, and the WEBS have not moved up yet. Belgium, at these levels, is a buy.

Netherlands—25^1/$_2$; and **Switzerland**—16. The WEBS in these countries are not very exciting. The economies are reasonably solid and improving. The value factors are mixed. The markets have lagged and should perform but need some time before they become buys.

France—22^7/$_8$; and **Germany**—21^3/$_4$. On a short-term basis, these countries are not compelling buys. The economics in both countries are improving. Their earnings outlook and stock market values are mixed. Both countries, under new governments, are extolling growth and full-employment policies.

Canada—14^1/$_8$. This country usually advances and declines with the outlook for commodity prices. Its market is heavy with resource-based companies. The country is also affected by the U.S. economy. With commodity prices lagging, Canada should be avoided.

Malaysia—6. The government of this emerging market country has rebuilt the level of foreign reserves that fled the country during the mid-1998 Asian crises. There are political risks in Malaysia. The country is nevertheless attractive and can be bought as a speculation.

United Kingdom—21^1/$_2$. The U.K. economy appears a little weak. Stock valuations appear high, and the earnings outlook is not very attractive. At the present price, the WEBS do not have a lot of risk, but there is no compelling reason to buy.

Sweden—23^1/$_2$. Valuations in Sweden look rather high. The currency does not look attractive. Also threatening is the European Monetary Union (EMU) question. The Left and Green parties are opposed to Sweden joining the EMU. If Sweden does not join, investors could lose interest in its equity markets, further worsening market performance in that country. Avoid.

Spain—$26^3/_4$. Spain is enthusiastic about its inclusion in the EMU and the benefits it has derived. The country is fairly priced on its fundamentals, and there is no compelling reason to buy. An overhanging political uncertainty is the general election in March 2000. The present government has presided over growth, but it may have trouble staying in office.

Table 10-2 shows the stocks and their weightings of each country WEBS.

TABLE 10-2 The Stocks of the 17 Different Country WEBS

WBJ	**Member Weightings**		Page 1 / 1	
MSCI WEBS AUSTRALIA IOPV			% capitalization weighted index %	
37 Members				
1) AMC	AN AMCOR LTD	2.088 %	21) NCP	AN NEWS CORP LTD	7.629 %
2) AMP	AN AMP LIMITED	5.341 %	22) NCPDP	AN NEWS CORP-PFD OR	4.807 %
3) AGL	AN AUST GAS LIGHT	.944 %	23) NDY	AN NORMANDY MINING	.651 %
4) BOR	AN BORAL LIMITED	1.273 %	24) NBH	AN NORTH LIMITED	1.147 %
5) BIL	AN BRAMBLES INDS	3.931 %	25) ORI	AN ORICA LTD	1.025 %
6) BHP	AN BROKEN HILL PROP	9.929 %	26) PDP	AN PAC DUNLOP LTD	.989 %
7) CCL	AN COCA-COLA AMATIL	1.853 %	27) PNI	AN PIONEER INTL LTD	1.750 %
8) CML	AN COLES MYER LTD	3.804 %	28) RIO	AU RIO TINTO LTD	3.434 %
9) CSR	AN CSR LIMITED	1.764 %	29) STO	AN SANTOS LTD	1.142 %
10) EML	AN EMAIL LTD	.489 %	30) SMI	AN SMITH (HOWARD)	1.431 %
11) FBG	AN FOSTERS BREWING	3.319 %	31) SRP	AN SOUTHCORP LTD	2.024 %
12) GPT	AN GEN PROP TRUST	1.065 %	32) SGP	AN STOCKLAND TST	1.067 %
13) GIO	AN GIO AUSTRALIA	.559 %	33) TAH	AN TABCORP HLDGS LT	1.597 %
14) GMF	AN GOODMAN FIELDER	.764 %	34) TLS	AN TELSTRA CORP	9.127 %
15) HAH	AN JAMES HARDIE IND	.897 %	35) WFT	AN WESTFIELD TRUST	1.981 %
16) LEI	AN LEIGHTON HLDGS	.323 %	36) WBC	AN WESTPAC BANKING	4.230 %
17) LLC	AN LEND LEASE CORP	3.322 %	37) WMC	AN WMC LTD	2.990 %
18) MIM	AN MIM HLDGS LTD	.851 %			
19) NAB	AN NATL AUST BANK	9.230 %			
20) NCM	AN NEWCREST MINING	.465 %			

Tables courtesy of MSLI.

157

TABLE 10-2 *(Continued)*

MSCI WEBS AUSTRIA IOPV   = capitalization weighted index =

	19 Members	
1) AMSI	AV AUSTRIA MIKRO SY	.738 %
2) ATBK	AV AUSTRIA TABAK	4.125 %
3) AAIR	AV AUSTRIAN AIRLINE	3.186 %
4) BAUS	AV BANK AUSTRIA AG	22.347 %
5) BHLDV	AV BAU HOLDING-VORZ	.395 %
6) BHLD	AV BAU HOLDING	3.257 %
7) OEBB	AV BBAG OEST BRAU	1.668 %
8) BOEH	AV BOEHLER-UDDEHOLM	4.441 %
9) BWTA	AV BWT AG	3.174 %
10) FLUG	AV FLUGHAFEN WIEN	4.497 %
11) EAGE	AV GENERALI HLDG	3.466 %
12) LENZ	AV LENZING AG	2.679 %
13) MAYR	AV MAYR-MELNHOF KAR	4.859 %
14) OEEW	AV OEST ELEKTRIZ-A	16.606 %
15) OMV	AV OMV AG	10.407 %
16) RADX	AV RHI AG	3.939 %
17) UNIB	AV UNIVERSALE BAU	.642 %
18) VATC	AV VA TECHNOLOGIE	3.772 %
19) WBST	AV WIENERBERGER BAU	4.652 %

TABLE 10-2 (Continued)

```
 INK          Member Weightings        Page  1 / 1
MSCI WEBS BELGIUM IOPV              ■ capitalization weighted index ■
    17    Members
 1) BAR     BB BARCO NV                 1.785 %
 2) BEK     BB BEKAERT NV               1.650 %
 3) CBR     BB CBR CIMENTERIES          3.863 %
 4) CMB     BB CMB CIE MARITIME         1.665 %
 5) COL     BB COLRUYT NV               4.260 %
 6) DIEA    BB D'IETEREN                5.113 %
 7) DEHT    BB DELHAIZE-LE LION         4.497 %
 8) ELB     BB ELECTRABEL SA           13.607 %
 9) ELC     BB ELECTRAFINA              1.747 %
10) FOR     BB FORTIS (B)              21.700 %
11) GVB     BB GLAVERBEL SA             1.387 %
12) GBL     BB GROUP BRUX LAMB          1.000 %
13) KBC     BB KBC BANCASSURANC        13.555 %
14) SOL     BB SOLVAY SA-A              4.855 %
15) TRC     BB TRACTEBEL               10.255 %
16) UCB     BB UCB SA                   4.689 %
17) UM      BB UNION MINIERE SA         3.150 %
```

TABLE 10-2 (Continued)

MSCI WEBS CANADA IOPV
69 Members

#			Weighting
1) A	CT	ABITIBI-CONSOLID	.868 %
2) AGU	CT	AGRIUM INC	.432 %
3) AC	CT	AIR CANADA	.247 %
4) AEC	CT	ALBERTA ENERGY	1.151 %
5) AL	CT	ALCAN ALUM	2.490 %
6) AXL	CT	ANDERSON EXPLOR	.523 %
7) BMO	CT	BANK MONTREAL	2.805 %
8) BNS	CT	BANK NOVA SCOTIA	3.254 %
9) ABX	CT	BARRICK GOLD CRP	2.051 %
10) BCE	CT	BCE INC	7.441 %
11) BTS/A	CT	BCT.TELUS-A SHS	.352 %
12) BBD/B	CT	BOMBARDIER INC B	3.331 %
13) CBJ	CM	CAMBIOR INC	.062 %
14) CCO	CT	CAMECO CORP	.403 %
15) CM	CT	CAN IMPL BK COMM	2.901 %
16) CNQ	CT	CAN NATURAL RES	.709 %
17) CXY	CT	CAN OCCI PETE	.828 %
18) CP	CT	CAN PACIFIC LTD	2.756 %
19) CTR/A	CT	CAN TIRE CORP -A	.935 %
20) CCQ/B	CM	CCL INDS B	.217 %
21) CLT	CT	COMINCO LTD	.489 %
22) DFS	CT	DOFASCO INC	.750 %
23) DTC	CT	DOMTAR INC	.557 %
24) ECO	CT	ECHO BAY MINES	.058 %
25) EBC/A	CT	EDPERBRASCAN-A	.775 %
26) ENB	CT	ENBRIDGE INC	1.224 %
27) EXE/A	CT	EXTENDICARE-CL A	.091 %
28) FFH	CT	FAIRFAX FINL HLD	.265 %
29) GOU	CT	GULF CANADA RES	.312 %
30) HBC	CM	HUDSONS BAY CO	.317 %
31) IMS	CT	IMASCO LTD	3.776 %
32) IMO	CT	IMPERIAL OIL	2.699 %
33) N	CT	INCO LTD	1.146 %
34) N/V	CT	INCO LTD-CL VBN	.180 %
35) LDM	CT	LAIDLAW INC	.771 %
36) MB	CT	MACMILLAN BLOED	.740 %
37) MG/A	CT	MAGNA INTL-A	1.087 %
38) MHG/B	CT	MDS INC-CL B	.421 %
39) MX	CT	METHANEX CORP	.175 %
40) MOL/A	CT	MOLSON INC-A SHS	.499 %

TABLE 10-2 (Continued)

MSCI WEBS CANADA IOPV
69 Members

#				
1) MCL	CT	MOORE CORP LTD	.308 %	
2) NA	CT	NATL BK CANADA	.725 %	
3) NNC	CT	NEWBRIDGE NETWRK	1.680 %	
4) NOR	CT	NORANDA INC	1.223 %	
5) NT	CT	NORTEL NETWORKS	16.090 %	
6) PCA	CT	PETRO-CANADA	.558 %	
7) PDG	CT	PLACER DOME INC	.901 %	
8) POC	CT	POCO PETRO LTD	.445 %	
9) POT	CT	POTASH CORP SAS	1.262 %	
10) POW	CT	POWER CORP CDA	1.279 %	
11) QBR/B	CT	QUEBECOR INC-B	.533 %	
12) RGO	CT	RANGER OIL LTD	.166 %	
13) RES	CT	RENAISSANCE ENGY	.595 %	
14) ROM	CT	RIO ALGOM LTD	.337 %	
15) RCI/B	CT	ROGERS COMM-B	.990 %	
16) RY	CT	ROYAL BK CANADA	3.800 %	
17) VO	CT	SEAGRAM CO LTD	4.618 %	
18) SBY	CT	SOBEYS INC	.178 %	
19) SPZ	CM	SPAR AEROSPACE	.054 %	
20) STE/A	CM	STELCO INC -A	.272 %	
21) SU	CT	SUNCOR ENERGY	1.173 %	
22) TLM	CT	TALISMAN ENERGY	1.121 %	
23) TEK/B	CT	TECK CORP-B	.301 %	
24) TOC	CT	THOMSON CORP	4.250 %	
25) TA	CT	TRANSALTA CORP	.879 %	
26) TRP	CT	TRANSCAN PIPELNE	2.200 %	
27) UDI	CT	UNITED DOM INDS	.858 %	
28) W	CT	WESTCOAST ENERGY	.667 %	
29) WN	CT	WESTON (GEORGE)	1.598 %	

161

TABLE 10-2 *(Continued)*

WBF   Member Weightings   Page 1 / 2
MSCI WEBS FRANCE IOPV
50   Members
                                         * capitalization weighted index *

#	Ticker	Name	Weight	#	Ticker	Name	Weight
1)	AC	FP ACCOR SA	1.374 %	21)	GT	FP GROUPE GTM	.300 %
2)	AI	FP AIR LIQUIDE	1.633 %	22)	NK	FP IMETAL	.410 %
3)	CGE	FP ALCATEL	3.258 %	23)	OR	FP L'OREAL	6.286 %
4)	CS	FP AXA S.A.	4.755 %	24)	LG	FP LAFARGE	1.608 %
5)	BNP	FP BANQ NATL PARIS	2.608 %	25)	MMB	FP LAGARDERE SCA	.656 %
6)	BB	FP BIC	.542 %	26)	LR	FP LEGRAND	.963 %
7)	EN	FP BOUYGUES	1.085 %	27)	MC	FP LVMH	3.638 %
8)	AN	FP CANAL PLUS	1.329 %	28)	ML	FP MICHELIN-B	.863 %
9)	CAP	FP CAP GEMINI SA	1.639 %	29)	PAT	FP PATHE	.443 %
10)	CA	FP CARREFOUR	4.626 %	30)	RI	FP PERNOD-RICARD	.706 %
11)	CO	FP CASINO GUICHARD	.589 %	31)	UG	FP PEUGEOT CITROEN	1.386 %
12)	CU	FP CLUB MEDITERRANE	.236 %	32)	PP	FP PINAULT-PRINTEMP	2.738 %
13)	PD	FP CPR SA	.109 %	33)	PE	FP PROMODES	2.077 %
14)	BN	FP DANONE	2.711 %	34)	RPP	FP RHONE-POULENC	2.423 %
15)	AQ	FP ELF AQUITAINE	6.641 %	35)	SA	FP SAGEM SA	.396 %
16)	BG	FP ERIDANIA BEGHIN	.560 %	36)	SAN	FP SANOFI-SYNTHELAB	2.547 %
17)	EF	FP ESSILOR INTL	.540 %	37)	SU	FP SCHNEIDER ELECTR	1.384 %
18)	RF	FP EURAFRANCE	.385 %	38)	ITA	FP SEITA	.515 %
19)	FTE	FP FRANCE TELECOM	8.060 %	39)	SID	FP SIDEL	.575 %
20)	GA	FP GEOPHYSIQUE	.053 %	40)	SC	FP SIMCO	.273 %

162

TABLE 10-2 *(Continued)*

WBF   Member Weightings Page 2 / 2
MSCI WEBS FRANCE IOPV
= capitalization weighted index =
50 Members

1) SW	FP SODEXHO ALLIANCE	.743 %
2) SGO	FP ST GOBAIN	2.399 %
3) LY	FP SUEZ LYONNAISE	3.258 %
4) TEC	FP TECHNIP	.320 %
5) HO	FP THOMSON CSF	.702 %
6) FP	FP TOTAL FINA SA-B	4.259 %
7) UL	FP UNIBAIL	.272 %
8) USI	FP USINOR	.666 %
9) FR	FP VALEO	1.036 %
10) EX	FP VIVENDI (EX-GEN	5.504 %

TABLE 10-2 (Continued)

MSCI WEBS GERMANY IOPV
40 Members   * capitalization weighted index *

1) ADS	GF ADIDAS-SALOMON	.734 %	21) LHA	GF LUFTHANSA-REG	1.125 %
2) ALV	GF ALLIANZ AG-REG	8.570 %	22) MAN	GF MAN AG	.544 %
3) AMB2	GF AMB AACHENER-BR	.698 %	23) MAN3	GF MAN AG-PFD	.175 %
4) COL	GF AXA COLONIA KONZ	.380 %	24) MMN	GF MANNESMANN AG	7.274 %
5) BAS	GF BASF AG	3.997 %	25) MRK	GF MERCK KGAA	.894 %
6) BAY	GF BAYER AG	4.489 %	26) MEO	GF METRO AG	2.057 %
7) BEI	GF BEIERSDORF	.903 %	27) MUV2	GF MUENCHENER RUE-R	4.668 %
8) GBF	GF BILFINGER & BERG	.160 %	28) PRS	GF PREUSSAG AG	1.518 %
9) BUD	GF BUDERUS AG	.322 %	29) RWE	GF RWE AG	2.458 %
10) CON	GF CONTL AG	.322 %	30) RWE3	GF RWE AG-N VTG PFD	.699 %
11) DCX	GF DAIMLERCHRYSLER	7.038 %	31) SAP	GF SAP AG	3.212 %
12) DBK	GF DEUTSCHE BK	5.275 %	32) SAP3	GF SAP AG-PFD	2.743 %
13) DTE	GF DEUTSCHE TELEKOM	11.755 %	33) SCH	GF SCHERING AG	1.032 %
14) DOU	GF DOUGLAS HOLDING	.202 %	34) SGL	GF SGL CARBON	.258 %
15) DRB	GF DRESDNER BANK	3.146 %	35) SIE	GF SIEMENS AG	5.513 %
16) HEI	GF HEIDEL ZMT	.761 %	36) TKA	GF THYSSEN KRUPP AG	1.125 %
17) HOT	GF HOCHTIEF AG	.415 %	37) VEB	GF VEBA AG	4.480 %
18) HVM	GF HYPOVEREINSBANK	3.434 %	38) VIA	GF VIAG AG	2.044 %
19) KAR	GF KARSTADT AG	.776 %	39) VOW	GF VOLKSWAGEN AG	2.272 %
20) LIN	GF LINDE AG	.963 %	40) VOW3	GF VOLKSWAGEN-PFD	.440 %

TABLE 10-2 (Continued)

MSCI WEBS HONG KONG IOPV
30   Members   * capitalization weighted index *

1) 23	HK BANK EAST ASIA	3.223 %	21) 78	HK REGAL HOTEL INTL	.101 %
2) 8	HK CABLE & WIRELESS	10.188 %	22) 69	HK SHANGRI-LA ASIA	.745 %
3) 293	HK CATHAY PAC AIR	3.898 %	23) 242	HK SHUN TAK HOLDING	.488 %
4) 1	HK CHEUNG KONG	5.739 %	24) 583	HK SOUTH CH MORN PO	2.886 %
5) 127	HK CHINESE ESTATES	.835 %	25) 16	HK SUN HUNG KAI PRO	7.448 %
6) 2	HK CLP HLDGS LTD	2.883 %	26) 19	HK SWIRE PACIF 'A'	4.271 %
7) 33	HK ELEC &ELTEK INTL	.670 %	27) 511	HK TELEVISION BROAD	2.015 %
8) 709	HK GIORDANO INTL	.988 %	28) 710	HK VARITRONIX INTL	1.051 %
9) 10	HK HANG LUNG DEV	2.497 %	29) 4	HK WHARF HLDG	4.942 %
10) 11	HK HANG SENG BK	8.714 %	30) 96	HK WING LUNG BANK	2.576 %
11) 44	HK HONG KG AIRCRAFT	.967 %			
12) 3	HK HONG KG CHINA GS	4.574 %			
13) 45	HK HONGKONG SHANGHA	1.567 %			
14) 54	HK HOPEWELL HLDGS	.394 %			
15) 13	HK HUTCHISON WHAMPO	15.717 %			
16) 14	HK HYSAN DEVELOP CO	1.592 %			
17) 179	HK JOHNSON ELEC	2.779 %			
18) 71	HK MIRAMAR HOT &INV	.920 %			
19) 17	HK NEW WORLD DEV	4.276 %			
20) 18	HK ORIENTAL PRESS G	.650 %			

165

TABLE 10-2 *(Continued)*

MSCI WEBS ITALY IOPV
37   Members
* capitalization weighted index *

#	Code	Name	Weight		#	Code	Name	Weight
1)	AZA	IM ALITALIA	.748 %		21)	MRNC	IM MONTEDISON-RNC	.275 %
2)	COMR	IM BANCA COMM ITAL	3.721 %		22)	OL	IM OLIVETTI	2.008 %
3)	BIN	IM BANCA INTESA SPA	3.079 %		23)	FICN	IM PARMALAT FINANZI	.791 %
4)	BINR	IM BANCA INTESA-RNC	.593 %		24)	P	IM PIRELLI SPA	1.797 %
5)	BPM	IM BANCA POP MILANO	.967 %		25)	R	IM RAS SPA	1.829 %
6)	BEN	IM BENETTON	1.620 %		26)	RR	IM RAS SPA-RNC	.896 %
7)	BUL	IM BULGARI SPA	.744 %		27)	RI	IM RINASCENTE	.660 %
8)	SEL	IM EDISON SPA	1.744 %		28)	SA	IM SAI SPA	.893 %
9)	ENI	IM ENI SPA	14.542 %		29)	SPI	IM SAN PAOLO-IMI	4.254 %
10)	F	IM FIAT SPA	3.806 %		30)	SIT	IM SIRTI SPA	.694 %
11)	FP	IM FIAT SPA -PFD	1.431 %		31)	SN	IM SNIA SPA	.505 %
12)	G	IM GENERALI ASSIC	7.353 %		32)	TI	IM TELECOM ITALIA	10.422 %
13)	INA	IM INA	3.432 %		33)	TIR	IM TELECOM ITAL-RNC	1.300 %
14)	IT	IM ITALCEMENTI	1.863 %		34)	TIM	IM TIM SPA	10.906 %
15)	IG	IM ITALGAS	1.052 %		35)	TIMR	IM TIM SPA-RNC	1.307 %
16)	MZI	IM MARZOTTO SPA	.276 %		36)	UC	IM UNICREDITO ITALI	4.318 %
17)	MS	IM MEDIASET SPA	3.237 %		37)	UI	IM UNIONE IMMOBILIA	.652 %
18)	MB	IM MEDIOBANCA	2.138 %					
19)	MNR	IM MONDADORI (ARN)	1.157 %					
20)	M	IM MONTEDISON SPA	1.508 %					

TABLE 10-2 (Continued)

MSCI WEBS JAPAN IOPV

186 Members

= capitalization weighted index =

#	Code		Name	Weight	#	Code		Name	Weight
1)	8341	JT	77 BANK LTD	.224 %	21)	4505	JT	DAIICHI PHARM	.199 %
2)	8572	JT	ACOM CO LTD	1.159 %	22)	6367	JT	DAIKIN INDS	.299 %
3)	2802	JT	AJINOMOTO CO INC	.443 %	23)	4631	JT	DAINIPPON INK	.188 %
4)	6113	JT	AMADA CO LTD	.203 %	24)	1925	JT	DAIWA HOUSE INDU	.263 %
5)	8322	JT	ASAHI BANK LTD	.543 %	25)	8601	JT	DAIWA SECS GRP	.672 %
6)	2502	JT	ASAHI BREWERIES	.353 %	26)	6902	JT	DENSO CORP	1.160 %
7)	3407	JT	ASAHI CHEM INDUS	.421 %	27)	9020	JT	EAST JAPAN RAIL	1.213 %
8)	5201	JT	ASAHI GLASS CO	.403 %	28)	6361	JT	EBARA CORP	.152 %
9)	8335	JT	ASHIKAGA BANK	.124 %	29)	4523	JT	EISAI CO LTD	.279 %
10)	8332	JT	BANK OF YOKOHAMA	.171 %	30)	6954	JT	FANUC LTD	.824 %
11)	8315	JT	BANK TOKYO-MITSU	3.169 %	31)	8317	JT	FUJI BANK LTD	1.031 %
12)	5108	JT	BRIDGESTONE CORP	1.118 %	32)	4901	JT	FUJI PHOTO FILM	.930 %
13)	7751	JT	CANON INC	1.692 %	33)	5803	JT	FUJIKURA LTD	.166 %
14)	6952	JT	CASIO COMPUTER	.176 %	34)	6702	JT	FUJITSU LTD	2.669 %
15)	8331	JT	CHIBA BANK LTD	.176 %	35)	5801	JT	FURUKAWA ELECT	.208 %
16)	7762	JT	CITIZEN WATCH	.216 %	36)	8334	JT	GUNMA BANK LTD	.165 %
17)	5007	JT	COSMO OIL CO	.088 %	37)	9042	JT	HANKYU CORP	.237 %
18)	8253	JT	CREDIT SAISON CO	.262 %	38)	8242	JT	HANKYU DEPT STOR	.092 %
19)	7912	JT	DAI NIPPON PRINT	.653 %	39)	6501	JT	HITACHI LTD	1.792 %
20)	8263	JT	DAIEI INC	.150 %	40)	7004	JT	HITACHI ZOSEN	.074 %

TABLE 10-2 *(Continued)*

#	Code	Member	Weight	#	Code	Member	Weight
1)	8357	JT HOKURIKU BANK	.075 %	21)	9041	JT KINKI NIPPON RAI	.385 %
2)	7267	JT HONDA MOTOR CO	2.281 %	22)	2503	JT KIRIN BREWERY CO	.758 %
3)	5336	JT INAX	.179 %	23)	7984	JT KOKUYO	.229 %
4)	8302	JT INDUS BK JAPAN	1.069 %	24)	6301	JT KOMATSU LTD	.408 %
5)	8238	JT ISETAN	.106 %	25)	4902	JT KONICA CORP	.102 %
6)	8264	JT ITO-YOKADO CO	1.780 %	26)	6326	JT KUBOTA CORP	.251 %
7)	8001	JT ITOCHU CORP	.225 %	27)	1861	JT KUMAGAI GUMI CO	.085 %
8)	9201	JT JAPAN AIRLINES	.368 %	28)	3405	JT KURARAY CO LTD	.289 %
9)	5014	JT JAPAN ENERGY	.076 %	29)	6370	JT KURITA WATER IND	.245 %
10)	8333	JT JOYO BANK	.216 %	30)	6971	JT KYOCERA CORP	.791 %
11)	8267	JT JUSCO LTD	.233 %	31)	4151	JT KYOWA HAKKO KOG	.172 %
12)	1812	JT KAJIMA CORP	.338 %	32)	6586	JT MAKITA CORP	.146 %
13)	9364	JT KAMIGUMI CO LTD	.149 %	33)	8002	JT MARUBENI CORP	.160 %
14)	1942	JT KANDENKO CO LTD	.077 %	34)	8252	JT MARUI CO LTD	.418 %
15)	9503	JT KANSAI ELEC PWR	1.029 %	35)	6752	JT MATSUS ELECTRIC	2.556 %
16)	4452	JT KAO CORPORATION	.708 %	36)	2202	JT MEIJI SEIKA	.180 %
17)	7012	JT KAWASAKI HVY IND	.179 %	37)	6479	JT MINEBEA CO LTD	.304 %
18)	5403	JT KAWASAKI STEEL	.215 %	38)	4010	JT MITSUB CHEM	.444 %
19)	9006	JT KEIHIN ELEC EXPR	.087 %	39)	8058	JT MITSUB CORP	.583 %
20)	1944	JO KINDEN CORP	.131 %	40)	6503	JT MITSUB ELEC CORP	.582 %

TABLE 10-2 *(Continued)*

INJ Member Weightings Page 3 / 5

MSCI WEBS JAPAN IOPV

186 Members

■ capitalization weighted index ■

#	Code		Name	Weight	#	Code		Name	Weight
1)	8802	JT	MITSUB ESTATE CO	.744 %	21)	8760	JT	NICHIDO FIRE & M	.115 %
2)	7011	JT	MITSUB HEAVY IND	.783 %	22)	7731	JT	NIKON CORP	.435 %
3)	9301	JT	MITSUB LOGISTICS	.131 %	23)	9062	JT	NIPPON EXPRESS	.339 %
4)	5711	JT	MITSUB MATERIALS	.152 %	24)	8754	JT	NIPPON FIRE & MA	.119 %
5)	3404	JT	MITSUB RAYON CO	.103 %	25)	5701	JT	NIPPON LIGHT MET	.069 %
6)	8402	JT	MITSUB TRUST &BK	.692 %	26)	2282	JT	NIPPON MEAT PACK	.184 %
7)	8031	JT	MITSUI & CO	.685 %	27)	5001	JT	NIPPON MITSUB OI	.382 %
8)	7003	JT	MITSUI ENG&SHIPB	.082 %	28)	3863	JT	NIPPON PAPER	.305 %
9)	8801	JT	MITSUI FUDOSAN	.295 %	29)	5401	JT	NIPPON STEEL CO	.831 %
10)	8752	JT	MITSUI MAR &FIRE	.261 %	30)	9101	JT	NIPPON YUSEN KAB	.266 %
11)	9104	JT	MITSUI OSK LINES	.146 %	31)	1820	JT	NISHIMATSU CONST	.142 %
12)	8401	JT	MITSUI TRUST & B	.103 %	32)	7201	JT	NISSAN MOTOR CO	.792 %
13)	8231	JT	MITSUKOSHI LTD	.134 %	33)	3105	JT	NISSHINBO INDS	.055 %
14)	6981	JO	MURATA MFG	1.044 %	34)	2897	JT	NISSIN FOOD PROD	.355 %
15)	8269	JT	MYCAL CORP	.077 %	35)	6988	JT	NITTO DENKO CORP	.362 %
16)	9048	JT	NAGOYA RAILROAD	.161 %	36)	5404	JT	NKK CORP	.143 %
17)	9044	JO	NANKAI ELEC RAIL	.179 %	37)	8604	JT	NOMURA SECS CO	1.399 %
18)	6701	JT	NEC CORP	1.206 %	38)	6471	JT	NSK LTD	.239 %
19)	5333	JT	NGK INSULATORS	.265 %	39)	6472	JT	NTN CORP	.125 %
20)	5334	JT	NGK SPARK PLUG	.127 %	40)	9432	JT	NTT CORP	7.397 %

TABLE 10-2 (Continued)

● INJ   Member Weightings   Page 4 / 5

MSCI WEBS JAPAN IOPV
186 **Members**

capitalization weighted index

#	Code		Member	Weight	#	Code		Member	Weight
1)	1802	JT	OBAYASHI CORP	.190 %	21)	4911	JT	SHISEIDO CO LTD	.334 %
2)	9007	JT	ODAKYU ELEC RAIL	.124 %	22)	8355	JT	SHIZUOKA BANK	.533 %
3)	3861	JT	OJI PAPER CO LTD	.391 %	23)	4004	JT	SHOWA DENKO K.K.	.086 %
4)	7733	JT	OLYMPUS OPTICAL	.405 %	24)	6758	JT	SONY CORP	3.290 %
5)	6645	JO	OMRON CORP	.244 %	25)	8318	JT	SUMITOMO BANK	1.978 %
6)	9532	JT	OSAKA GAS CO	.491 %	26)	4005	JT	SUMITOMO CHEM CO	.449 %
7)	6773	JT	PIONEER ELECTRON	.249 %	27)	8053	JT	SUMITOMO CORP	.367 %
8)	8314	JT	SAKURA BANK LTD	.722 %	28)	5802	JT	SUMITOMO ELEC IN	.688 %
9)	4501	JT	SANKYO CO LTD	.646 %	29)	1911	JO	SUMITOMO FOREST	.093 %
10)	6764	JT	SANYO ELECTRIC	.516 %	30)	6302	JT	SUMITOMO HVY IND	.152 %
11)	2501	JT	SAPPORO BREWER	.107 %	31)	8753	JT	SUMITOMO MARINE	.306 %
12)	9076	JT	SEINO TRANSPORTA	.078 %	32)	5713	JT	SUMITOMO MET MIN	.098 %
13)	8268	JT	SEIYU	.062 %	33)	5405	JT	SUMITOMO MET IND	.207 %
14)	4204	JT	SEKISUI CHEM CO	.141 %	34)	5233	JT	TAIHEIYO CEMENT	.162 %
15)	1928	JT	SEKISUI HOUSE	.407 %	35)	1801	JT	TAISEI CORP	.134 %
16)	6753	JT	SHARP CORP	1.000 %	36)	4535	JT	TAISHO PHARM	.500 %
17)	7309	JO	SHIMANO INC	.309 %	37)	8233	JT	TAKASHIMAYA CO	.112 %
18)	1803	JT	SHIMIZU CORP	.255 %	38)	4502	JT	TAKEDA CHEMICAL	2.725 %
19)	4063	JT	SHIN-ETSU CHEM	.520 %	39)	3401	JT	TEIJIN LIMITED	.203 %
20)	4507	JT	SHIONOGI & CO	.220 %	40)	9001	JT	TOBU RAILWAY CO	.149 %

TABLE 10-2 (Continued)

INJ   Member Weightings   Page 5 / 5

MSCI WEBS JAPAN IOPV   * capitalization weighted index *

186 **Members**

#	Code		Name	Weight		#	Code		Name	Weight
1)	9506	JT	TOHOKU ELEC PWR	.403 %		21)	8380	JT	YAMAGUCHI BANK	.105 %
2)	8321	JT	TOKAI BANK	.530 %		22)	7951	JT	YAMAHA CORP	.134 %
3)	8751	JT	TOKIO MAR & FIRE	1.152 %		23)	4503	JT	YAMANOUCHI PHARM	.578 %
4)	9681	JT	TOKYO DOME CORP	.069 %		24)	9064	JT	YAMATO TRANSPORT	.604 %
5)	9501	JT	TOKYO ELEC PWR	1.797 %		25)	2212	JT	YAMAZAKI BAKING	.167 %
6)	8035	JT	TOKYO ELECTRON	.921 %		26)	6841	JT	YOKOGAWA ELEC	.082 %
7)	9531	JT	TOKYO GAS CO LTD	.374 %						
8)	5423	JT	TOKYO STEEL MFG	.061 %						
9)	9005	JT	TOKYU CORP	.162 %						
10)	7911	JT	TOPPAN PRINTING	.477 %						
11)	3402	JT	TORAY INDUSTRIES	.369 %						
12)	4042	JT	TOSOH CORP	.107 %						
13)	5938	JT	TOSTEM CORP.	.269 %						
14)	5332	JT	TOTO LTD	.180 %						
15)	5901	JT	TOYO SEIKAN	.279 %						
16)	3101	JT	TOYOBO LTD	.128 %						
17)	6201	JT	TOYODA AUTO LOOM	.205 %						
18)	7203	JT	TOYOTA MOTOR	6.230 %						
19)	4208	JT	UBE INDS LTD	.104 %						
20)	8270	JT	UNY CO LTD	.172 %						

TABLE 10-2 *(Continued)*

MSCI WEBS MALAYSIA IOPV

* capitalization weighted index *

47   Members

#	Code		Name	Weight
1)	AMM	MK	AMMB HLDG BHD	1.228 %
2)	ASM	MK	AMSTEEL CORP BHD	.644 %
3)	BG	MK	BERJAYA GROUP	.970 %
4)	CAHB	MK	COMMERCE ASSET	2.756 %
5)	EOL	MK	EDARAN OTOMOBIL	1.864 %
6)	EKR	MK	EKRAN BERHAD	.109 %
7)	GHP	MK	GOLDEN HOPE PLAN	1.548 %
8)	GUIN	MK	GUINNESS ANCHOR	1.298 %
9)	HLB	MK	HIGHLANDS & LOWL	.904 %
10)	HLP	MK	HONG LEONG PROPE	.595 %
11)	HUM	MK	HUME INDS MALAY	.665 %
12)	IOI	MK	IOI CORP BHD	.401 %
13)	KJC	MK	KIAN JOO CAN FAC	.409 %
14)	KLK	MK	KUALA LUMPUR KEP	1.260 %
15)	LGH	MK	LAND & GENERAL	.275 %
16)	LUH	MK	LEADER UNIVERSAL	.353 %
17)	MNM	MK	MAGNUM CORP BHD	2.325 %
18)	MAY	MK	MALAYAN BANKING	10.481 %
19)	MCB	MK	MALAYAN CEMENT	.317 %
20)	MISF	MK	MALAYSIA INTL-F	3.373 %
21)	MMC	MK	MALAYSIA MINING	.816 %
22)	MRC	MK	MALAYSIAN RES CO	1.014 %
23)	MAS	MK	MALAYSIAN AIRLIN	.775 %
24)	MPI	MK	MALAYSIAN PAC IN	1.461 %
25)	MBFC	MK	MBF CAPITAL BHD	.409 %
26)	MPU	MK	MULTI-PURPOSE	.838 %
27)	NESZ	MK	NESTLE (MALAY)	1.751 %
28)	NST	MK	NEW STRAITS TIME	1.039 %
29)	ORH	MK	ORIENTAL HOLDING	1.090 %
30)	PMC	MK	PAN MALAYSIA	.777 %
31)	PEP	MK	PERLIS PLANTS	.673 %
32)	PROT	MK	PROTON	1.436 %
33)	PBKF	MK	PUB BANK-FOREIGN	1.848 %
34)	RHB	MK	RASHID HUSSAIN	.673 %
35)	RNB	MK	RESORTS WORLD	5.187 %
36)	RHBC	MK	RHB CAPITAL BHD	1.882 %
37)	ROTH	MK	ROTHMANS PALL MA	3.370 %
38)	SHELL	MK	SHELL REFINING	.884 %
39)	SDY	MK	SIME DARBY BERHD	3.855 %
40)	TCM	MK	TAN CHONG MOTOR	1.054 %

TABLE 10-2 (*Continued*)

```
INM      Member Weightings   Page  2 / 2
MSCI WEBS MALAYSIA IOPV          * capitalization weighted index *
   47   Members
1) TRI   MK TECH RES INDS      1.434 %
2) T     MK TELEKOM MALAYSIA  13.038 %
3) TNB   MK TENAGA NASIONAL   11.010 %
4) TIM   MK TIME ENGINEERING    .248 %
5) UMWH  MK UMW HLDG BHD       1.597 %
6) UEM   MK UNITED ENGIN       2.189 %
7) YTL   MK YTL CORP BHD       3.439 %
```

TABLE 10-2 *(Continued)*

MSCI WEBS MEXICO IOPV   * capitalization weighted index *

34   Members

#	Symbol	Name	Weight
1)	ALFA MM	ALFA SA-A	2.358 %
2)	APASCO MM	APASCO SA	2.003 %
3)	BANACL MM	BANACCI-L	.143 %
4)	BANACO MM	BANACCI-O	2.814 %
5)	CEMEXA MM	CEMEX SA-A	1.676 %
6)	CEMEXB MM	CEMEX SA-B	2.011 %
7)	CEMEXCP MM	CEMEX SA-CPO	1.008 %
8)	CIFRA MM	CIFRA SA-C	1.405 %
9)	CIFRAV MM	CIFRA SA-V	8.121 %
10)	CCMUBC MM	CONTROLA COM-UBC	1.157 %
11)	CORPGEO MM	CORP GEO	.516 %
12)	CYDSA MM	CYDSA SA DE CV	.312 %
13)	DESCB MM	DESC SA-B	1.830 %
14)	ICA MM	EMP ICA	.571 %
15)	FEMSUBD MM	FOMENTO ECON-UBD	4.118 %
16)	CARSOA1 MM	GRUPO CARSO-A1	4.045 %
17)	CONT MM	GRUPO CONTL-*	1.057 %
18)	ELEKTRA MM	GRUPO ELEKTR-CPO	.746 %
19)	GFNORTO MM	GRUPO F BANORT-O	.466 %
20)	GFPB MM	GRUPO F BBV-B	.731 %
21)	GFBO MM	GRUPO FIN BANC-O	1.764 %
22)	BIMBO MM	GRUPO IND BIMB-A	3.872 %
23)	MASECB MM	GRUPO IND MAS-B	.787 %
24)	GMEXIB MM	GRUPO MEXICO-B	3.068 %
25)	GMC MM	GRUPO MODELO-C	9.612 %
26)	TV MM	GRUPO TELEV-CPO	5.742 %
27)	GHBC MM	HERDEZ-B	.151 %
28)	PENOLES MM	INDUS PENOLES-CP	1.926 %
29)	KCMA MM	KIMBERLY-CLA M-A	4.758 %
30)	SAVIA MM	SAVIA-A	4.882 %
31)	TELMEXL MM	TELEF MEXICO-L	19.285 %
32)	TELMEX MM	TELEF MEXICO-A	4.716 %
33)	TAMSA MM	TUBOS DE ACERO	.839 %
34)	VITROA MM	VITRO SA-SER A	.583 %

TABLE 10-2 *(Continued)*

INN   Member Weightings   Page 1 / 1

MSCI WEBS NETHERLND IOPV

25   **Members**

* capitalization weighted index *

1) AA	NA ABN AMRO HLDG	4.809 %	21) VMFN	NA STORK NV	.531 %
2) AEGN	NA AEGON NV	9.056 %	22) TPG	NA TNT POST GROUP	3.019 %
3) AHLN	NA AHOLD NV	4.196 %	23) UN	NA UNILEVER NV-CVA	7.111 %
4) AKZO	NA AKZO NOBEL	4.222 %	24) VEDR	NA VEDIOR NV-CVA	.725 %
5) BUH	NA BUHRMANN NV	.838 %	25) WLSNC	NA WOLTERS KLUWER-C	2.274 %
6) ELSNC	NA ELSEVIER	2.289 %			
7) GVKN	NA GETRONICS NV	2.159 %			
8) HAGN	NA HAGEMEYER NV	1.998 %			
9) HEIN	NA HEINEKEN NV	3.929 %			
10) HBG	NA HOLLANDSCHE BETN	.686 %			
11) OVEN	NA HOOGOVENS-CVA	1.444 %			
12) IHCN	NA IHC CALAND NV	.444 %			
13) INTNC	NA ING GROEP NV	9.428 %			
14) KLM	NA KLM	1.745 %			
15) KPN	NA KPN (KONIN) NV	4.180 %			
16) NLYN	NA NEDLLOYD NV	2.350 %			
17) OCEN	NA OCE NV	1.690 %			
18) PAKN	NA PAKHOED NV	.798 %			
19) PHIL	NA PHILIPS ELECTRON	4.355 %			
20) RD	NA ROYAL DUTCH PETR	25.355 %			

175

TABLE 10-2 (*Continued*)

INR   Member Weightings   Page 1 / 1
MSCI WEBS SINGAPORE IOPV
* capitalization weighted index *
29   Members

#	Code	Member	Weight
1)	CIT	SP CITY DEVELOPS	4.516 %
2)	COMF	SP COMFORT GROUP	2.529 %
3)	CREAF	SP CREATIVE TECH LT	1.313 %
4)	CNC	SP CYCLE & CARRIAGE	1.375 %
5)	DBSL	SP DBS LAND	3.634 %
6)	DBSF	SP DEV BK SING-F	9.538 %
7)	FCC	SP FIRST CAP CORP	.470 %
8)	FNN	SP FRASER & NEAVE	2.534 %
9)	HPAR	SP HAW PAR CORP	.863 %
10)	HPL	SP HOTEL PROPS	.498 %
11)	INCH	SP INCHCAPE MOTORS	.372 %
12)	KEP	SP KEPPEL CORP	4.109 %
13)	NATS	SP NATSTEEL LTD	.427 %
14)	NOL	SP NEPTUNE ORIENT	3.261 %
15)	OCBCF	SP OCBC FOREIGN	10.137 %
16)	OUE	SP OVERSEAS UNI ENT	1.083 %
17)	PWAY	SP PARKWAY HLDGS	1.069 %
18)	ROB	SP ROBINSON & CO	.407 %
19)	SCI	SP SEMBCORP INDUS	3.096 %
20)	SLH	SP SHANGRI-LA HOTEL	1.668 %
21)	SIAF	SP SINGAP AIR-FORGN	11.903 %
22)	SPH	SP SINGAP PRESS HGS	4.408 %
23)	STE	SP SINGAP TECH ENG	3.782 %
24)	ST	SP SINGAP TELECOMM	14.175 %
25)	STRTR	SP STRAITS TRADING	2.199 %
26)	UIC	SP UNITED INDL CORP	2.043 %
27)	UOL	SP UNITED O/S LAND	2.218 %
28)	UOBF	SP UNITED O/S BK-F	4.224 %
29)	VMS	SP VENTURE MFG	1.275 %

TABLE 10-2 (*Continued*)

MSCI WEBS SPAIN IOPV   * capitalization weighted index *

36 **Members**

#	Code		Member	Weight
1)	ACX	SM	ACERINOX SA	1.504 %
2)	ACE	SM	ACESA	2.342 %
3)	ACS	SM	ACS ACTIVIDADES	.691 %
4)	AGS	SM	AGUAS BARCELONA	2.075 %
5)	AGI	SM	AGUILA SA (EL)	.541 %
6)	ARG	SM	ARGENTARIA	4.434 %
7)	AZC	SM	ASTURIANA ZINC	.710 %
8)	AEA	SQ	AZUCARERA EBRO	.990 %
9)	BBV	SM	BANCO BILBAO VIZ	9.287 %
10)	SCH	SM	BSCH	14.606 %
11)	ALB	SM	CORP FIN ALBA	1.630 %
12)	CTF	SM	CORTEFIEL SA	1.334 %
13)	DRC	SM	DRAGADOS	1.439 %
14)	ENC	SM	EMP NAC CELULOSA	.411 %
15)	ELE	SM	ENDESA SA	4.215 %
16)	ECR	SM	ERCROS SA	.256 %
17)	FAE	SQ	FAES	.613 %
18)	FCC	SM	FOMENTO DE CONST	2.550 %
19)	CTG	SM	GAS NATURAL SDG	4.374 %
20)	IBE	SM	IBERDROLA SA	4.444 %
21)	MAP	SM	MAPFRE	1.108 %
22)	MVC	SM	METROVACESA	.544 %
23)	VDR	SM	PORTLAND VALDERR	.984 %
24)	PSG	SM	PROSEGUR SECUR-R	.412 %
25)	PUL	SM	PULEVA, S.A.	.519 %
26)	REP	SM	REPSOL SA	5.307 %
27)	SOL	SM	SOL MELIA SA	1.023 %
28)	TAB	SM	TABACALERA-A	2.625 %
29)	TEF	SM	TELEFONICA SA	20.065 %
30)	TPZ	SQ	TELEPIZZA	.508 %
31)	UNF	SM	UNION FENOSA	2.554 %
32)	URA	SM	URALITA	.432 %
33)	URB	SM	URBIS	.830 %
34)	VAL	SM	VALLEHERMOSO SA	1.571 %
35)	VIS	SM	VISCOFAN ENVOL	1.059 %
36)	ZOT	SM	ZARDOYA OTIS	1.220 %

TABLE 10-2 *(Continued)*

WBQ   Member Weightings Page 1 / 1
MSCI WEBS SWEDEN IOPV
31 Members   * capitalization weighted index *

#	Ticker	Name	Weight	#	Ticker	Name	Weight
1)	AGAA	SS AGA AB-A	1.662 %	21)	SKFB	SS SKF AB-B	1.679 %
2)	AGAB	SS AGA AB-B	1.747 %	22)	SSABA	SS SSAB-A	.720 %
3)	ATCOA	SS ATLAS COPCO-A	1.855 %	23)	SSABB	SS SSAB-B	.315 %
4)	ATCOB	SS ATLAS COPCO-B	.732 %	24)	SCAB	SS SVENSKA CELL-B	3.100 %
5)	DROTB	SS DROTT AB-B	.470 %	25)	SHBA	SS SVENSKA HAN-A	4.002 %
6)	ELUXB	SS ELECTROLUX AB-B	4.068 %	26)	SHBB	SS SVENSKA HAN-B	.473 %
7)	LMEB	SS ERICSSON LM-B	24.159 %	27)	SWMA	SS SWEDISH MATCH AB	.753 %
8)	SLTA	SS ESSELTE AB-A	.470 %	28)	TRELB	SS TRELLEBORG-B	1.442 %
9)	SLTB	SS ESSELTE AB-B	.476 %	29)	VOLVA	SS VOLVO AB-A	2.437 %
10)	FSPAA	SS FORENINGSSPARBAN	4.242 %	30)	VOLVB	SS VOLVO AB-B	4.864 %
11)	HMB	SS HENNES & MAURI-B	10.572 %	31)	WMB	SS WM-DATA AB-B	2.678 %
12)	NCOMB	SS NETCOM AB-B	2.533 %				
13)	OMG	SS OM GRUPPEN AB	.617 %				
14)	SANDB	SS SANDVIK AB-B	2.013 %				
15)	SANDA	SS SANDVIK AB-A	3.841 %				
16)	SECUB	SS SECURITAS AB-B	2.862 %				
17)	SEBA	SS SKANDI ENSKIL-A	4.290 %				
18)	SDIA	SS SKANDIA FORSAKRI	7.047 %				
19)	SKAB	SS SKANSKA AB-B	1.989 %				
20)	SKFA	SS SKF AB-A	1.603 %				

TABLE 10-2 (Continued)

```
⊞  INL        Member  Weightings   Page   1 / 1
   MSCI WEBS SWISS IOPV                * capitalization weighted index *
   32   Members
```

#	Ticker	Name	Weight	#	Ticker	Name	Weight
1)	ABBN	SE ABB LTD	4.319 %	21)	SCHN	SE SCHINDLER HLDG-R	1.167 %
2)	ADEN	SE ADECCO SA-REG	3.070 %	22)	RUKN	SE SCHW RUECKVER-R	4.084 %
3)	ALUN	SE ALUSUISSE-LON RG	4.148 %	23)	SGSN	SE SGS SURV-R	.041 %
4)	BAER	SE BAER HLDG	2.563 %	24)	SIK	SE SIKA FINANZ-B	.656 %
5)	BCV	SE BANQ CANT VAU-B	1.852 %	25)	SUN	SE SULZER AG-REG	.299 %
6)	CSGN	SE CS GROUP-REG	6.075 %	26)	UHR	SE SWATCH GROUP-B	1.162 %
7)	EMS	SE EMS-CHEMIE HLDG	3.171 %	27)	SCMN	SE SWISSCOM AG-REG	4.612 %
8)	FI/N	SE FISCHER(GEO) -R	.156 %	28)	TAGN	SE TAG HEUER INTL-R	.577 %
9)	FORN	SE FORBO-R	1.461 %	29)	UBSN	SE UBS AG-REG	8.569 %
10)	HOL	SE HOLDERBANK-B	2.026 %	30)	VALN	SE VALORA HLDG AG	1.762 %
11)	HOLN	SW HOLDERBANK-R	2.703 %	31)	VON	SE VONTOBEL HLDG-B	1.010 %
12)	JEL	SE JELMOLI-BEARER	1.732 %	32)	ZUAN	SE ZURICH ALLIED AG	4.056 %
13)	JELN	SE JELMOLI-R	.245 %				
14)	MOV	SE MOEVENPICK HLD-B	.159 %				
15)	NESN	SE NESTLE SA-R	4.466 %				
16)	NOVN	SE NOVARTIS-REG	14.423 %				
17)	ROG	SE ROCHE HLDG-GENUS	14.980 %				
18)	RO	SE ROCHE HOLDING AG	2.723 %				
19)	SRN	SE SAIRGROUP-REG	1.026 %				
20)	SCHP	SE SCHINDLER HLD-PC	.153 %				

TABLE 10-2 (*Continued*)

MSCI WEBS U.K. IOPV   * capitalization weighted index *

96   **Members**

No.	Code	Member	Weight
1) ANL	LN	ABBEY NATL	1.464 %
2) ADZ	LN	ALLIED ZURICH	1.177 %
3) AW/	LN	ANGLIAN WATER	.162 %
4) AWA	LN	ARJO WIGGINS	.239 %
5) ABF	LN	ASSOC BR FOOD	.444 %
6) AZN	LN	ASTRAZENECA PLC	3.891 %
7) BAA	LN	BAA PLC	.588 %
8) BARC	LN	BARCLAYS PLC	2.429 %
9) BASS	LN	BASS PLC	.863 %
10) BBA	LN	BBA GROUP	.369 %
11) BG/	LN	BG PLC	1.360 %
12) BICC	LN	BICC PLC	.063 %
13) BCI	LN	BLUE CIRCLE INDS	.457 %
14) BOC	LN	BOC GROUP PLC	.677 %
15) BOOT	LN	BOOTS CO PLC	.718 %
16) BWTH	LN	BOWTHORPE PLC	.169 %
17) BPA	LN	BP AMOCO PLC	11.277 %
18) BPB	LN	BPB PLC	.231 %
19) BA/	LN	BRIT AEROSPACE	.873 %
20) BAY	LN	BRIT AIRWAYS PLC	.456 %
21) BATS	LN	BRIT AMER TOBACC	.819 %
22) BLND	LN	BRIT LAND CO PLC	.364 %
23) BSY	LN	BRIT SKY BROADCA	.864 %
24) BS/	LN	BRIT STEEL	.343 %
25) BT/A	LN	BRIT TELECOM PLC	5.688 %
26) BMAH	LN	BURMAH CASTROL	.262 %
27) CW/	LN	CABLE & WIRELESS	1.669 %
28) CBRY	LN	CADBURY SCHWEPPE	.862 %
29) CRN	LN	CARADON PLC	.100 %
30) CCM	LN	CARLTON COMM	.290 %
31) CNA	LN	CENTRICA PLC	.610 %
32) CGU	LN	CGU PLC	.891 %
33) CVY	LN	COATS VIYELLA	.060 %
34) CPG	LN	COMPASS GROUP	.293 %
35) DLAR	LN	DE LA RUE PLC	.082 %
36) DGE	LN	DIAGEO PLC	2.108 %
37) EMI	LN	EMI GROUP PLC	.476 %
38) GEC	LN	GEN ELEC PLC	1.756 %
39) GKN	LN	GKN PLC	.716 %
40) GLXO	LN	GLAXO WELLCOME	4.736 %

TABLE 10-2 (*Continued*)

🇬🇧 INU Member Weightings Page 2 / 3

MSCI WEBS U.K. IOPV * capitalization weighted index *

96 Members

#	Ticker		Name	Weight
1)	GAA	LN	GRANADA GROUP	1.118 %
2)	GUS	LN	GREAT UNIV STORE	.534 %
3)	HFX	LN	HALIFAX GROUP	1.507 %
4)	HNS	LN	HANSON PLC	.408 %
5)	HPW	LN	HEPWORTH PLC	.070 %
6)	HG/	LN	HILTON GROUP PLC	.255 %
7)	HSBA	LN	HSBC HLDGS PLC	4.635 %
8)	ICI	LN	IMPERIAL CH INDS	.582 %
9)	ISYS	LN	INVENSYS PLC	1.054 %
10)	KGF	LN	KINGFISHER PLC	.874 %
11)	LAND	LN	LAND SECURITIES	.266 %
12)	LSMR	LN	LASMO PLC	.215 %
13)	LGEN	LN	LEGAL & GEN GRP	.894 %
14)	LLOY	LN	LLOYDS TSB GROUP	4.285 %
15)	LMI	LN	LONMIN PLC	.135 %
16)	MKS	LN	MARKS & SPENCER	1.048 %
17)	MEPC	LN	MEPC PLC	.211 %
18)	MSY	LN	MISYS PLC	.044 %
19)	NGG	LN	NATL GRID GROUP	.579 %
20)	NPR	LN	NATL POWER PLC	.536 %
21)	NXT	LN	NEXT PLC	.268 %
22)	PSON	LN	PEARSON PLC	.814 %
23)	PO/	LN	PENINS & ORIENT	.731 %
24)	PILK	LN	PILKINGTON PLC	.143 %
25)	PFG	LN	PROVIDENT FIN	.291 %
26)	PRU	LN	PRUDENTL CORP	1.756 %
27)	RTK	LN	RAILTRACK GRP	.540 %
28)	RNK	LN	RANK GROUP PLC	.279 %
29)	REED	LN	REED INTL PLC	.396 %
30)	RTO	LN	RENTOKIL INITIAL	.443 %
31)	RTR	LN	REUTERS GRP PLC	1.373 %
32)	REX	LN	REXAM PLC	.139 %
33)	RIO	LN	RIO TINTO PLC-R	1.381 %
34)	RMC	LN	RMC GROUP PLC	.342 %
35)	RR/	LN	ROLLS-ROYCE	.463 %
36)	RSA	LN	ROYAL & SUN ALLI	.764 %
37)	RBOS	LN	ROYAL BK SCOTLAN	.962 %
38)	SFW	LN	SAFEWAY PLC	.317 %
39)	SBRY	LN	SAINSBURY PLC	.688 %
40)	SDR	LN	SCHRODERS PLC	.477 %

TABLE 10-2 (*Continued*)

```
🏴  INU        Member Weightings        Page  3 / 3
    MSCI WEBS U.K. IOPV               # capitalization weighted index #
    96   Members
 1) SCTN   LN SCOTTISH & NEWCA       .447 %
 2) SSE    LN SCOTTISH & SOUTH       .232 %
 3) SPW    LN SCOTTISH POWER         .526 %
 4) SB/    LN SMITHKLINE BEECH      4.066 %
 5) SMIN   LN SMITHS INDS PLC        .380 %
 6) STJ    LN ST JAMES'S PLACE       .055 %
 7) TWOD   LN TAYLOR WOODROW         .102 %
 8) TSCO   LN TESCO PLC             1.073 %
 9) TW/    LN THAMES WATER           .228 %
10) TI/    LN TI GROUP PLC           .290 %
11) ULVR   LN UNILEVER PLC          1.830 %
12) UBIS   LN UNITED BISCUITS        .088 %
13) UU/    LN UNITED UTILITIES       .376 %
14) VOD    LN VODAFONE AIRTOUC      6.074 %
15) WLMS   LN WILLIAMS PLC           .256 %
16) WLY    LN WOLSELEY PLC           .335 %
```

182

A

THE STOCKS OF THE SELECT SECTOR SPDRs

BASIC INDUSTRIES SELECT SECTOR SPDR (XLB)

E. I. DuPont de Nemours (DD)—Earnings estimate, fiscal year 2000: $3.00. P/E on estimated earnings: 27 times. DuPont is the number-one chemical company in the United States. Among the products the company produces are pharmaceuticals, pigments, chemicals, and specialty fibers used in clothing and rugs. The company produces many household name goods, such as Dacron, Lycra, and Teflon.

Monsanto Co. (MTC)—Earnings estimate, fiscal year 2000: $1.27. P/E on estimated earnings, 32 times. Monsanto is a giant chemical manufacturing and basic materials company that is branching out into food technology. The company is finding solutions for food needs by applying scientific applications. Its drug division makes, among other things, products to treat insomnia and arthritis.

Dow Chemical (DOW)—Earnings estimate, 2000: $5.61. P/E on estimated earnings, 22 times. Dow mostly specializes in plastics, in which it is a world leader. It is the number-two chemical company in the United States. Like the other chemical companies, Dow is diversifying into the life sciences and biotechnology markets.

International Paper Company (IP)—Earnings estimate, 2000: $2.66. P/E on estimated earnings, 20 times. Forest products, such as paper and packaging, are the main output of this company. IP is also a worldwide distributor of paperboard and office supplies. Other operations include oil and gas.

Alcoa (AA)—Earnings estimate, 2000: $3.45. P/E on estimated earnings, 19 times. This is the world's number-one aluminum manufacturer, with operations in over 30 countries. Products made include chemicals, cans, and automotive parts. AA also supplies the packaging, construction, and aerospace industries.

PPG Industries, Inc. (PPG)—Earnings estimate, 2000: $4.05. P/E on estimated earnings, 16 times. PPG manufactures the Olympic line of stains and coatings for architectural, automotive, and industrial use. PPG also makes car windshields and other glass products. The company manufactures products in 16 countries.

Weyerhaeuser Company (WY)—Earnings estimate, 2000: $3.39. P/E on estimated earnings, 20 times. WY is the world's largest private owner of softwood timber. Its forest products include lumber, plywood, doors, pulp, and containerboards. The company has expanded its overseas operations, too.

Air Products and Chemicals, Inc. (APD)—Earnings estimate, 2000: $2.51. P/E on estimated earnings, 17 times. APD produces industrial gases and chemicals. Other areas of activity includes power generation and gas treatment. The company has operations in 30 countries.

Barrick Gold Corporation (ABX)—Earnings estimate, 2000: $0.84. P/E on estimated earnings, 20 times. Barrick Gold mines and explores for gold and other minerals in the United States, Canada, Chile, and Peru. The company has reserves of more than 70 million ounces of gold.

Alcan Aluminium, Ltd. (AL)—Earnings estimate, 2000: $2.13. P/E on estimated earnings, 16 times. Note the extra *i* in the name spelling. It is the British way. About 90 percent of AL's sales comes from selling aluminum in ingot and fabricated forms. Recent earnings have suffered from the Brazilian economic crises and weaker conditions in Europe.

Tenneco, Inc. (TEN)—Earnings estimate, 2000: $2.80. P/E on estimated earnings, 9 times. This company is a manufacturer of automotive parts, cartons, and specialty packaging. Its auto parts are sold in over 100 countries. TEN makes Hefty and Baggies plastic bags, aluminum foil, and polystyrene foam. The company operates in more than 32 countries.

Union Carbide (UK)—Earnings estimate, 2000: $2.50. P/E on estimated earnings, 21 times. This giant chemical company receives about 70 percent of its sales revenue from special and intermediary chemicals. The product range is very wide: latex for paint and adhesives, specialty coatings, and polyolefins, among many other items.

Praxair, Inc. (PX)—Earnings estimate, 2000: $2.94. P/E on estimated earnings, 17 times. The company produces and sells specialty gases and high-performance surface coatings. PX is the largest industrial gases company in North and South America. It has also developed gas applications for many industries, from electronics to medicine.

Avery Dennison Corp. (AVY)—Earnings estimate, 2000: $2.80. P/E on estimated earnings, 22 times. Avery Dennison makes pressure-sensitive materials and adhesives for central systems and office products. Its wide variety of products has mainly to do with fastening, from mailing labels that blend in to Hi-Lite markers that stand out.

Georgia Pacific (GP)—Earnings estimate, 2000: $3.43. P/E on estimated earnings, 14 times. Georgia Pacific makes and distributes building products. The company also produces pulp and paper products. Building products sales have been up with increased home building, boosting earnings.

Rohm and Haas Company (ROH)—Earnings estimate, 2000: $2.36. P/E on estimated earnings, 19 times. ROH manufactures specialty chemicals, plastic additives, building products, and other items. Their Electronic Research Division helped the company achieve a record earnings year in 1998.

Owens Illinois, Inc. (OI)—Earnings estimate, 2000: $2.41. P/E on estimated earnings, 13 times. The company manufactures glass and plastic containers, labels, plastic beverage containers, and other items. OI has more than 130 locations around the world.

Ecolab, Inc. (ECL)—Earnings estimate, 2000: $1.47. P/E on estimated earnings, 29 times. ECL makes and markets cleaning and maintenance products for the hospitality, industrial, and institutional markets. The company has an 8700-member sales-and-service force worldwide.

Champion International. Corp. (CHA)—Earnings estimate, 2000: $3.25. P/E on estimated earnings, 16 times. The company manufactures paper for business communications, commercial printing, and newspapers. They also produce lumber, pulp, and plywood. CHA has launched a new high-brightness paper to meet copying, faxing, and desktop printing needs.

Sealed Air Corporation (SEE)—Earnings estimate, 2000: $2.13. P/E on estimated earnings, 29 times. This company manufactures specialty packaging materials and systems, including polyurethane packaging systems and foams. SEE is a global company, and it was named the Packaging Education Founder's Leader of the Year for 1998.

Allegheny Teledyne (ALT)—Earnings estimate, 2000: $1.86. P/E on estimated earnings, 11 times. ALT is a group of technology manufacturing companies in the field of specialty metals, aerospace and electronic, and industrial and consumer products. The company includes stainless steel and silicon electrical steels in its range of products.

Nucor Corp. (NUE)—Earnings estimate, 2000: $3.41. P/E on estimated earnings, 13 times. Nucor manufactures steel products and has operating facilities in eight states. They make metal building systems, steel bearing products, steel joists and joist girders, and other products. NUE is committed to building steel manufacturing facilities and operating them productively.

Crown Cork and Seal Company (CCK)—Earnings estimate, 2000: $2.70. P/E on estimated earnings, 12 times. Crown is the world's leading manufacturer of packaging products for consumer goods. CCK makes plastic containers for beverage, processed good, household, personal care, and other products. The company operates 223 plants in 49 countries.

Eastman Chemical Co. (EMN)—Earnings estimate, 2000: $3.13. P/E on estimated earnings, 18 times. Eastman is a leading international chemical company producing more than 400 chemicals and plastics. Their products are used in automobiles, tools, medical parts, and other products.

Reynolds Metals Co. (RLM)—Earnings estimate, 2000: $4.27. P/E on estimated earnings, 14 times. RLM is a leader in the aluminum industry. They just opened a new service center in Chicago that produces a whole line of customized aluminum, stainless steel, and nickel products.

Temple Inland, Inc. (TIN)—Earnings estimate, 2000: $3.82. P/E on estimated earnings, 18 times. Temple Inland Forest Group, which operates the Building Products Group, is one of the major subsidiaries of Temple Inland, Inc. They own forests; manufacture building materials, paperboard, and packaging; and offer financial services. TIN operates 113 banking centers.

Williamette Industries, Inc. (WLL)—Earnings estimate, 2000: $2.79. P/E on estimated earnings, 16 times. The company makes paper bags, corrugated containers, market pulp, all sorts of printing papers, and other wood products. WLL plans to acquire Darbo S.A., a private French company with a strong brand name.

Newmont Mining Corporation (NEM)—Earnings estimate, 2000: $0.46. P/E on estimated earnings, 39 times. Newmont is involved in the production of gold, the development of gold properties, and exploration for gold worldwide. NEM is the world's second-largest gold producer, and the largest in North America.

Mead Corporation (MEA)—Earnings estimate, 2000: $2.64. P/E on estimated earnings, 15 times. This company manufactures and sells paper, pulp, paperboard, and other wood products. MEA manufactures and distributes school and office supplies. Their packaging division is a leading supplier worldwide of multiple packaging.

Morton Intl. (MII)—Earnings estimate, 2000: $1.88. P/E on estimated earnings, 22 times. Specialty chemicals are the core of Morton's business. They sell products around the globe, from chemicals for recycling newsprint to coatings used to paint furniture and photoresists used in electronic devices. MII is also the industry leader in salt.

Sigma Aldrich Corp. (SIAL)—Earnings estimate, 2000: $1.95. P/E on estimated earnings, 16 times. The company has two core businesses. Chemicals generate 80 percent of its revenues. Metals generate the other 20 percent. Nearly 50 percent of Sigma's chemical sales comes from products they manufacture. Almost all metals sales come from their own manufacturing processes.

Phelps Dodge Corp. (PD)—Earnings estimate, 2000: $1.87. P/E on estimated earnings, 32 times. PD is involved in smelting and refining and the production of copper and copper products. It produces 30 percent of the copper in the United States as well as gold, silver, and other minerals. PD also operates manufacturing businesses such as Phelps Dodge Magnet wire and Columbian Chemicals.

Placer Dome, Inc. (PDG)—Earnings estimate, 2000: $0.30. P/E on estimated earnings, 33 times. This company is the number-two gold-mining firm, producing about 2.5 million ounces annually. PDG operates 15 gold mines in Australia, Canada, Chile, Papua New Guinea, and the United States. The company also operates a copper mine in Chile and explores in over 30 countries.

Englehard Corp. (EC)—Earnings estimate, 2000: $1.57. P/E on estimated earnings, 14 times. EC produces catalysts for the automotive, food-processing, petroleum, and pharmaceutical industries. The company produces pigments and additives used in paper, plastics, ink, and paints. Other products include conductive pastes and electroplating materials.

Hercules, Inc. (HPC)—Earnings estimate, 2000: $2.80. P/E on estimated earnings, 13 times. Hercules supplies industrial and commercial users with water treatment programs. They also make naturally grown ingredients for food and beverages. HPC is a worldwide supplier of specialty chemical products.

Westvaco Corp. (W)—Earnings estimate, 2000: $2.01. P/E on estimated earnings, 15 times. Westvaco produces printing papers, graphic paperboard, packaging materials, envelopes, specialty chemicals, and other products. Their markets range from the boarding used for decorative and industrial laminations to specialty lumber and real estate development. They also convert timber into construction lumber.

Great Lake Chemical (GLK)—Earnings estimate, 2000: $2.74. P/E on estimated earnings, 17 times. GLK produces bromine derivatives, including flame retardants and methyl bromide, drilling fluids, cleaning solvents, chlorine, leaded gasoline and other petroleum additives, and other products. The company has shares in control of about 75 percent of global production of methyl bromide. Their bromide products line includes flame retardants.

Homestake Mining Company (HM)—Earnings estimate, 2000: $0.06. P/E on estimated earnings, 9 times. Homestake is an international gold mining company with operations in the United States, Canada, Australia, and Chile. They also explore in Latin America and Eastern Europe. From 16 operating mines, Homestake currently produces about 2.3 million ounces of gold annually.

USX U.S. Steel Group (X)—Earnings estimate, 2000: $3.22. P/E on estimated earnings, 11 times. This is the largest steelmaker in the United States. They operate steel manufacturing plants in Fairfield, Alabama; Pittsburgh, Pennsylvania; and Gary, Indiana, and produce sheet, tubular, plate, and semifinished steel. The company also provides consulting and mineral resource management services and is involved in real estate development.

Nalco Chemical Co. (NLC)—Earnings estimate, 2000: $2.33. P/E on estimated earnings, 15 times. This company is the largest producer in the world of specialty chemicals and services for water and industrial process treatment. Many industries are served by NLC: paper, chemicals, refining, mining, petroleum, and others. NLC recently announced the acquisition of Bycosin AB., a European water treatment company.

Louisiana Pacific Corp. (LPX)—Earnings estimate, 2000: $1.72. P/E on estimated earnings, 12 times. LPX is a major manufacturer of building materials, industrial wood products, and pulp. One of their companies, Greenstone, is the nation's largest and fastest-growing manufacturer of cellulose insulation, one of nature's best insulation materials.

Bemis Co., Inc. (BMS)—Earnings estimate, 2000: $2.37. P/E on estimated earnings, 16 times. Bemis is the largest flexible packaging company in North America and a major manufacturer of pressure-sensitive materials used for labels, decoration, and sign. The company's technologies have grown more complex, and they now produce packaging machinery.

FMC Corp. (FMC)—Earnings estimate, 2000: $6.35. P/E on estimated earnings, 9 times. The company is one of the world's leading producers of chemicals and machinery for industry and agriculture. FMC is involved in energy systems, food and transportation equipment, agricultural products, specialty chemicals, and industrial chemicals.

Inco, Ltd. (N)—Earnings estimate, 2000: $0.03. P/E on estimated earnings, NA. Inco is one of the world's leading producers of nickel and is an important producer of copper, precious metals, and cobalt. The demand for the company's products keeps growing as living standards around the world improve.

Boise Cascade Corp. (BCC)—Earnings estimate, 2000: $2.20. P/E on estimated earnings, 20 times. Boise Cascade is a major distributor of office products and building materials. The company owns and manages over 2 million acres of timberland in the United States. BCC also has international operations.

Freeport McMoran Copper Gold (FCX)—Earnings estimate, 2000: $0.78. P/E on estimated earnings, 19 times. FCX is one of the largest and lowest-cost copper and gold producers. They also are involved in mineral development and mining and smelting of ore. Through subsidiaries, the company smelts and refines copper in Spain.

Ball Corporation (BLL)—Earnings estimate, 2000: $3.32. P/E on estimated earnings, 13 times. This company has interests in the food and beverage packaging industry. Through subsidiaries, it designs and manufactures spacecraft and space systems and communications and antenna systems.

Timkin Co. (TKR)—Earnings estimate, 2000: $1.85. P/E on estimated earnings, 10 times. Timkin is a leading manufacturer of alloy steels, serving the automotive, railway, machinery, and aerospace industries. The company also produces highly engineered bearings.

Worthington Industries, Inc. (WTHG)—Earnings estimate, 2000: $1.07. P/E on estimated earnings, 11 times. Worthington is one of North America's premier suppliers of steel and plastic products, and employs about 12,000 people. The company operates 66 production facilities in 22 states and 8 countries.

W. R. Grace and Co. (GRA)—Earnings estimate, 2000: $1.68. P/E on estimated earnings, 10 times. Grace is a leading global supplier of specialty chemical, construction, and container products. The company supplies the food, consumer products, petroleum refinery, and construction industries.

Bethlehem Steel Corp. (BS)—Earnings estimate, 2000: $1.00. P/E on estimated earnings, 12 times. Bethlehem produces a wide variety of steel mill products, including hot-rolled, cold-rolled, and coated sheets, tin mill products, carbon and alloy plates, and other products. BS also produces and sells coke and iron ore.

Potlach Corp. (PCH)—Earnings estimate, 2000: $1.94. P/E on estimated earnings, 21 times. This a diversified forest products company with more than 1.5 million acres of timberland in Arkansas, Idaho, and Minnesota.

Battle Mountain Gold (BMG)—Earnings estimate, 2000: $0.09 (loss). BMG explores for, mines, and processes gold and associated metals internationally. Annual gold production is about 750 million ounces. The company operates mines in four countries.

Cyprus Amax Minerals Co. (CYM)—Earnings estimate, 2000: $0.07 (loss). Cyprus Amax is a leading producer of copper and coal, the world's largest producer of molybdenum, and owns a 32 percent interest in Kinrosa Gold Corporation. They employ more than 7000 people worldwide.

Asarco, Inc. (AR)—Earnings estimate, 2000: $1.35 (loss). AR is a fully integrated miner, smelter, and refiner of copper in the United States and Peru. Asarco is also a significant producer of molybdenum and produces solvent extraction refined copper cathodes.

THE CONSUMER SERVICES SELECT SECTOR SPDR (XLV)
Time Warner, Inc. (TWX)—Earnings estimate, 2000: $0.70. P/E on estimated earnings, 94 times. TWX is a media and entertainment company with interests in television production and broadcasting, cable television programming, book publishing, magazine publishing, and cable TV systems.

Walt Disney (DIS)—Earnings estimate, 2000: $0.87. P/E on estimated earnings, 34 times. DIS is a worldwide entertainment company, operating theme parks and resorts, broadcasting, and other endeavors. Disney also produces filmed entertainment. They have an interest in the Internet company Infoseek.

McDonalds Corporation (MCD)—Earnings estimate, 2000: $1.92. P/E on estimated earnings, 25 times. The company franchises, develops, operates, and services a worldwide chain of fast-food restaurants. MCD has been expanding recently, and higher sales reflect this aggressive marketing.

Carnival Corp. (CCR)—Earnings estimate, 2000: $1.92. P/E on estimated earnings, 25 times. Carnival operates cruise lines under the name Carnival Cruise Lines, Cunard Lines, Holland America Lines, Seaborn Cruise Line, and Winstar Cruises. The company also operates a tour business.

Media One Group, Inc. (UMG)—Earnings estimate, 2000: $1.30 (loss). UMG is engaged in cable and telecommunications operations, service operations, multimedia connections, and wireless communications.

Viacom (VIA.B)—Earnings estimate, 2000: $0.01 (loss). This company is one of the leading media companies in the world. Among the subsidiaries it owns are MTV Networks, which owns MTV and VH-l, Nickelodeon, and Showtime. Viacom also has an interest in Comedy Central.

CBS Corp. (CBS)—Earnings estimate, 2000: $0.86. P/E on estimated earnings, 48 times. The company has the number-one spot in television ratings through its CBS Television Network. CBS owns MarketWatch.com, an Internet company. They also own 14 television stations.

Comcast Corp. (CMCK)—Estimated earnings, last 12 months: $2.86. P/E on earnings, 12 times. The company is a diversified global leader in entertainment services and telecommunications. It operates cable television and telephone services, cellular and direct-to-home satellite television, and personal computer services.

Gannett, Inc. (GCI)—Earnings estimate, 2000: $3.58. P/E on estimated earnings, 20 times. Gannett publishes *USA Today*. It offers a direct marketing program, built on over 28 years of successful programs. The company also engages in information management services such as telemarketing.

Cendant Corp. (CD)—Earnings estimate, 2000: $1.26. P/E on estimated earnings, 15 times. Cendant offers services in travel shopping, home improvement, credit card packages, car rentals, tax services, and real estate brokerage.

Columbia HCA Healthcare Corp. (COL)—Earnings estimate, 2000: $1.47. P/E on estimated earnings, 17 times. Operating 220 hospitals and surgery centers nationwide, COL is the largest in the United States. They also have operations in Spain, Switzerland, and the United Kingdom.

Seagram Company, Ltd. (VO)—Earnings estimate, 2000: $0.01 (loss). Seagram is engaged in marketing and producing wines, coolers, beers, distilled spirits, and mixes. They also distribute motion pictures, television products, and operate theme parks.

Clear Channel Communications, Inc. (CCU)—Earnings estimate, 2000: $0.66. P/E on estimated earnings, 104 times. CCU owns or operates 206 radio stations and 18 domestic television stations. They are also involved in outdoor advertising and other media activities.

IMS Health, Inc. (RX)—Earnings estimate, 2000: $1.02. P/E on estimated earnings, 29 times. RX is a leading worldwide provider of information and decision-support services to the healthcare industry and also to the pharmaceutical sector. They also provide venture capital to growing health-care companies.

Aetna, Inc. (AET)—Earnings estimate, 2000: $5.53. P/E on estimated earnings, 16 times. The company is a leading provider of health and retire-ment benefit plans and financial services. AET has 16 million members in its healthcare organization. They also market a variety of retirement plans.

Interpublic Group of Companies, Inc. (IPG)—Earnings estimate, 2000: $2.91. P/E on estimated earnings, 27 times. IPG offers strategic directions as well as centralized functional services, including finance and negotia-tions support, real estate expertise, legal counsel, and investor relations.

McGraw-Hill Co., Inc.—Earnings estimate, 2000: $2.11. P/E on esti-mated earnings, 24 times. McGraw-Hill is one of the world's premier pub-lishers and is expanding in the technology and computer fields. Their PRIMIS subsidiary is the leading customized publisher, with 18.5 percent of the market.

Service Corporation Intl.—Earnings estimate, 2000: $1.44. P/E on esti-mated earnings, 13 times. The company operates 3442 funeral service loca-tions, 433 cemeteries, and 191 crematoria. In addition to its death-care services, the company provides financial services.

Omnicom Group (OMC)—Earnings estimate, 2000: $2.24. P/E on esti-mated earnings, 32 times. OMC is a worldwide advertising and marketing services company ranking among the top in creative excellence. Omnicom operates as three agency networks: BBDO Worldwide, DDB Needham Worldwide, and TBWA International network.

Tenent Healthcare Corp. (THC)—Earnings estimate, 2000: $2.02. P/E on estimated earnings, 10 times. This company is a for-profit hospital man-ager with 130 facilities in 22 states. It also operates psychiatric facilities and home healthcare rehabilitation centers. Tenent is one of the largest investor-owned hospital chains in the United States.

United Healthcare Corp. (UNH)—Earnings estimate, 2000: $3.49. P/E on estimated earnings, 19 times. UNH provides a number of healthcare ser-vices and products, including health maintenance organizations, preferred provider organizations, and point of service plans. It also offers other health products.

Tribune Co. (TRB)—Earnings estimate, 2000: $3.29. P/E on estimated earnings, 24 times. The company has businesses in 12 of the nation's largest markets. Tribune reaches about 75 percent of households daily through newspapers, broadcasting, and news media.

Tricon Global Restaurants, Inc. (YUM)—Earnings estimate, 2000: $3.02. P/E on estimated earnings, 16 times. In the number of units, Tricon is the world's largest quick-service restaurant business. It owns the KFC, Pizza Hut, and Taco Bell chains, among other properties.

Marriott International, Inc. (MAR)—Earnings estimate, 2000: $1.94. P/E on estimated earnings, 19 times. MAR is involved in the food and facilities management business, as well as hotel and senior living facilities and food distribution center operations.

Healthsouth Corporation (HRC)—Earnings estimate, 2000: $1.26. P/E on estimated earnings, 9 times. HRC is a market leader in rehabilitative healthcare services, both inpatient and outpatient. It has over 1000 patient facilities, located in all 50 states. The company has also purchased hospital centers.

New York Times (NYT)—Earnings estimate, 2000: $1.88. P/E on estimated earnings, 18 times. NYT operates *The New York Times* newspaper, and it has interests in other newspapers, broadcasting, information services, magazines, and forest products. *The New York Times* is circulated in all 50 states and around the globe.

R. R. Donnelley and Sons Co. (DNY)—Earnings estimate, 2000: $2.46. P/E on estimated earnings, 15 times. DNY is the largest commercial printer in the United States, serving about 20 percent of the market. The company offers services in digital and print media to 26 countries on 5 continents.

Dun and Bradstreet Corp. (DNB)—Earnings estimate, 2000: $1.95. P/E on estimated earnings, 17 times. This company supplies commercial credit information to the general public and businesses. Moody's Investor Services, which offers ratings services, is one of its major divisions.

H & R Block, Inc. (HRB)—Earnings estimate, 2000: $2.49. P/E on estimated earnings, 19 times. HRB operates a worldwide network of tax preparers. There is an H & R Block office within about 10 miles of 80 percent of American homes. The company is also the leading tax helper in Canada.

Dow Jones and Company (DJ)—Earnings estimate, 2000: $2.33. P/E on estimated earnings, 21 times. The company publishes *The Wall Street Journal* and *Barron's*, two highly regarded and widely read financial papers. In addition, it publishes other financial papers and distributes them worldwide.

Times Mirror Co. (TMC)—Earnings estimate, 2000: $3.40. P/E on estimated earnings, 17 times. This is a major newspaper publisher and information company. It has interests in professional information and consumer media. TMC publishes newspapers nationally, including in such media centers as California and New York.

Knight Ridder, Inc. (KRI)—Earnings estimate, 2000: $3.45. P/E on estimated earnings, 14 times. KRI is one of the largest newspaper publishers in the United States, publishing papers in over 30 markets. The company has products in print and online, and also has interests in newsprint mills.

Hilton Hotels Corp. (HLT)—Earnings estimate, 2000: $0.94. P/E on estimated earnings, 13 times. Hilton franchises, owns, and manages over 200 hotels, including major hotels in New York City and Chicago. The company is also active in gaming interests and owns casinos in many states, including Nevada.

HRC Manor Care, Inc. (HCR)—Earnings estimate, 2000: $2.21. P/E on estimated earnings, 12 times. HCR operates assisted living and skilled nursing facilities. It also offers a full range of services through over 200 healthcare facilities, and owns pharmacy facilities.

Humana, Inc. (HUM)—Earnings estimate, 2000: $0.92. P/E on estimated earnings, 15 times. This is one of the biggest managed healthcare companies that is publicly traded. Over 8 million people participate in its health plan services. It operates in many states, including Florida, Georgia, and Texas.

Deluxe Corp. (DLX)—Earnings estimate, 2000: $2.95. P/E on estimated earnings, 12 times. DLX is the largest player in the check printing business. Deluxe also is a leading processor of interchange connections and a third-party processor of ATM transactions.

American Greetings Corp. (AM)—Earnings estimate, 2000: $2.51. P/E on estimated earnings, 11 times. The company is the number-two greeting card company in the United States. AM distributes its cards in various languages in more than 80 countries, through 100 outlets, including drugstores and large retail outlets.

Wendy's International, Inc. (WEN)—Earnings estimate, 2000: $1.44. P/E on estimated earnings, 20 times. The company operates or franchises more than 5000 Wendy's restaurants and owns other fast-food chains. Wendy's operates all over the world, including Canada and Latin America.

Mirage Resorts, Inc. (MIR)—Earnings estimate, 2000: $1.23. P/E on estimated earnings, 14 times. MIR is one of the largest U.S. gaming companies, owning and operating casinos all over the world. Among the places the company owns properties are Las Vegas, Atlantic City, and Biloxi, MS.

Darden Restaurants, Inc. (DRI)—Earnings estimate, 2000: $1.06. P/E on estimated earnings, 20 times. Darden is a major company in the low-cost dining segment of the restaurant business. Two of the better-known chains owned by the company are Red Lobster and Olive Garden.

King World Productions, Inc. (KWP)—Earnings estimate, 2000: $2.20. P/E on estimated earnings, 14 times. KWP distributes first-run television shows including "Wheel of Fortune," "Jeopardy," and "The Oprah Winfrey Show." It also distributes television magazine shows and is active in other program syndications.

Meredith Corp. (MDP)—Earnings estimate, 2000: $1.83. P/E on estimated earnings, 18 times. Meredith is a diversified media company that serves the home and family market. Among other magazines, the company publishes *Better Homes and Gardens* and *The Ladies Home Journal.*

Harrah's Entertainment, Inc. (HET)—Earnings estimate, 2000: $1.65. P/E on estimated earnings, 12 times. HET operates gambling casinos and other gambling interests in Nevada, New Jersey, Louisiana, and other locales; it also operates casinos on riverboats.

Shared Medical Systems (SMS)—Earnings estimate, 2000: $3.72. P/E on estimated earnings, 16 times. This company provides information systems such as patient management, managed care, financial, and clinical data interchange services. SMS also offers consulting and customer education services.

Jostens, Inc.—Earnings estimate, 2000: $1.91. P/E on estimated earnings, 11 times. Jostens manufactures and distributes products and services that recognize achievements. A large part of their business is in school-related products, such as graduation rings and related items.

COMPANIES IN THE CONSUMER STAPLES SELECT SPDR (XLP)
Merck and Co., Inc. (MRK)—Earnings estimate, 2000: $2.78. P/E on estimated earnings, 23 times. The company conducts business in pharmaceuticals and laboratory and specialty chemicals. Operating in 48 countries, MRK has 171 companies. It conducts research in such major areas as cancer therapy and biomaterials.

Coca-Cola Co. (KO)—Earnings estimate, 2000: $1.61. P/E on estimated earnings, 39 times earnings. KO is the world's largest soft-drink company. It is also the world's largest producer of juice and juice products. The company makes Coca-Cola, Fanta, Sprite, TAB, and other beverage products.

Pfizer, Inc. (PFE)—Earnings estimate, 2000: $2.94. P/E on estimated earnings, 32 times. Pfizer is a drug company that fights a disease that afflicts millions of people: depression. The company spent over $2.0 billion in 1998 on research into depression and other illnesses.

Bristol Meyers Squibb Co. (BMY)—Earnings estimate, 2000: $2.31. P/E on estimated earnings, 28 times. BMY is one of the largest pharmaceutical companies in the world. They produce medical devices, toiletries, and medications. A large part of their business comes from foreign operations.

Philip Morris Companies, Inc. (MO)—Earnings estimate, 2000: $3.73. P/E on estimated earnings, 11 times. MO is one of the largest tobacco companies in the world, controlling 45 percent of the U.S. market and 12 percent of the world market. Tobacco accounts for about 72 percent of the company's profits.

Watson Pharmaceuticals, Inc. (WPI)—Earnings estimate, 2000: $2.11. P/E on estimated earnings, 16 times. This company develops, manufactures, and sells off-patent and proprietary pharmaceutical products. It develops drugs in the primary care area, women's health, and other areas.

Procter and Gamble Co. (PG)—Earnings estimate, 2000: $3.18. P/E on estimated earnings, 36 times. PG manufactures and markets consumer products, such as Crest toothpaste, Pampers diapers, and Tide detergent. The products are sold in over 140 countries. The company is now developing its markets in places such as China, Brazil, and Russia.

Johnson and Johnson (JNJ)—Earnings estimate, 2000: $3.37. P/E on estimated earnings, 37 times. JNJ offers prescription drugs, professional products, and a broad line of health-related consumer products. Among the company's products are Tylenol and Band-Aid adhesive bandages.

Eli Lilly and Company (LLY)—Earnings estimate, 2000: $2.67. P/E on estimated earnings, 38 times. Among other products, this company makes the well-known antidepressant drug Prozac. It produces animal health products and also operates a large pharmacy benefit management firm.

Schering Plough Corp. (SGP)—Earnings estimate, 2000: $1.61. P/E on estimated earnings, 35 times. A leader in making prescription pharmaceuticals, animal health products, and consumer products, SGP makes Claritin antihistamines and Claritin D decongestant.

Abbott Laboratories (ABT)—Earnings estimate, 2000: $1.88. P/E on estimated earnings, 23 times. ABT offers a wide range of prescription pharmaceuticals, infant and adult nutrition items, and hospital and laboratory products. The company also is a manufacturer of products for hospitals and blood banks.

American Home Products (AHP)—Earnings estimate, 2000: $2.05. P/E on estimated earnings, 38 times. This company is a leading manufacturer of prescription pharmaceuticals and medical products. AHP makes such popular brands as Anacin and Advil. Its foreign operations are significant.

Warner Lambert Co. (WLA)—Earnings estimate, 2000: $2.32. P/E on estimated earnings, 35 times. WLA makes Trident chewing gum, Halls cough drops, and Listerine mouthwash. It is also one of the world's leading makers of prescription drugs.

Pepsico Inc. (PEP)—Earnings estimate, 2000: $1.39. P/E on estimated earnings, 25 times. PEP makes and distributes Pepsi Cola, Diet Pepsi, Mountain Dew, Slice, Mug, and other popular brands of beverages. Its snack food division produces Fritos brand corn chips and other products.

Gillette Company (G)—Earnings estimate, 2000: $1.55. P/E on estimated earnings, 27 times. This company makes and markets Gillette and Sensor blades and razors and other popular consumer items, including Braun electric shavers. G produces Oral-B and other dental products and a variety of cosmetics.

Unilever NV (UN)—Earnings estimate, 2000: $3.57. P/E on estimated earnings, 33 times. UN manufactures and distributes brand-name toothpaste, hair care, and deodorant products. It's a worldwide company and also distributes cosmetics and fragrances.

Medtronic, Inc. (MDT)—Earnings estimate, 2000: $2.19. P/E on estimated earnings, 33 times. This is a medical technology company. Among its products are cardiac pacemakers and defibrillators. Other products offered are stents, heart valves, and neurological products.

Anheuser Busch Co., Inc. (BUD)—Earnings estimate, 2000: $3.15. P/E on estimated earnings, 22 times. BUD owns the largest U.S. brewery. It makes Budweiser, Bud Light, Michelob, and many other beverage products. The company owns breweries across the United States.

Safeway, Inc. (SWY)—Earnings estimate, 2000: $2.14. P/E on estimated earnings, 22 times. Safeway is a large food and drug retailer, marketing primarily through its supermarket chain. It operates stores in California, Oregon, and Washington, and even spreads across the United States to the mid-Atlantic region.

Kimberly-Clark Corp. (KMB)—Earnings estimate, 2000: $3.18. P/E on estimated earnings, 17 times. Brand names such as Huggies, Kleenex, Kotex, and Scott are produced by this major company. KMB focuses on consumer products and personal care items.

Walgreen Co. (WAG)—Earnings estimate, 2000: $0.70. P/E on estimated earnings, 38 times. Walgreen is a large retail drugstore chain that operates throughout the United States. Prescriptions account for a large percentage of sales. Nonprescription drugs and general merchandise are also significant contributors.

Pharmacia and Upjohn, Inc. (PNU)—Earnings estimate, 2000: $2.06. P/E on earnings estimate, 26 times. The company is a leading international pharmaceutical firm, deriving most of its revenues from Europe and the United States. PNU markets prescription drugs and consumer healthcare items.

Colgate Palmolive Co. (CL)—Earnings estimate, 2000: $3.29. P/E on estimated earnings, 30 times. This is a leading global consumer products company. It manufactures and markets oral care, household, animal care, and other products. Colgate, Palmolive, Ajax, Fab, and Protex are among its famous brands.

Sara Lee Corp. (SLE)—Earnings estimate, 2000: $1.33. P/E on estimated earnings, 18 times. SLE produces baked goods sold under the Sara Lee name throughout the world. It also produces consumer products such as Hanes, L'eggs, and Playtex, among others.

Campbell Soup Co. (CPB)—Earnings estimate, 2000: $2.02. P/E on estimated earnings, 21 times. Campbell is a major producer of soups and makes other grocery food products. Among its products are Campbell's soups, Swanson and Hungry Man frozen foods, and Franco-American spaghetti sauces.

CVS Corp. (CVS)—Earnings estimate, 2000: $1.76. P/E on estimated earnings, 29 times. This company owns a chain of drugstores which operate under the name CVS. It derives most of its revenues from pharmacy operations and has also been successful in the managed care area.

H. J. Heinz Co. (HNZ)—Earnings estimate, 2000: $2.87. P/E on estimated earnings, 16 times. HNZ makes and markets the well-known Heinz ketchup. It also produces StarKist tuna, Weight Watchers frozen dinners, Ken-L-Ration dog good, and other products.

Baxter International, Inc. (BAX)—Earnings estimate, 2000: $3.21. P/E on estimated earnings, 19 times. BAX is a world leader in producing and distributing medical products and equipment. The company markets blood and circulatory-system products and technologies.

Guidant Corp. (GDT)—Earnings estimate, 2000: $1.62. P/E on estimated earnings, 29 times. This company produces medical devices for coronary artery disease prevention and cardiac rhythm management. It also has an interest in the cardiac pacemaker market.

Albertsons, Inc. (ABS)—Earnings estimate, 2000: $3.06. P/E on estimated earnings, 17 times. ABS operates one of the largest drug and food chains in the United States. The company has stores in northern, western, and midwestern states, many of which have in-house bakeries and delicatessens.

Kroger Co. (KR)—Earnings estimate, 2000: $2.72. P/E on estimated earnings, 20 times. KR owns and operates supermarkets throughout the United States. It also operates food processing facilities to supply private-label items to its stores. Kroger operates convenience stores, too.

ConAgra, Inc. (CAG)—Earnings estimate, 2000: $1.63. P/E on estimated earnings, 15 times. A major U.S. food processor, the company is also involved in branded grocery and frozen food products. It makes items such as Monfort and Armour meats and Country Pride chicken.

Cardinal Health, Inc. (CAH)—Earnings estimate, 2000: $2.52. P/E on estimated earnings, 22 times. Cardinal distributes health products, pharmaceuticals, and medical/surgical supplies on the wholesale level. It is one of the largest pharmacy services to hospitals.

Bestfoods (BFO)—Earnings estimate, 2000: $2.70. P/E on estimated earnings, 18 times. This baking concern makes and markets some of the best-known brands in the United States. Some of their products are Entemann's, Orowheat, Skippy's peanut butter, Hellman's dressings, and Mazola oils.

Kellogg Co. (K)—Earnings estimate, 2000: $1.61. P/E on estimated earnings, 19 times. Here is one of the leading producers of cereal. It operates worldwide. Some of its familiar product names are Corn Flakes, Rice

Krispies, and Special K. Kellogg also produces Pop-Tarts toaster pastries and many other products.

UST, Inc. (UST)—Earnings estimate, 2000: $2.85. P/E on estimated earnings, 11 times. Among the market leaders in smokeless tobacco, UST offers the brand names Copenhagen and Skoal. It also produces wines and various types of cigars.

Quaker Oats (OAT)—Earnings estimate, 2000: $2.92. P/E on estimated earnings, 23 times. OAT manufactures and markets hot cereals, such as Quick and Quaker Oats. The company also produces rice and pasta foods, Rice-A-Roni, Pasta Roni, for instance, and the Gatorade sports drinks.

Pioneer Hi-Bred Intl. (PHB)—Earnings estimate, 2000: $1.28. P/E on estimated earnings, 29 times. This is a leading breeder and producer of hybrid seed corn. It owns and operates conditioning plants for seed corn and also offers microorganisms for livestock production.

Winn-Dixie Stores (WIN)—Earnings estimate, 2000: $1.39. P/E on estimated earnings, 25 times. WIN is a large food retailer, concentrated primarily in the Sunbelt. The company has over 20 manufacturing facilities and a number of warehouses and distribution centers to support its stores.

Wrigley (Wm.) Jr. (WWY)—Earnings estimate, 2000: $3.00. P/E on estimated earnings, 28 times. WWY is a major producer of chewing gum. Important items include Doublemint, Juicy Fruit, Big Red, and Extra. The company also produces Freedent and Hubba Bubba bubble gum.

Sysco Corp. (SYY)—Earnings estimate, 2000: $1.19. P/E on estimated earnings, 26 times. This company is a major distributor and marketer of food products, serving over 200,000 customers. SYY distributes frozen foods, meats, fully prepared entrees, fruits, vegetables, and other products.

Rite Aid (RAD)—Earnings estimate, 2000: $1.78. P/E on estimated earnings, 14 times. RAD operates a large chain of retail drugstores. In addition to drugs and prescription items, the stores offer cosmetics, designer fragrances, frozen meals, small appliances, and other products.

Ralston Purina (RAL)—Earnings estimate, 2000: $1.50. P/E on estimated earnings, 19 times. This is a major producer of dry dog and cat foods. It produces Dog Chow, Cat Chow, and other products. They also produce battery products, which are sold under the Eveready and Energizer names.

American Stores (ASC)—Earnings estimate, 2000: $1.69. P/E on estimated earnings, 20 times. Here is a leading retailer, with drugstores, super drug centers, and combination food-drug stores. They sell private-label merchandise under the names Value Wise and Lady Lee, among others.

Archer-Daniels-Midland (ADM)—Earnings estimate, 2000: $0.82. P/E on estimated earnings, 18 times. ADM is a merchandiser of agricultural commodities, including wheat, corn, and oilseeds. Wheat flour is sold mostly to large bakeries, flour is sold to pasta manufacturers, and the company carries on many other distributing activities.

Boston Scientific (BSX)—Earnings estimate, 2000: $1.38. P/E on estimated earnings, 28 times. The company makes medical devices for radiology, cardiology, and other fields. BSX sells catheters and other items used in coronary and vascular angioplasty and many other items.

Becton, Dickinson (BDX)—Earnings estimate, 2000: $1.72. P/E on estimated earnings, 17 times. BDX makes and distributes therapeutic and diagnostic items used in hospitals, doctors' offices, research labs, and elsewhere. Their medical products include insulin injection systems, among other products.

Avon Products (AVP)—Earnings estimate, 2000: $1.96. P/E on estimated earnings, 26 times. A major global direct seller of beauty care and related items, this company distributes products under the Anew, Avon Color, Far Away, Rare Gold, and other brand names.

Clorox Co. (CLX)—Earnings estimate, 2000: $3.66. P/E on estimated earnings, 25 times. Clorox dominates the worldwide bleach market. It also is a diversified consumer products company, operating a full line of retail products from charcoal briquets to salad dressings.

Coca-Cola Enterprises (CCE)—Earnings estimate, 2000: $0.47. P/E on estimated earnings, 68 times. CCE is the largest bottler of Coca-Cola beverage products in the world. The company also produces sparkling waters, juices, isotonics, and teas. It distributes Dr. Pepper and other brands.

Fortune Brands (FO)—Earnings estimate, 2000: $2.38. P/E on estimated earnings, 17 times. Fortune sells hardware and home improvement products through its Master Brand Industries subsidiary. Some of the names it makes are Moen, Master Lock, and Waterloo, and there are many others.

Fort James (FJ)—Earnings estimate, 2000: $2.94. P/E on estimated earnings, 12 times. FJ is a leader in consumer and commercial tissue products. Mardi Gras, Green Forest, and So-Dri are some of the names the company makes. Many of its products come from recycled paper.

General Mills (GIS)—Earnings estimate, 2000: $3.95. P/E on estimated earnings, 20 times. This major company produces packaged consumer food products: Big G cereals, Betty Crocker baking mixes, Bugles snacks and Bisquick baking mixes are among its brand names.

Hershey Foods (HSY)—Earnings estimate, 2000: $2.60. P/E on estimated earnings, 20 times. This company is a leading producer of confectionery and chocolate products. HSY also produces dry pasta products. Among its products are Hershey's Krackle, Kit Kat wafer bars, and Reeses' Pieces candies.

St. Jude Medical (STJ)—Earnings estimate, 2000: $2.02. P/E on estimated earnings, 17 times. A major producer of mechanical heart valves, St. Jude also leads in the pacemaker market. STJ offers both mechanical and tissue replacement heart valves.

Mallinckrodt Incorporated (MKG)—Earnings estimate, 2000: $2.58. P/E on estimated earnings, 13 times. The company services specialty markets in healthcare and chemicals. MKG offers X-ray contrast media, diagnostic and therapeutic products for hospitals, and other products.

Longs Drug Stores (LDG)—Earnings estimate, 2000: $2.02. P/E on estimated earnings, 17 times. LDG operates drugstores, most of them in the western United States and Hawaii. The company is adding stores for its own pharmacy network and the pharmacies in which it participates.

Alberto-Culver (ACV)—Earnings estimate, 2000: $1.60. P/E on estimated earnings, 16 times. This is a health and beauty aids company. It also operates a large chain of professional beauty supply stores. Among its products are Alberto VO5, CONSORT hair care, and FDS deodorant spray.

Bard (C.R.), (BCR)—Earnings estimate, 2000: $2.59. P/E on estimated earnings, 16 times. This company is a leader in manufacturing and distributing medical products. It offers a wide range of equipment for hospitals, physicians, nursing homes, and other segments of the healthcare market.

Bausch & Lomb (BOL)—Earnings estimate, 2000: $3.24. P/E on estimated earnings, 20 times. BOL is a leading player in the contact lens market, marketing its products around the world. Among its other offerings are ReNu, Sensitive Eyes, and Boston solutions products.

Allergan, Inc. (AGN)—Earnings estimate, 2000: $2.95. P/E on estimated earnings, 35 times. Allergan offers treatment for dermatological and neuromuscular disorders, and is a leader in ophthalmic drugs. Its products are offered under the Betagan, Propine, and other brand names.

ALZA Corp. (AZA)—Earnings estimate, 2000: $1.89. P/E on estimated earnings, 24 times. This company ranks among the leaders in the controlled-release drug delivery systems field. Its delivery system allows the drugs to release at a controlled rate. It also makes patches for smoke cessation.

International Flavors & Fragrances (IFF)—Earnings estimate, 2000: $1.96. P/E on estimated earnings, 21 times. This company leads in making aromas, with products from soaps and detergents to cosmetic creams and lotions. It also makes flavorings for beverages.

Supervalu (SVU)—Earnings estimate, 2000: $1.91. P/E on estimated earnings, 13 times. Here is one of the nation's largest food distribution companies and the eleventh-largest food retailer. SVU supplies 2700 stores, and it operates, among other names, Save-A-Lot and Scott's Foods.

Biomet (BMET)—Earnings estimate, 2000: $1.48. P/E on estimated earnings, 27 times. BMET is active in orthopedics, serving physicians directly. It makes and distributes products such as hip systems, knee systems, glove liners, and hip positioners for the medical industry.

Adolph Coors Co. (RKY)—Earnings estimate, 2000: $2.67. P/E on estimated earnings, 18 times. This is a holding company for Coors Brewing Co. Coors makes and markets high-quality malt-based beverages. Some of the products made are Coors and Keystone beers and Zima Clearmalt.

AFLAC, Inc. (AFL)—Earnings estimate, 2000: $2.25. P/E on estimated earnings, 20 times. AFLAC offers supplemental cancer insurance as well as other forms of health coverage. Much of its revenue comes from Japan. AFL offers policies that help defray out-of-pocket expenses connected with cancer treatment.

RJR Holdings (RJR)—Earnings estimate, 2000: $3.70. P/E on estimated earnings, 8 times. This company's U.S. tobacco business is run by its wholly owned subsidiary. The company makes cigarettes—Winston, Camel, Doral, Monarch, and others—and sells its products worldwide.

Brown-Forman Corp. (BF.B)—Earnings estimate, 2001: $3.43. P/E on estimated earnings, 18 times. This is a distiller and importer of alcoholic beverages. Its major brands include Jack Daniels Tennessee Whiskey, Southern Comfort, Korbel, and Bolla. Brown-Forman also makes Lenox china.

Great Atlantic and Pacific Tea Company (GAP)—Earnings estimate, 2001: $2.61. P/E on estimated earnings, 12 times. This company operates supermarkets and the larger superstores in Canada and throughout the

United States. It operates under the names A&P, Waldbaum's, Food Emporium, and others.

COMPANIES IN THE CYCLICAL/TRANSPORT SELECT SECTOR SPDR (XLY)

Wal-Mart Stores (WMT)—Earnings estimate, 2001: $1.34. P/E on estimated earnings, 32 times. Wal-Mart operates a chain of discount department stores, discount store-supermarket combinations, and wholesale clubs. It has long been a leader in using retail information technology.

Sears, Roebuck and Company (S)—Earnings estimate, 2000: $4.10. P/E on estimated earnings, 11 times. Sears is a leading retailer of home and automotive products, apparel, and other products and services. It operates throughout the United States and Canada.

May Department Stores (MAY)—Earnings estimate, 2001: $2.82. P/E on estimated earnings, 14 times. May is a leading retail chain in the United States. The company operates stores under the Lord & Taylor, Foley's, Robinsons-May, Famous-Barr, and other names.

Lowe's Companies (LOW)—Earnings estimate, 2001: $2.07. P/E on estimated earnings, 26 times. Here you have a retailer of building materials and supplies, lumber appliances, and hardware across the United States. LOW offers do-it-yourself and home improvement centers.

Dayton Hudson (DH)—Earnings estimate, 2001: $2.68. P/E on estimated earnings, 23 times. DH operates Target discount stores and Mervyn's department stores. Target is an upscale discount store, while Mervyn's is a moderately priced, promotional, family-type store.

Home Depot (HD)—Earnings estimate, 2001: $1.68. P/E on estimated earnings, 36 times. HD operates a chain of retail warehouse-type stores. They sell a variety of products for the do-it-yourself, home-remodeling, and home improvement markets.

Ford Motor Company (F)—Earnings estimate, 2000: $5.53. P/E on estimated earnings, 9 times. Ford, of course, is a major automobile manufacturer, producing cars and trucks, many vehicle components, and replacement parts. It also has a major financial services operation.

The Gap (GPS)—Earnings estimate, 2001: $2.12. P/E on estimated earnings, 32 times. This is a specialty retailer that operates The Gap Stores, Old Navy Clothing Co., and Banana Republic. GPS offers sophisticated, high-quality sportswear and dress clothes at reasonable prices.

Best Buy Corporation (BBY)—Earnings estimate, 2001: $1.85. P/E on estimated earnings, 37 times. BBY operates across the United States, selling retail consumer electronics, home office equipment, entertainment software, and appliances. It offers a customer savings on PC and Internet service packages.

Network Appliances, Inc. (NTAP)—Earnings estimate, 2001: $0.99. P/E on estimated earnings, 56 times. This company provides data access solutions and network storage. Its network file servers, or filers, and Web-catching solutions afford quick access to network-stored data.

Kansas City Southern Industries, Inc. (KSU)—Earnings estimate, 2000: $3.21. P/E on estimated earnings, 17 times. KSU provides rail freight transportation. Its rail network links markets in the United States, Canada, and Mexico. It also owns the money management firms Janus Capital Corp. and Berger Associates, Inc.

General Motors (GM)—Earnings estimate, 2000: $8.70. P/E on estimated earnings, 7 times. The world's largest manufacturer of cars and trucks, GM also has important defense and electronics, aerospace, and finance operations. They even produce locomotives, among their many other products.

Burlington Northern Santa Fe (BNI)—Earnings estimate, 2000: $2.78. P/E on estimated earnings, 11 times. This company operates a large rail system in the United States and northern Canada. BNI can boast a diversified traffic base and an efficient and cost-saving computer system.

Costco Companies (COST)—Earnings estimate, 2001: $2.68. P/E on estimated earnings, 27 times. COST operates an international chain of membership warehouses, mostly under the Costco Wholesale name. Its warehouses offer a large product range, from groceries and appliances to televisions and auto supplies.

Penney (J.C.) (JCP)—Earnings estimate, 2001: $3.42. P/E on estimated earnings, 14 times. J.C. Penney is a leading retailer with department stores and catalog operations across the United States. JCP also has major drugstore interests and is a mass marketer of health and life insurance.

Norfolk Southern (NSC)—Earnings estimate, 2000: $2.28. P/E on estimated earnings, 13 times. Norfolk Southern operates a rail transportation service in the eastern United States and provides motor carrier services. Its North American Van Lines subsidiary provides relocation services.

NIKE (NKE)—Earnings estimate, 2000: $2.02. P/E on estimated earnings, 29 times. NIKE makes athletic footwear, apparel, and accessory products for men, women, and children; the company has worldwide operations.

Masco Corp. (MAS)—Earnings estimate, 2000: $1.82. P/E on estimated earnings, 15 times. This is a U.S. leader of brand-name consumer products for home building and improvement. The company is also a world-leading faucet manufacturer, operating under such names as Peerless and Brass-Craft.

Union Pacific (UNP)—Earnings estimate, 2000: $4.00. P/E on estimated earnings, 14 times. Union Pacific is a leading rail system company, with operations in more than 20 states. Its Overnite Transporation subsidiary offers less-than-truckload services in the United States, Canada, and Mexico.

TJX Companies (TJX)—Earnings estimate, 2001: $1.84. P/E on estimated earnings, 16 times. This company operates off-regular-price apparel specialty stores in the United Kingdom, Canada, and the United States. Its store names include Marshalls, T. J. Maxx, and Home Goods.

Federated Department Stores (FD)—Earnings estimate, 2001: $3.73. P/E on estimated earnings, 13 times. Federated operates department stores in the United States, with such familiar names as Jordan Marsh, Bloomingdale's, The Bon Marche, Broadway, Burdine, and Macy's.

Kohl's Corporation (KSS)—Earnings estimate, 2001: $1.73. P/E on estimated earnings, 40 times. Kohl's operates specialty department stores, mostly in the Midwest. These stores offer moderately priced apparel, shoes, accessories, home products and housewares.

AMR Corporation (AMR)—Earnings estimate, 2000: $6.17. P/E on estimated earnings, 10 times. AMR's principal subsidiary is American Airlines. One of the world's largest airlines, American has a dominant position in Latin America travel. The company also has a position in a major computer reservation system.

CSX Corporation (CSX)—Earnings estimate, 2000: $3.62. P/E on estimated earnings, 12 times. The company provides rail, shipping, barge, and logistics services. It operates a major railroad that extends from the eastern seaboard to the western gateways of Chicago.

Staples, Inc. (SPLS)—Earnings estimate, 2001: $0.89. P/E on estimated earnings, 32 times. Staples is a leader in office products superstores and is a leading office products distributor. It has over 900 retail stores in the United States, Canada, the United Kingdom, and Germany.

FDX Corp. Holding Company (FDX)—Earnings estimate, 2000: $2.44. P/E on estimated earnings, 22 times. FDX is a leader in global express distribution. It offers time-certain deliveries within 24 to 48 hours among markets comprising more than 90 percent of the world's gross domestic product. FDX owns Federal Express and RPS, Inc.

Delta Air Lines (DAL)—Earnings estimate, 2000: $6.98. P/E on estimated earnings, 8 times. DAL is a major international carrier. It extends its service worldwide through marketing alliances with Swissair, Sabena, and Austrian Airlines. Delta is one of the industry's lowest-cost carriers.

V.F. Corporation (VFC)—Earnings estimate, 2000: $3.64. P/E on earnings estimate, 10 times. This company manufactures and markets knitwear and sportswear, jeans, intimate apparel, and other items. Some of its brand names are Lee, Wrangler, Vanity Fair, and Jantzen.

Kmart Corporation (KM)—Earnings estimate, 2001: $1.41. P/E on earnings estimate, 10 times. Kmart operates discount stores in the United States and Puerto Rico, and operates stores in Canada as well. They stock major brand names and sell them at a discount. Kmart also sells food, snack, and household products.

Goodyear Tire & Rubber (GT)—Earnings estimate, 2000: $4.80. P/E on earnings estimate, 11 times. Goodyear is a leading manufacturer of tires and other automotive products worldwide. The company also makes plastic and rubber products and chemicals, and operates an oil pipeline.

Genuine Parts (GPC)—Earnings estimate, 2000: $2.35. P/E on earnings estimate, 14 times. GPC is a leading wholesale distributor of office products, industrial parts and supplies, and automotive replacement parts. It operates NAPA warehouse distribution centers in the United States.

Southwest Airlines (LUV)—Earnings estimate, 2000: $1.62. P/E on estimated earnings, 19 times. Southwest is a low-cost airline, focusing on short-haul, point-to-point service. The company has one of the lowest cost structures in the industry, partly because it offers only unrestricted coach seats.

Sherwin-Williams (SHW)—Earnings estimate, 2000: $1.94. P/E on estimated earnings, 13 times. SHW is a market leader in manufacturing paints and is also an important marketer of wall coverings and other products. Sherwin-Williams owns Pratt & Lambert, Inc., which is a major merchandiser.

The Limited (LTD)—Earnings estimate, 2001: $1.98. P/E on estimated earnings, 22 times. The Limited is a specialty retailer of women's apparel in the United States. The company also has a major interest in Intimate Brands and Abercrombie & Fitch. Its other stores include Victoria's Secret and Bath & Body Works.

Nordstrom, Inc. (JWN)—Earnings estimate, 2001: $1.86. P/E on estimated earnings, 18 times. The company is a leading retailer of major brand names and operates throughout the United States. Some of the brands carried are Calvin Klein, Esprit, Guess?, and Mossimo.

Newell Company (NWL)—Earnings estimate, 2000: $2.38. P/E on estimated earnings, 18 times. This consumer products firm offers brand names in housewares, home furnishings, hardware, and office products. Its home furnishings brands include Levolor window coverings and Pyrex kitchen utensils.

Maytag Corporation (MYG)—Earnings estimate, 2000: $4.26. P/E on estimated earnings, 16 times. Maytag produces home appliances under the Maytag, Magic Chef, Admiral, and Jenn-Air brand names. Its floor-care products division manufactures under the Hoover name.

Mattel, Inc. (MAT)—Earnings estimate, 2000: $1.85. P/E on estimated earnings, 12 times. Mattel is a major toy maker whose product line includes Barbie dolls, Fisher Price preschool items, Disney-related products, Tyco Toys, and Hot Wheels miniature vehicles.

ITT Industries (IIN)—Earnings estimate, 2000: $2.75. P/E on estimated earnings, 13 times. This company is split into two divisions: ITT Hartford Group is involved in insurance, and ITT Corporation is involved in gaming, hotels, entertainment, and education. The company has operations around the globe.

Harcourt General (H)—Earnings estimate, 2000: $2.82. P/E on estimated earnings, 17 times. Harcourt General is a major publisher, is a major owner of the Neiman Marcus group, and owns National Education Corp. National Education is a global leader in information technology.

Tandy Corporation (TAN)—Earnings estimate, 2000: $1.65. P/E on estimated earnings, 27 times. A leading retailer of consumer electronics products, Tandy sells its products through RadioShack and Computer City stores. The stores carry electronic parts, digital satellite systems, personal computers, and other products.

Williams Companies, Inc. (WMB)—Earnings estimate, 2000: $1.38. P/E on estimated earnings, 31 times. WMB transports by pipeline natural gas and petroleum products, trades natural gas, and performs the gathering and processing of natural gas.

Halliburton Company (HAL)—Earnings estimate, 2000: $1.46. P/E on estimated earnings, 30 times. HAL is a leading company in the oilfield services business and also a major factor in the engineering and construction industry. The company also finds solutions in the management of producing fields.

Phillips Petroleum (P)—Earnings estimate, 2000: $2.43. P/E on estimated earnings, 20 times. This is one of the largest integrated oil companies in the United States. The company explores for and produces crude oil and natural gas all over the globe. It also produces chemicals.

Occidental Petroleum (OXY)—Earnings estimate, 2000: $0.67. P/E on estimated earnings, 29 times. OXY is an oil and natural gas exploration and production company with activities all over the world. The company also operates chemical manufacturing facilities worldwide.

Enron Corporation (ENE)—Earnings estimate, 2000: $2.71. P/E on estimated earnings, 29 times. This is a leading wholesale marketer of natural gas and nonregulated electricity. It also sells natural gas liquids all over the world and engages in crude oil exploration and other activities.

USX-Marathon Group, Marathon Oil (MRO)—Earnings estimate, 2000: $1.85. P/E on estimated earnings, 17 times. MRO explores and produces energy worldwide and refines and markets energy in the United States. In volume, it is one of the biggest refiners of products in the United States.

Unocal Corporation Delaware (UCL)—Earnings estimate, 2000: $1.45. P/E on estimated earnings, 28 times. UCL is a giant independent exploration and production company. It does oil and gas production in the Gulf of Mexico and Asia. The company has agricultural business and other interests.

Sonat, Incorporated (SNT)—Earnings estimate, 2000: $1.74. P/E on estimated earnings, 20 times. Sonat develops, explores for and produces oil and natural gas, transmits natural gas, and distributes natural gas and electric power. The company is a giant in intrastate gas transmission.

Union Pacific Resources Group, Inc. (UPR)—Earnings estimate, 2000: $0.46. P/E on estimated earnings, 32 times. This company is one of the largest independent energy companies in North America. Its oil and gas activities are conducted throughout the United States, including the Texas Gulf Coast.

Texaco, Inc. (TX)—Earnings estimate, 2000: $2.88. P/E on estimated earnings; 21 times. TX has vast international oil and gas operations, including a venture with the Saudi Arabia Oil Company. The company's efforts include the deep water Gulf of Mexico and the Louisiana salt domes.

Schlumberger, Ltd. (SLB)—Earnings estimate, 2000: $1.77. P/E on estimated earnings, 35 times. This company is a leader in the fragmented oil and gas equipment and services industry. Among other activities, it provides drilling service and computerized wireline services to the petroleum industry.

Burlington Resources, Inc. (BR)—Earnings estimate, 2000: $2.36. P/E on estimated earnings, 31 times. A major portion of BR's reserves are centered in the San Juan Basin in northwest New Mexico and southwest Colorado. The company produces, explores for, and develops oil and gas.

Coastal Corporation (CGP)—Earnings estimate, 2000: $2.68. P/E on estimated earnings, 14 times. Coastal operates a major gas pipeline business. It also operates in oil and gas production and power generation. Other operations include refining and mining coal.

Apache Corporation (APA)—Earnings estimate, 2000: $1.38. P/E on estimated earnings, 28 times. Apache is engaged in the production, exploration, processing, and marketing of natural gas and oil. Most of the company's operations are in North America.

Anadarko Petroleum Corporation (APC)—Earnings estimate, 2000: $0.47. P/E on estimated earnings, 76 times. APC is one of the world's largest oil and gas companies. The company drills in known oil and gas areas, mostly in the Anadarko Basin of Oklahoma.

Ashland Incorporated (ASH)—Earnings estimate, 2000: $4.23. P/E on estimated earnings, 9 times. The company makes and markets Valvoline motor oil and operates the SuperAmerica gasoline and convenience stores. ASH also is a major investor in a publicly traded coal unit.

Amerada Hess Corporation (AHC)—Earnings estimate, 2000: $2.22. P/E on estimated earnings, 27 times. AHC is heavily involved in exploring and producing oil and natural gas in the United States and the North Sea. Also among its holdings is a refinery in the Virgin Islands.

Consolidated Natural Gas Company (CNG)—Earnings estimate, 2000: $3.89. P/E on estimated earnings, 15 times. This is one of the largest natural gas companies in the United States. CNG is involved in all aspects of natural gas, including exploration and production, purchasing, gathering, and transmission.

Columbia Energy Group (CG)—Earnings estimate, 2000: $4.18. P/E on estimated earnings, 15 times. Columbia produces, transmits, and distributes natural gas. The company is involved in many projects, among which is a pipeline network that serves 15 states and the District of Columbia.

Baker Hughes, Inc. (BHI)—Earnings estimate, 2000: $0.84. P/E on estimated earnings, 38 times. A leader in the oil services and oil well equipment industry, it produces and is a major supplier of drill bits and is a major producer of drilling fluids.

Atlantic Richfield Company (ARC)—Earnings estimate, 2000: $3.26. P/E on estimated earnings, 26 times. ARC is a major oil producer and operates in Alaska and elsewhere. The company markets gasoline in California and throughout the U.S. West Coast. It also is involved in chemical and coal operations.

McDermott International, Inc. (MDR)—Earnings estimate, 2001: $2.02. P/E on estimated earnings, 13 times. This company operates in three main areas: power generation, marine construction, and industrial operations. A subsidiary supplies equipment to power generators.

Herlmerich and Payne (HP)—Earnings estimate, 2000: $1.14. P/E on estimated earnings, 20 times. HP does contract drilling, oil and gas exploration and production, natural gas marketing, and real estate. The company is one of the industry's leading land drillers.

Rowan Companies, Inc. (RDC)—Earnings estimate, 2000: $0.44. P/E on estimated earnings, 38 times. The company offers contract aviation services, builds heavy equipment and offshore drilling rigs, and contracts for oil and natural gas drilling. It also manufactures cranes and drilling trucks.

Kerr-McGee Corporation (KMG)—Earnings estimate, 2000: $2.55. P/E on estimated earnings, 20 times. KMG is an oil and natural gas exploration and production company. It also is involved in chemical production and coal mining. Titanium dioxide pigment accounts for much of its chemical operating profits.

THE COMPANIES OF THE FINANCIAL SELECT SECTOR (XLF)

American International Group, Inc. (AIG)—Earnings estimate, 2000: $4.55. P/E on estimated earnings, 26 times. This company is a leader in providing property, casualty, and life insurance as well as other insurance and financial services products. The company operates throughout the world.

Bank of New York Co., Inc. (BK)—Earnings estimate, 2000: $1.92. P/E on estimated earnings, 19 times. BK operates a number of corporate trust and custody operations for other banks and financial institutions. The company is a leading global bank and offers an array of financial services.

Associates First Capital Corp. (AFS)—Earnings estimate, 2000: $2.38. P/E on estimated earnings, 17 times. AFS offers consumer and commercial finance along with leasing and related services, home equity lending, personal lending, and credit cards.

Allstate Corporation (ALL)—Earnings estimate, 2000: $3.51. P/E on estimated earnings, 10 times. Allstate is a major property-liability insurer in the United States and one of the largest life insurers. It writes business in the United States, Canada, Puerto Rico, and other locales.

American Express Company (AXP)—Earnings estimate, 2000: $6.09. P/E on estimated earnings, 22 times. American Express offers charge card and travelers check products. It also offers travel-related services, financial advisory services, and international banking services.

Southtrust Corporation (SOTR)—Earnings estimate, 2000: $2.87. P/E on estimated earnings, 13 times. This bank holding company provides a range of banking services in over 600 locations. It has offices in Alabama, Florida, Georgia, Mississippi, North Carolina, and other states.

Paine Webber Group, Inc. (PWJ)—Earnings estimate, 2000: $3.68. P/E on estimated earnings, 11 times. PWJ is also a holding company. It supplies investment services through its broker-dealer subsidiary, Paine Webber, Inc. Its services include retail sales, capital transactions, and asset management.

Chase Manhattan Corp. (CMB)—Earnings estimate, 2000: $5.84. P/E on estimated earnings, 14 times. Wholesale banking services, including global corporate finance, global capital market, and other services, are offered by this major bank. Its retail businesses include major commercial bank services.

Banc One Corp. (ONE)—Earnings estimate, 2000: $4.53. P/E on estimated earnings, 13 times. Another major bank, Banc One has offices in Ohio, Indiana, Louisiana, Texas, and other states. Its affiliates engage in merchant processing, consumer finance, mortgage banking, and other activities.

BankAmerica Corp. (BAC)—Earnings estimate, 2000: $5.50. P/E on estimated earnings, 13 times. Major bank BAC offers retail deposit, credit card, home mortgage, manufactured housing, and auto loan financing. The company also provides capital-raising and other services.

Wells Fargo and Company (WFC)—Earnings estimate, 2000: $2.57. P/E on estimated earnings, 17 times. WFC offers banking services to institutions and retail clients. Among its services are credit products, financial services, investment management, and brokerage services.

Citigroup (C)—Earnings estimate, 2000: $2.97. P/E on estimated earnings, 16 times. Citigroup is one of the biggest credit card companies in the world and also a major financial services company. It offers brokerage services under the Solomon Smith Barney name.

Freddie Mac (FRE)—Earnings estimate, 2000: $3.27. P/E on estimated earnings, 17 times. FRE is a government-mandated company that buys conventional residential mortgages from mortgage bankers and banks and uses them to generate fees and interest income. It is involved in financing one out of six homes in the United States.

Washington Mutual (WM)—Earnings estimate, 2000: $3.88. P/E on estimated earnings, 9 times. This company has more than 2000 thrift facilities across the United States, mostly in the West and the South. It also offers traditional commercial and consumer banking, mutual funds, and other services.

Merrill Lynch and Company, Inc. (MER)—Earnings estimate, 2000: $5.46. P/E on estimated earnings, 14 times. This is a major worldwide diversified broker and financial services concern. MER has a large in-house money management operation, which, standing alone, would be a leading enterprise.

National City Corp. (NCC)—Earnings estimate, 2000: $5.07. P/E on estimated earnings, 13 times. This leading bank holding company operates in Ohio, Kentucky, Indiana, and other states. In addition to corporate and retail banking, it offers trust services, merchant banking, and other services.

Morgan Stanley, Dean Witter, Discover & Company (MWD)—Earnings estimate, 2000: $6.98. P/E on estimated earnings, 14 times. This major financial firm receives revenues from investment banking, commissions, credit cards, and other sources. It services institutions and retail customers.

Fleet Financial Group, Inc. (FLT)—Earnings estimate, 2000: $3.20. P/E on estimated earnings, 13 times. This major banking and trust organization operates throughout the United States. The company has a major brokerage operation and functions in cash management and mortgage products, among other activities.

First Union Corporation (FTU)—Earnings estimate, 2000: $3.85. P/E on estimated earnings, 11 times. This leading bank holding company operates full-service branches throughout the United States. It is also active in investment banking and has brokerage operations.

First National Mortgage Association (FNM)—Earnings estimate, 2000: $4.16. P/E on estimated earnings, 16 times. This company, known as Fannie Mae, is a U.S. government-sponsored company. It buys a variety of mortgages, creating a secondary market for mortgage lenders.

U.S. Bancorp (USB)—Earnings estimate, 2000: $2.46. P/E on estimated earnings, 13 times. USB is a bank holding company operating in banking offices throughout the United States. The company provides banking, trust, investment, and payment systems products to consumers and institutions.

SunTrust Banks, Inc. (STI)—Earnings estimate, 2000: $4.29. P/E on estimated earnings, 15 times. Another leading bank holding company, STI operates full-service branches in the United States, particularly the South. Its primary business is traditional deposit and credit services, but it provides other services.

Fifth Third Bancorp (FITB)—Earnings estimate, 2000: $2.75. P/E on estimated earnings, 23 times. This diversified financial services company offers commercial services, retail banking, investment advisory services, and Midwest payments systems. It operates in Ohio, Kentucky, Indiana, and other states.

Wachovia Corporation (WB)—Earnings estimate, 2000: $5.52. P/E on estimated earnings, 15 times. A bank holding company with branches in North Carolina, Georgia, and other states, Wachovia offers general commercial banking, trust and investment management, and other services.

The Charles Schwab Corporation (SCH)—Earnings estimate, 2000: $0.82. P/E on estimated earnings, 63 times. Schwab is one of the nation's largest financial services firms, operating branches throughout the United States. It offers mutual funds and is the leader in online brokerage services.

CIGNA Corporation (CI)—Earnings estimate, 2000: $6.00. P/E on estimated earnings, 15 times. This company is a leader in the property-casualty and group life/health insurance fields. Cigna markets a full line of group life and health insurance products and operates a managed-care operation.

American General Corporation (AGC)—Earnings estimate, 2000: $5.13. P/E on estimated earnings, 14 times. AGC is a leading insurance-based financial services company. It offers retirement services, consumer finance, and life insurance. It sells term insurance to customers in their homes.

MBNA Corporation (KRB)—Earnings estimate, 2000: $1.41. P/E on estimated earnings, 21 times. KRB is a leading lender through bank credit cards and a leading issuer of affinity cards. The company also provides financial transaction processing services and retail deposit services.

J.P. Morgan & Company, Inc. (JPM)—Earnings estimate, 2000: $9.49. P/E on estimated earnings, 15 times. This bank holding company owns Morgan Guaranty Trust, a major U.S. bank. It is a leader in finance and advisory services for clients and for its own account.

Mellon Bank Corporation (MEL)—Earnings estimate, 2000: $2.03. P/E on estimated earnings, 17 times. This major bank has subsidiaries in Pennsylvania, Massachusetts, Delaware, and other states. Its efforts are in consumer investment, trust and custody, and other services.

PNC Bank Corporation (PNC)—Earnings estimate, 2000: $4.24. P/E on estimated earnings, 13 times. This leading banking company has branch offices in Pennsylvania, New Jersey, Kentucky, and other states. The bank offers asset management, mortgage banking, and other services.

Marsh & McLennan Companies, Inc. (MMC)—Earnings estimate, 2000: $3.93. P/E on estimated earnings, 19 times. This is a leading company in the insurance brokerage business. MMC advises clients in risk assessment and assists them in the implementation of risk transfers to insurance companies or other funding methods.

Firstar Corporation (FSR)—Earnings estimate, 2000: $1.48. P/E on estimated earnings, 18 times. This bank holding company has offices in Wisconsin, Iowa, Illinois, and other states. It offers commercial and industrial loans, commercial real estate loans, and other types of loans and credit card services.

Household International, Inc. (HI)—Earnings estimate, 2000: $3.51. P/E on estimated earnings, 13 times. HI is a leading consumer financial services provider, operating in the United States, Canada, and the United

Kingdom. It offers secured and unsecured lending products, mostly to individual customers.

State Street Corporation (STT)—Earnings estimate, 2000: $4.39. P/E on estimated earnings, 15 times. Here is a leading bank holding company that operates worldwide. The company offers investment management, commercial lending, and financial assets services.

The Hartford Financial Services Group (HIG)—Earnings estimate, 2000: $4.36. P/E on estimated earnings, 13 times. This leading worldwide company offers financial and insurance products. Among other offerings, its life insurance products provide individual and group life and disability insurance.

KeyCorp (KEY)—Earnings estimate, 2000: $2.65. P/E on estimated earnings, 12 times. This is a nationwide financial services company that performs a range of services. KeyCorp offers transaction processing and advisory services, international banking, venture capital, and other services.

BB and T Corporation (BBT)—Earnings estimate, 2000: $2.17. P/E on estimated earnings, 16 times. This bank holding company operates more than 580 branches in North Carolina, South Carolina, Virginia, and other states. It also operates over 40 community banks and thrifts, as well as insurance companies.

Northern Trust Corporation (NTR)—Earnings estimate, 2000: $3.88. P/E on estimated earnings, 25 times. NTR is a Chicago-based bank holding company with locations all over the world. It provides financial services, including trust banking, retirement and investment management, and other services.

BankBoston Corporation (BKB)—Earnings estimate, 2000: $3.49. P/E on estimated earnings, 14 times. This bank holding company is a leader throughout the United States. BKB specializes in global and individual banking, investment management, commercial real estate lending, and other activities.

Comerica Incorporated (CMA)—Earnings estimate, 2000: $4.58. P/E on estimated earnings, 13 times. A bank holding company, CMA operates banking subsidiaries in Michigan, California, Texas, and other locales. It is involved in business, individual, and investment banking.

The Chubb Corporation (CB)—Earnings estimate, 2000: $4.80. P/E on estimated earnings, 14 times. Chubb is a leading property-casualty insurer.

It operates in the commercial lines, personal lines, and reinsurance. Premiums are divided into commercial casualty, executive protection, and other areas.

Conseco, Incorporated (CNG)—Earnings estimate, 2000: $4.54. P/E on estimated earnings, 6 times. This holding company owns and operates annuity, life, and health insurance companies. Its premiums come from annuities, supplemental health insurance, and other sources.

The Progressive Corporation (PGR)—Earnings estimate, 2000: $6.79. P/E on estimated earnings, 20 times. PGR is a leading underwriter of auto lines for the nonstandard market and other specialty personal lines coverage. Most of its business comes from underwriting private passenger automobiles.

Providian Financial Corporation (PVN)—Earnings estimate, 2000: $4.85. P/E on estimated earnings, 20 times. This leading insurance company provides life, annuity, accident and health, and property-casualty insurance. Its financial subsidiaries issue credit cards and perform other financial services.

Loews Corporation (LTR)—Earnings estimate, 2000: $7.65. P/E on estimated earnings, 10 times. This major, diversified company derives much of its revenue from life and property-casualty insurance. It offers professional and specialty lines, general liability, and other forms of insurance.

Regions Financial Corporation (RGBK)—Earnings estimate, 2000: $0.87. P/E on estimated earnings, 15 times. This bank holding company has recently extended its five-state franchise westward into Arkansas. It has over 600 offices stretching from Florida across the Southeast to East Texas.

Jefferson-Pilot (JP)—Earnings estimate, 2000: $4.12. P/E on estimated earnings, 16 times. JP provides a number of products and services: individual life insurance, annuities and investment products, and group insurance, to name only a few. In life insurance it offers whole life, term, and annuity and endowment products.

Franklin Resources (BEN)—Earnings estimate, 2000: $2.24. P/E on estimated earnings, 18 times. This is one of the largest mutual fund management companies in the United States. It offers many types of funds: tax-free income, U.S. government fixed-income, U.S. equity, global equity, and others.

Aon Corporation (AOC)—Earnings estimate, 2000: $2.55. P/E on estimated earnings, 16 times. This is a leading insurance broker and an underwriter of many insurance products. AON has worldwide operations and offices in more than 60 countries.

Capital One Financial Corporation (COF)—Earnings estimate, 2000: $2.16. P/E on estimated earnings, 25 times. Here is a major issuer of Visa and MasterCard credit cards. It was a pioneer of balance transfer products, which allow customers to move credit card balances.

Transamerica Corporation (TA)—Earnings estimate, 2000: $4.45. P/E on estimated earnings, 17 times. This company is a giant in the insurance, real estate services, leasing, and finance marketplaces. In the area of finance, it markets annuities, both fixed and variable, and many mutual funds.

UNUM Corporation (UNM)—Earnings estimate, 2000: $3.86. P/E on estimated earnings, 14 times. This company's disability insurance products include short-term disability, long-term disability reinsurance, and group disability. It also offers life insurance and group pension products.

The St. Paul Companies, Inc. (SPC)—Earnings estimate, 2000: $2.85. P/E on estimated earnings, 10 times. SPC is a leading property-liability insurer with subsidiaries in businesses such as medical liability insurance and reinsurance. It is also a player in the asset management business.

SLM Holding Corporation (SLM)—Earnings estimate, 2000: $3.52. P/E on estimated earnings, 13 times. This company is a major provider of financial services for educational needs and a source for student loans. It buys student loans from various lenders and makes a secondary market in them.

Summit Bancorp (SUB)—Earnings estimate, 2000: $3.09. P/E on estimated earnings, 13 times. This major bank holding company operates in New Jersey and eastern Pennsylvania, among other places. It also offers asset management and discount brokerage services.

Mercantile Bancorporation, Inc. (MTL)—Earnings estimate, 2000: $3.32. P/E on estimated earnings, 17 times. Mercantile is a major bank holding company that operates banks in Missouri, Kansas, Illinois, and other places. The company is a traditional banker, possessing a large base of customers.

Lincoln National Corporation (LNC)—Earnings estimate, 2000: $3.41. P/E on estimated earnings, 15 times. LNC is active in three main businesses: life insurance, annuity, and asset management operations. It offers life insurance through five companies, Lincoln National Life being one of the major firms.

Lehman Brothers Holdings, Inc. (LEH)—Earnings estimate, 2000: $6.60. P/E on estimated earnings, 10 times. This major investment banking firm serves institutional, corporate, individual, and government clients worldwide. Lehman is also well-known for its capital-raising activities.

Union Planters Corporation (UPC)—Earnings estimate, 2000: $3.40. P/E on estimated earnings, 14 times. This bank holding company operates primarily in the southeastern and central United States. As with all commercial banks, it derives most of its revenues from net interest income

MBIA, Incorporated (MBI)—Earnings estimate, 2000: $5.33. P/E on estimated earnings, 12 times. MBIA is a leading insurer of municipal bonds, and insures bonds traded in the secondary market. Among the insured bond mix are general obligation bonds, utility bonds, and healthcare bonds.

Provident Companies, Inc. (PVT)—Earnings estimate, 2000: $2.80. P/E on estimated earnings, 14 times. This company is a leading provider of noncancelable disability insurance for individuals. It also offers life insurance, pension products, and group disability policies.

Torchmark Corporation (TMK)—Earnings estimate, 2000: $2.84. P/E on estimated earnings, 7 times. TMK is a financial services company. It serves the life and health insurance industry. It also markets and manages a family of mutual funds under Waddell & Reed and other names.

Republic New York Corporation (RNB)—Earnings estimate, 2000: 4.31. P/E on estimated earnings, 16 times. This leading banker offers a wide range of banking and financial services worldwide. It serves corporations, financial institutions, government units, and individuals.

Synovus Financial Corporation (SNV)—Earnings estimate, 2000: $0.90. P/E on estimated earnings, 22 times. This bank holding company has branches in Georgia, Florida, Alabama, and other states. It also has an interest in a commercial and private-label card processing company.

Golden West Financial Corporation (GDW)—Earnings estimate, 2000: $8.80. P/E on estimated earnings, 10 times. A major thrift, GDW avoided many of the problems of the industry in the 1980s. It concentrates on high-end customers, lending only to the most creditworthy home buyers.

Countrywide Credit Industries, Inc. (CCR)—Earnings estimate, 2001: $4.16. P/E on estimated earnings, 10 times. This is a leading independent residential mortgage lender and servicer. It is also involved in refinancing. CCR charges fees or points to borrowers when they take out a loan.

SAFECO Corporation (SAFC)—Earnings estimate, 2000: $3.22. P/E on estimated earnings, 13 times. SAFECO underwrites property-casualty insurance, life and health insurance, and surety insurance. It also functions in the investment management and commercial lending areas.

Cincinnati Financial Corporation (CINF)—Earnings estimate, 2000: $1.59. P/E on estimated earnings, 23 times. This leading insurer provides vehicle and equipment leasing through its Cincinnati Financial Corp. CFC-1 division. The company also provides life, fire, and other insurance.

Huntington Bancshares, Inc. (HBAN)—Earnings estimate, 2000: $2.15. P/E on estimated earnings, 16 times. This regional bank holding company operates more than 600 offices, mostly in Ohio, Michigan, Florida, and a few other states. It offers checking and savings accounts, a discount brokerage, and other services.

MGIC Investment Corporation (MTG)—Earnings estimate, 2000: $4.22. P/E on estimated earnings, 13 times. A major holding company, MGIC helps Americans afford new homes by providing insurance to lenders. MGIC receives the biggest part of its revenues from premiums earned on mortgage insurance.

Bear Stearns (BSC)—Earnings estimate, 2000: $4.56. P/E on estimated earnings, 10 times. Bear Stearns is a leading broker and member of the New York Stock Exchange. It is also a major investment banker. The company also offers research, trading capabilities, asset management, and other services.

THE STOCKS OF THE INDUSTRIAL SELECT SECTOR SPDR (XLI)

Tyco International Ltd. (TYC)—Earnings estimate, 2000: $3.93. P/E on estimated earnings, 25 times. Tyco is a leader in making fire protection systems. It also provides electronic security services and makes such other items as disposable medical and flow control products.

Waste Management International (WME)—Earnings estimate, 2000: $3.24. P/E on estimated earnings, 10 times. This company offers waste management and related services. It is global in scope, with operations in Asia, South America, and the Middle East.

Textron, Inc. (TXT)—Earnings estimate, 2000: $4.56. P/E on estimated earnings, 19 times. This leading diversified company offers financial services and also operates in the aircraft, automotive, and other industrial markets. It is a major maker of light and midsized business jets.

Minnesota Mining and Manufacturing Company (MMM)—Earnings estimate, 2000: $4.44. P/E on estimated earnings, 20 times. 3M operates worldwide, producing industrial, consumer, and healthcare products. It is a leader in coating and bonding technology for consumer products.

Illinois Tool Works, Inc. (ITW)—Earnings estimate, 2000: $3.32. P/E on estimated earnings, 24 times. A leading specialty products company, ITW produces primarily for the auto, food, and construction industries. It makes fasteners, components, assemblies and systems, and other products.

Emerson Electric Company (EMR)—Earnings estimate, 2000: $3.29. P/E on estimated earnings, 19 times. This diversified manufacturer makes a large number of electrical and electronic products. Among its many offerings are process control instrumentation, valves and systems, and industrial machinery.

General Electric (GE)—Earnings estimate, 2000: $3.64. P/E on estimated earnings, 32 times. Here is one of the all-time leaders in aircraft engines, medical systems, power systems, and a host of other products. A large portion of GE's revenues comes from its financial services division.

Allied Signal, Inc. (ALD)—Earnings estimate, 2000: $3.10. P/E on estimated earnings, 20 times. Allied Signal mostly serves the aerospace and automotive industries, making gas turbine engines and other products, ranging from fibers and chemicals to plastic and other engineered materials.

Corning, Inc. (GLW)—Earnings estimate, 2000: $2.20. P/E on estimated earnings, 33 times. Corning is involved in specialty materials, consumer products, and fiber optics. It manufactures optical fiber, cable, hardware, and components for the global telecommunications industry.

Caterpillar, Inc. (CAT)—Earnings estimate, 2000: $3.88. P/E on estimated earnings, 15 times. CAT stands in the forefront among manufacturers of earth-moving machinery and equipment. It is also a producer of diesel, turbine, and natural gas engines. CAT makes a full range of machinery, from small tractors to big, big trucks.

Johnson Controls, Inc. (JCI)—Earnings estimate, 2000: $4.63. P/E on estimated earnings, 14 times. JCI produces automotive interior systems, building controls systems, and other products. Its largest source of revenues is its automotive operations, with plastics and batteries contributing a lesser amount.

Ingersoll-Rand Company (IR)—Earnings estimate, 2000: $3.92. P/E on estimated earnings, 15 times. This leading maker of capital goods has as its primary business the design and manufacture of compressed air systems. International operations account for a sizable percentage of IR's sales.

Honeywell, Inc. (HON)—Earnings estimate, 2000: $5.51. P/E on estimated earnings, 21 times. This company produces automation and control systems for industry, aerospace, homes, and buildings. HON is known for its residential thermostats and climate control systems. International operations are important for Honeywell.

Case Corporation (CSE)—Earnings estimate, 2000: $1.64. P/E on estimated earnings, 28 times. Case is a leader in farm equipment manufacture and also produces light and medium-size construction equipment. CSE makes replacement parts and also engages in finance.

Cummins Engine Company, Inc. (CUM)—Earnings estimate, 2000: $4.49. P/E on estimated earnings, 12 times. CUM is a leader in manufacturing diesel engines for heavy-duty trucks and is also involved in midrange engines. Most of its sales are in the United States, but international business is growing.

Crane Company (CR)—Earnings estimate, 2000: $2.53. P/E on estimated earnings, 10 times. This diversified company makes engineered products for the aerospace, fluid-handling, automatic merchandising, and construction businesses. Most of its operations are in the United States

Briggs & Stratton Corporation (BGG)—Earnings estimate, 2000: $4.47. P/E on estimated earnings, 13 times. BGG makes small gasoline engines. Most of its engine sales are to manufacturers of lawn and garden equipment. Briggs & Stratton also makes pressure washers, which can be used to clean driveways, patios, and other areas.

Cooper Industries, Inc. (CBE)—Earnings estimate, 2000: $3.79. P/E on estimated earnings, 14 times. Cooper makes electrical products, tools and hardware, and automotive products. Its products are marketed under the Edison, Crouse-Hinds, Halo, and other brand names.

Browning-Ferris Industries, Inc. (BFI)—Earnings estimate, 2000: $2.39. P/E on estimated earnings, 17 times. This company produces solid waste collection, processing, and other disposal services for government, residential, industrial, and commercial customers.

Foster Wheeler Corporation (FWC)—Earnings estimate, 2000: $0.82. P/E on estimated earnings, 15 times. This excellent company provides design, engineering, and construction services. Its main customers are in the chemical, petroleum refining, power, generating, and other industries.

Fluor Corporation (FLR)—Earnings estimate, 2000: $2.50. P/E on estimated earnings, 16 times. Fluor operates worldwide as a leading provider of engineering, construction, and other services. The company serves process industrial, power, government, and diversified customers.

Danaher Corporation (DHR)—Earnings estimate, 2000: $2.07. P/E on estimated earnings, 27 times. Here is a leader in making hand tools and process and environmental controls. DHR's products are sold under the Sears Craftsman, Ammco, Coats, and other brand names.

Eaton Corporation (ETN)—Earnings estimate, 2000: $7.04. P/E on estimated earnings, 13 times. Eaton manufactures products for the electrical and electronic controls and vehicular components market. Components are supplied for trucks, automobiles, and other vehicles.

Deere & Company (DE)—Earnings estimate, 2000: $2.11. P/E on estimated earnings, 18 times. Deere stands out in the production of farm equipment. It also makes construction machinery and lawn and garden equipment. Deere also provides credit, insurance, and healthcare products.

Dana Corporation (DCN)—Earnings estimate, 2000: $4.91. P/E on estimated earnings, 9 times. Dana makes systems and controls for the vehicular, industrial, and off-highway original equipment markets. It is also a major supplier to related aftermarkets.

Dover Corporation (DOV)—Earnings estimate, 2000: $1.92. P/E on estimated earnings, 20 times. Dover makes and markets products to the building, petroleum, electronics, aerospace, and other industries. The company operates internationally, but mostly in the United States.

Pall Corporation (PLL)—Earnings estimate, 2000: $1.06. P/E on estimated earnings, 19 times. PLL operates worldwide, producing fine disposable filters and other fluid clarification equipment. It serves the fluid processing, healthcare, and aeropower industries.

Parker Hannifin Corporation (PH)—Earnings estimate, 2000: $3.08. P/E on estimated earnings, 14 times. This company produces motion and control components for industrial and aerospace markets. Currently, PH is expanding its foreign operations.

Navistar International Corporation (NAV)—Earnings estimate, 2000: $5.18. P/E on estimated earnings, 9 times. This outstanding industrial-sector company makes medium- and heavy-duty truck and school bus chassis and diesel engines. It finances new retail sales of NAV trucks and other vehicles through its finance subsidiary.

National Service Industries, Inc. (NSI)—Earnings estimate, 2000: $2.88. P/E on estimated earnings, 12 times. This company makes lighting equipment, textile rentals, chemicals, and envelopes. Its lighting equipment subsidiary is Lithonia Lighting, a major player in the industry,

NACCO Industries (NC)—Earnings estimate, 1999: $6.51. P/E on 1999 earnings, 8 times. This is a leader in manufacturing forklift trucks. Its Hamilton Beach/Proctor-Silex division makes small electrical appliances, such as blenders, food processors, mixers, electric knives, and the like.

PACCAR, Inc. (PCAR)—Earnings estimate, 2000: $5.44. P/E on estimated earnings, 10 times. This heavy-duty truck manufacturer produces the Peterbilt and Kenworth brands. It makes Leyland Trucks in Europe, and also produces industrial winches and sells general automotive parts.

Foster Wheeler Corporation (FWC)—Earnings estimate, 2000: $0.82. P/E on estimated earnings, 15 times. Foster Wheeler provides engineering services and products internationally. Among the industries it serves are petroleum, petrochemical, and other concerns.

Milacron, Inc. (MZ)—Earnings estimate, 2000: $2.22. P/E on estimated earnings, 8 times. This company is the broadest-line supplier of equipment, tooling, and supplies to the plastics processing industry in the world. MZ also supplies extrusion, mold basis, and mold-making supplies.

Harnischfeger Industries, Inc. (HPH)—Earnings estimate, 2000: $0.11. P/E on estimated earnings, 18 times. HPH is a frontrunner in the manufacture of papermaking machinery. It is also a major player in producing mining machinery and equipment and material-handling equipment.

THE STOCKS OF THE TECHNOLOGY SELECT SECTOR SPDR (XLK)
Hewlett-Packard Company (HWP)—Earnings estimate, 2000: $4.04. P/E on estimated earnings, 28 times. This standout of the tech sector makes computer products, including printers, workstations, and servers. HWP also offers a service and support network. It operates all over the world.

International Business Machines Corporation (IBM)—Earnings estimate, 2000: $4.43. P/E on estimated earnings, 30 times. IBM is a major worldwide computer firm. It offers computer hardware equipment, application and system software for client/server environments, and other services.

Lucent Technologies, Inc. (LU)—Earnings estimate, 2000: $1.45. P/E on estimated earnings, 48 times. This is one of the leading designers, developers, and manufacturers of telecommunications systems, software, and related products. LU operates in over 75 countries.

Compaq Computer Corporation (CPQ)—Earnings estimate, 2000: $1.28. P/E on estimated earnings, 20 times. This is a worldwide manufacturer of desktop and portable computers and PC servers. Compaq offers clustering and Internetworking solutions in its systems products group.

MCI Worldcom (WCOM)—Earnings estimate, 2000: $2.82. P/E on estimated earnings, 31 times. This worldwide company supplies businesses and individuals with Internet, local, long-distance, data, and communications services. Its services include 800 calls, calling cards, and debit cards.

Cisco Corporation (CSC)—Earnings estimate, 2000: $0.92. P/E on estimated earnings, 72 times. Cisco supplies data networking products to corporate clients and public service provider markets. It produces routers, LAN switches, frame relay/ATM, and remote access concentrators.

American Telephone and Telegraph Company (T)—Earnings estimate, 2000: $2.35. P/E on estimated earnings, 24 times. This company produces services and products for the communications industry. It offers voice, data, and video telecommunications to individuals, businesses, and government.

Microsoft Corporation (MSFT)—Earnings estimate, 2000: $1.54. P/E on estimated earnings, 60 times. Microsoft develops, manufactures, licenses, sells, and supports software products. Its operating systems software and other products are offered to both businesses and individuals.

Intel Corporation (INTC)—Earnings estimate, 2000: $2.70. P/E on estimated earnings, 24 times. This worldwide company designs, manufactures, and sells computer components and related products. Among its offerings are microprocessors, chipsets, and graphics products.

Dell Computer (DELL)—Earnings estimate, 2000: $0.98. P/E on estimated earnings, 42 times. This company is a leader in the direct marketing of personal computers, including desktops, notebooks, and servers. It has used its direct approach to penetrate the corporate and international markets as well.

America OnLine, Inc. (AOL)—Earnings estimate, 2000: $0.57. P/E on estimated earnings, 224 times. AOL provides interactive communications and services through its worldwide online system. It offers electronic mail services, interactive conversations, guest interviews, and other features on its Web sites.

Xerox Corporation (XRX)—Earnings estimate, 2000: $3.12. P/E on estimated earnings, 18 times. This company focuses on the global document market and offers photocopiers with the latest digital, multifunctional features. Customers can finance purchases through its Xerox credit subsidiaries.

United Technologies Corporation (UTX)—Earnings estimate, 2000: $3.34. P/E on estimated earnings, 20 times. This company makes aircraft jet engines, helicopters, flight systems, elevators, escalators, air-conditioning equipment, and automotive products. Its brand names include Otis and Carrier.

Texas Instruments Incorporated (TXN)—Earnings estimate, 2000: $3.98. P/E on estimated earnings, 36 times. This leading maker of semiconductors also turns out digital products. Among its offerings are microprocessors, microcontrollers, and application processors.

Sprint Corp. FON Group (FON)—Earnings estimate, 2000: $2.13. P/E on estimated earnings, 23 times. Sprint is a top U.S. long-distance carrier. It is active in 100 percent state-of-the-art wireless network technology. The company also serves markets in Hawaii, Alaska, Puerto Rico, and other locales.

Motorola, Inc. (MOT)—Earnings estimate, 2000: $2.89. P/E on estimated earnings, 34 times. MOT is a front-running competitor in cellular telephone systems, semiconductors, paging equipment, and other electronics products. Foreign operations account for a large percentage of revenues.

Northern Telecom Ltd. (NT)—Earnings estimate, 2000: $2.68. P/E on estimated earnings, 33 times. NT is a worldwide producer of telecommunications equipment. Most of the company's revenues comes from the United States, but some comes from Canada and Europe.

FMC Corporation (FMC)—Earnings estimate, 2000: $1.30. P/E on estimated earnings, 45 times. This is an outstanding manufacturer of industrial, specialty, and agricultural chemicals, as well as petroleum, food, and transportation machinery. In addition, FMC is a world leader in producing natural soda ash and derivatives.

Electronic Data Systems Corporation (EDS)—Earnings estimate, 2000: $2.22. P/E on estimated earnings, 27 times. This company is a successful provider of a number of information technology services. Among them are management consulting, systems development, and systems integration.

Boeing Company (BA)—Earnings estimate, 2000: $1.79. P/E on estimated earnings, 24 times. This well-respected company makes commercial airplanes, space systems, and military aircraft. Its defense operations include Airborne Warnings and Control Systems.

Sun Microsystems (SUNW)—Earnings estimate, 2000: $1.67. P/E on estimated earnings, 43 times. Sun sells servers and operating systems software and makes workstations for the technical, engineering, and scientific markets. It is the producer of JavaSoft, a programming language.

Oracle Corporation (ORCL)—Earnings estimate, 2000: $1.27. P/E on estimated earnings, 30 times. Oracle makes computer software products used in database management, applications development, and decision support. It offers customers guidance in the development of company applications.

Amgen, Inc. (AMGN)—Earnings estimate, 2000: $2.10. P/E on estimated earnings, 32 times. The leading company in the biotechnology industry offers Epogen and Neupogen, versions of natural hormones. It has marketing rights to Neupogen in the United States, Canada, and Australia.

Compuware Corporation (CPWR)—Earnings estimate, 2000: $1.55. P/E on estimated earnings, 23 times. CPWR develops, markets, and maintains a support system for a line of software products. It also provides services for planning and developing computer systems.

Applied Materials, Inc. (AMAT)—Earnings estimate, 2000: $2.68. P/E on estimated earnings, 29 times. AMAT makes water fabrication equipment for the semiconductor industry. Its products are sold in North America, Japan, Korea, Europe, and the Pacific Rim.

Tellabs, Inc. (TLAB)—Earnings estimate, 2000: $1.59. P/E on estimated earnings, 49 times. This leading communications company makes, markets, and sevices voice equipment worldwide. It produces echo cancellers and T-coders, high-bit digital subscriber line products, and other items.

3Com Corporation (COMS)—Earnings estimate, 2001: $1.39. P/E on estimated earnings, 19 times. This enterprise makes a variety of products, including adapters, hubs, and routers for Ethernet. Its sales are divided between network adapters and systems products. Systems products include LAN switches and network servers.

Eastman Kodak Company (EK)—Earnings estimate, 2000: $5.63. P/E on estimated earnings, 12 times. Kodak stands at the forefront of changes in the photography industry. Traditional chemical-based photography is now being augmented with digital technology.

First Data Corporation (FDC)—Earnings estimate, 2000: $1.97. P/E on estimated earnings, 24 times. A top independent data services firm, First Data is involved in almost all facets of the credit card business. It also provides back-office processing services to the mutual fund industry.

Computer Associates International, Inc. (CA)—Earnings estimate, 2001: $3.17. P/E on estimated earnings, 17 times. CA designs, develops, markets, and supports standardized computer software products. It also provides a number of software products for information systems.

Automatic Data Processing, Inc. (AUD)—Earnings estimate, 2000: $1.30. P/E on estimated earnings, 33 times. A leading provider of data processing services in the employer, brokerage, deal, and claims segments, AUD also offers a line of products to help customers estimate claims such as auto and bodily injury.

Pitney Bowes, Inc. (PBI)—Earnings estimate, 2000: $2.60. P/E on estimated earnings, 26 times. This company makes mailing systems and copying systems. It also offers management services, lease financing, and financing for the company's equipment.

Lockheed Martin Corporation (LMT)—Earnings estimate, 2000: $2.16. P/E on estimated earnings, 17 times. This company is involved in many manufacturing industries, including space and strategic missiles, aeronautics, and electronics. It also makes the orbiter's external tank for NASA.

Raytheon Company (RTN)—Earnings estimate, last 12 months: $1.19. P/E on estimated earnings, 17 times. Raytheon makes air defense missiles, radar systems, and other electronics items for the military. Its Raytheon Engineers & Constructors is a global engineering, construction, operation, and maintenance operation.

Sprint Corp. PCS Group (PCS)—Earnings estimate, 2000: $3.91 (loss). Sprint operates a nationwide digital wireless network in the United States. It serves over 150 metropolitan markets and has licensed coverage of almost 270 million people in all 50 states, Puerto Rico, and the U.S. Virgin Islands.

BMC Software, Inc. (BMCS)—Earnings estimate, 2001: $2.46. P/E on estimated earnings, 25 times. This company markets software to enhance database management and data communications products. Its products boost data communications speed and efficiency and provide other advantages.

Nextel Communications, Inc. (NXTL)—Earnings estimate, 2000: $3.03 (loss). Nextel excels in mobile radio communications services and operates a national digital wireless network. Its international subsidiary holds rights to operate in Mexico, Brazil, Argentina, and other places.

Paychex, Inc. (PAYX)—Earnings estimate, 2001: $0.87. P/E on estimated earnings, 36 times. This company provides payroll accounting services to small businesses. Among other services, it prepares payroll checks, internal accounting records, and federal, state, and local payroll tax returns.

Unisys Corporation (UIS)—Earnings estimate, 2000: $1.79. P/E on estimated earnings, 25 times. This top supplier of information services and technology solutions operates in more than 100 countries. It offers hardware and software technologies, network integration, and other services.

Solectron Corporation (SLR)—Earnings estimate, 2001: $3.02. P/E on estimated earnings, 23 times. Solectron provides integrated manufacturing services to original producers in the electronics industry. Its products include complex printed circuit boards.

Seagate Technology, Inc. (SEG)—Earnings estimate, 2001: $2.22. P/E on estimated earnings, 11 times. This group provides mass storage products for computers and related equipment, including disc drives. Seagate designs and manufacturers disc drive components, recording heads, motors, and more.

Rockwell International Corporation (ROK)—Earnings estimate, 2000: $3.28. P/E on estimated earnings, 17 times. ROK supplies semiconductor chips for personal computers and modems. It turns out products for personal wireless communications for home and office.

Micron Technology, Inc. (MU)—Earnings estimate, 2000: $0.95. P/E on estimated earnings, 58 times. Micron makes semiconductor memories and other semiconductor components. It also manufactures dynamic random access memories and static random access memories components.

Computer Sciences Corporation (CSC)—Earnings estimate, 2000: $1.50. P/E on estimated earnings, 47 times. Here is a company that provides an array of services, including information technology consulting, systems integration, and technical services. It has operations around the globe.

General Dynamics Corporation (GD)—Earnings estimate, 2000: $3.69. P/E on estimated earnings, 18 times. GD supplies weapons systems and services to the U.S. government. Among other products, it supplies nuclear submarines to the U.S. Navy and assault vehicles to the Marine Corps.

Gateway 2000, Inc. (GTW)—Earnings estimate, 2000: $3.50. P/E on estimated earnings, 20 times. A leader in supplying personal computers, Gateway sells to users, mostly more sophisticated customers, both individuals and corporations, through direct sales channels.

Scientific-Atlanta (SFA)—Earnings estimate, 2000: $1.18. P/E on estimated earnings, 33 times. Communications systems and satellite-based video and data communications networks are the domain of SFA. It also makes transmission products such as radio frequency amplifiers.

Silicon Graphics, Inc. (SGI)—Earnings estimate, 2000: $0.21. P/E on estimated earnings, 76 times. SGI makes workstations, servers, and supercomputer systems incorporating three-dimensional graphics. They have a software division that supplies applications used by creative professionals.

Thomas & Betts Corporation (TNB)—Earnings estimate, 2000: $3.66. P/E on estimated earnings, 12 times. This manufacturer is a leader in electrical and electronic components. Its products include fittings and accessories for electrical raceways, fastening products, and power connectors.

Raychem Corporation (RYC)—Earnings estimate, 2000: $2.01. P/E on estimated earnings, 18 times. RYC makes a variety of products based on materials science. Its electronics segment makes electrical and electronic interconnection systems, among other products.

Thermo Electron Corp. (TMO)—Earnings estimate, 2000: $1.19. P/E on estimated earnings, 15 times. TMO makes instruments to measure air pollution, radioactivity, and toxic substances. It also makes biomedical products and instruments used to detect explosives and narcotics.

TRW Incorporated (TRW)—Earnings estimate, 2000: $5.05. P/E on estimated earnings, 11 times. TRW is a top company in producing services and high-technology products to the space, automotive, and defense markets. Auto safety restraint systems contribute a large part of their automotive revenues.

KLA-Tencor Corp. (KLAC)—Earnings estimate, 2000: $1.66. P/E on estimated earnings, 42 times. This first-rate company manufactures yield monitoring and process control systems. Its water inspection systems include wafer inspection tools used to find, count, and characterize defects on wafers.

W.W. Grainger, Inc. (GWW)—Earnings estimate, 2000: $2.85. P/E on estimated earnings, 17 times. This nationwide company distributes maintenance, repair, and operating supplies and provides related information for the commercial, industrial, contractor, and institutional markets.

Equifax, Inc. (EFX)—Earnings estimate, 2000: $1.85. P/E on estimated earnings, 18 times. Equifax serves the information and processing needs of the financial services and other industries. It provides risk management services such as employee prescreening, drug screening, and laboratory testing.

General Instrument Corp. (GIC)—Earnings estimate, 2000: $1.16. P/E on estimated earnings, 40 times. This company excels in developing systems, technology, and products solutions for the delivery of data. It also provides addressable systems and subscriber terminals for the cable television industry.

LSI Logic Corporation (LSI)—Earnings estimate, 2000: $1.86. P/E on estimated earnings, 26 times. LSI leads in supplying customer performance semiconductors. It also markets to customers in the consumer, communications, and computer industries.

Novell, Inc. (NOVL)—Earnings estimate, 2000: $0.72. P/E on estimated earnings, 41 times. This company offers an array of network solutions with distributed network, Internet, and intranet products. Its customers include both large and small enterprises.

National Semiconductor Corp. (NSM)—Earnings estimate, 2001: $1.95. P/E on estimated earnings, 14 times. NSM makes a full line of semiconductors, including digital, analog, and mixed-signal integrated circuits. It is one of the leading suppliers of LAN Ethernet products.

Northrup Grumman Corporation (NOC)—Earnings estimate, 2000: $6.98. P/E on estimated earnings, 10 times. Here is a producer of military and commercial aircraft subassemblies and defense electronics systems. The U.S. government and Boeing are major customers.

Polaroid Corporation (PRD)—Earnings estimate, 2000: $1.92. P/E on estimated earnings, 11 times. Polaroid is, of course, a leader in photography and related products. In the digital imaging area, its products include film for medical imaging systems and other medical applications.

PeopleSoft, Inc. (PSFT)—Earnings estimate, 2000: $0.31. P/E on estimated earnings, 51 times. This software firm makes and sells human resource management, financial, and other applications for use by industry. It also offers application products for reporting and workflow tools.

Parametric Technology Corporation (PMTC)—Earnings estimate, 2000: $1.02. P/E on estimated earnings, 14 times. This group makes, markets, and supports a line of integrated software products for the automation of the mechanical design-through-manufacturing process.

Cabletron Systems, Inc. (CS)—Earnings estimate, 2000: $0.54. P/E on estimated earnings, 25 times. CS makes Internetworking products, including hardware and software solutions for networks. The interconnection products include multiport repeaters to increase the speed of data transmission.

PE Biosystems Group (PEB)—Earnings estimate, 2000: $3.33. P/E on estimated earnings, 36 times. Here is a company that makes and markets life science systems for the pharmaceutical, agricultural, forensics, and chemical industries. It plans to develop glass and quartz microstructures for bioanalytical applications.

Andrew Corporation (ANDW)—Earnings estimate, 2000: $1.01. P/E on estimated earnings, 20 times. This company's main products are coaxial cables, special-purpose antennas, antennas, and earth stations for satellite communication systems, radar, and communication devices.

Autodesk, Inc. (ADSK)—Earnings estimate, 2001: $2.27. P/E on estimated earnings, 11 times. ADSK is a maker and marketer of computer-aided design and drafting software. Its products enable users to interactively create, store, and edit a wide variety of drawings.

Adobe Systems, Inc. (ADBE)—Earnings estimate, 2000: $3.27. P/E on estimated earnings, 27 times. Adobe develops and supports software used to create, display, print, and communicate electronic documents. It supports technologies that are embedded within original equipment makers.

Apple Computer, Inc. (AAPL)—Earnings estimate, 2000: $3.01. P/E on estimated earnings, 17 times. Apple is a maker of personal computers and related equipment. It makes the PowerBook portable computer, develops and markets application software, and develops computer servers.

Advanced Micro Devices, Inc. (AMD)—Earnings estimate, 2000: $0.61. P/E on estimated earnings, 27 times. This leading company produces semi-conductors used by the computer and telecommunications industries. Its applications solutions products include integrated circuits to manage system functions.

Ceridian Corportion (CEN)—Earnings estimate, 2000: $1.31. P/E on estimated earnings, 24 times. Ceridian provides payroll processing and other employer services. It also is a leading provider of audience research to the radio industry. A subsidiary allows truck drivers to pay for fuel through credit cards.

Tektronix, Inc. (TEK)—Earnings estimate, 2001: $2.25. P/E on estimated earnings, 12 times. This is a market leader in making oscilloscopes. They also produce printers, X terminals, television systems, picture monitors, signal generators, and other products.

Data General Corporation (DGN)—Earnings estimate, $0.28. P/E on estimated earnings, 53 times. This technology stalwart makes computer systems and related technologies. Its product line includes AViion servers and CLARiion storage products, and peripheral products such as monitors, printers, and disk storage.

IKON Office Solutions, Inc. (IKN)—Earnings estimate, 2001: $0.94. P/E on estimated earnings, 14 times. IKON is a leading office technology company, and rents, sells, and leases photocopiers and other equipment. Among other products, it distributes office, paper, and supply systems.

EGG&G, Inc. (EGG)—Earnings estimate, 2001: $2.43. P/E on estimated earnings, 23 times. The company develops and manufactures hardware and associated software for applications in medical diagnostics and medical research. It also produces X-ray imaging applied to airport security.

B.F. Goodrich Company (GR)—Earnings estimate, 2001: $3.42. P/E on estimated earnings, 7 times. This excellent tech company provides aircraft systems, components, and services, and also makes specialty chemicals. Its aerospace segment provides aircraft landing systems, sensors, integrated systems, and other products.

Harris Corporation (HRS)—Earnings estimate, 2000: $2.51. P/E on estimated earnings, 15 times. HRS is a producer of sophisticated communications and information processing equipment, office automation equipment, and semiconductors. Sales to the U.S. government are an important source of revenue.

Moore Corporation, Ltd. (MCL)—Earnings estimate, 2001: $1.05. P/E on estimated earnings, 5 times. Moore is a leading supplier of business forms and related items. It also produces direct marketing products, custom packaging, and database management products and services.

Millipore Corporation (MIL)—Earnings estimate, 2000: $1.65. P/E on estimated earnings, 21 times. This company serves the semiconductor and pharmaceutical/healthcare industries and the analytical laboratory market. It makes industrial and medical-use filters.

THE STOCKS OF THE UTILITIES SELECT SECTOR SPDR (XLU)

Bell Atlantic Corporation (BEL)—Dividends paid the last 12 months: $1.54. Yield to market price: 2.30 percent. This telephone company also offers cellular services and has international telecommunications interests. It operates mostly on the East Coast, serving New York, Maine, and other locales.

BellSouth Corporation (BLS)—Dividends paid the last 12 months: $0.76. Yield to market price: 1.60 percent. This is one of the largest telephone holding companies in the United States. It provides service to communities in the Southeast. The company also has interests in international cellular operations in such foreign countries as Argentina and Australia.

SBC Communications, Inc. (SBC)—Dividends paid the last 12 months: $0.97. Yield to market price: 1.70 percent. This major telephone holding company serves California, Texas, and a number of other locales. It also serves many non-U.S. markets, including Mexico, Chile, and France. SBC owns cable television systems as well.

PECO Energy Company (PE)—Dividends paid the last 12 months: $1.00. Yield to market price: 2.3 percent. This electric and gas utility serves Philadelphia and surrounding northeastern Maryland. It also is active in such ventures as the development of a digital wireless network.

PG&E Corporation (PCG)—Dividends paid the last 12 months: $1.20. Yield to market price: 3.6 percent. PCG provides electricity and related services in northern and central California. Along with affiliates, it owns and operates natural gas transmission pipelines in the United States, Canada, and Australia.

FPL Group, Inc. (FPL)—Dividend paid the last 12 months: $2.08. Yield to market price: 3.7 percent. An electric utility holding company, FPL provides electricity along Florida's east and lower west coasts. It also has formed an investment group that looks for energy investments worldwide.

Texas Utilities Company (TXU)—Dividends paid the last 12 months: $2.30. Yield to market price: 5.2 percent. This energy holding company supplies electric, natural gas, and other energy services to customers, mostly in Texas. It also owns and operates one of the largest pipelines in the United States.

U S WEST Communications Group (USW)—Dividends paid the last 12 months: $2.14. Yield to market price: 3.8 percent. These shares track the local telephone operations of regional Bell operating company U S WEST. Its Carrier unit provides network access to long-distance and wireless companies.

The Southern Company (SO)—Dividends paid the last 12 months: $1.34. Yield to market price: 4.8 percent. SO serves the southeastern United States and southwestern England. It also has an interest in a major power producer. Among its domestic subsidiaries are Georgia Power, Gulf Power, and Savannah Electric & Power.

ALLTEL Corporation (AT)—Dividends paid the last 12 months: $1.22. Yield to market price: 1.6 percent. A diversified company, ALLTEL has operations in telephone service, information services, product distribution, and cellular. In telephone service the company operates primarily in the western United States.

Edison International (EIX)—Dividends paid the last 12 months: $1.08. Yield to market price: 4.1 percent. This company is involved in electric power generation, financial investments, and real estate development. Edison International is the holding company for Southern California Edison.

Duke Energy Corporation (DUK)—Dividends paid the last 12 months: $2.20. Yield to market price: 3.9 percent. One of the largest transporters and marketers of natural gas in the United States, Duke also provides electricity to about 2 million customers in North and South Carolina.

GTE Corporation (GTE)—Dividends paid the last 12 months: $1.88. Yield to market price: 2.4 percent. This is a leading telephone holding company with interests in wireless and defense communications, finance, insurance, and other areas. It offers local telephone exchange across the United States.

Consolidated Edison Company of N.Y., Inc. (ED)—Dividends paid the last 12 months: $2.14. Yield to market price: 4.9 percent. Con Ed serves New York City, Westchester County, and other areas with electricity. It also provides gas and steam in parts of its service area.

Ameritech Corporation (AIT)—Dividends paid the last 12 months: $1.27. Yield to market price: 1.7 percent. A leading holding company that supplies midwestern states with telephone service, Ameritech is also involved in cable television and long-distance services. It now offers wireless long-distance service.

Ameren Corporation (AEE)—Dividends paid the last 12 months: $2.54. Yield to market price: 6.4 percent. Through Union Electric Company and CIPSCO Incorporated, the company's wholly owned subsidiaries, AEE supplies natural gas and electricity to customers in Illinois and Missouri.

Sempra Energy (SRE)—Dividends paid the last 12 months: $1.56. Yield to market price: 6.8 percent. SRE is a holding company offering energy services in the United States, Canada, Mexico, and other Latin American countries. It offers a full range of value-added natural gas and electric services and products.

Carolina Power & Light Company (CPL)—Dividends paid the last 12 months: $2.00. Yield to market price: 4.6 percent. This company serves customers in eastern and western North Carolina and central South Carolina. It provides electricity at retail and wholesale to over a million customers.

AES Corporation (AES)—Earnings, 1999: $1.23. AES generates electricity and sells it to customers in the United States, England, Northern Ireland, Argentina, and elsewhere. It has recently increased its portfolio of generating assets by developing and constructing new plants.

American Electric Power Company, Inc. (AEP)—Dividends paid the last 12 months: $2.40. Yield to market price: 6.5 percent. A major utility holding company operating in Ohio, Indiana, Michigan, Virginia, and other Southern states, AEP also offers installation, maintenance, and engineering services.

Unicom Corporation (UCM)—Dividends paid the last 12 months: $1.60. Yield to market price: 3.9 percent. This utility holding company serves residential, commercial, and industrial customers in northern Illinois. It also offers district cooling services to offices and other buildings in Chicago.

Public Service Enterprise Group, Inc. (PEG)—Dividends paid the last 12 months: $2.16. Yield to market price: 5.1 percent. A company that supplies electric and gas service to New Jersey, PEG also operates nonutility businesses. It provides energy management consulting for businesses in the Northeast.

PacifiCorp (PPW)—Dividends paid the last 12 months: $1.08. Yield to market price: 5.6 percent. PPW owns electric and telephone utilities and is engaged in telecommunications ventures, natural gas, and finance. It owns a natural gas gathering, processing, storage, and marketing operation.

Dominion Resources, Inc. (D)—Dividends paid the last 12 months: $2.58. Yield to market price: 5.7 percent. Dominion supplies electric service in Virginia and North Carolina. It also provides nonutility electric power generation outside of Virginia and is active in all phases of natural gas.

FirstEnergy Corporation (FE)—Dividends paid the last 12 months: $1.50. Yield to market price: 5.0 percent. This holding company supplies electricity to over 2 million customers in northern and central Ohio and western Pennsylvania. Some of the cities served are Toledo and Cleveland, Ohio.

Entergy Corporation (ETR)—Dividends paid the last 12 months: $1.20. Yield to market price: 3.8 percent. ETR supplies electricity to retail customers in Arkansas, Texas, Louisiana, and Mississippi, and internationally to England, Australia, and Argentina.

DTE Energy Company (DTE)—Dividends paid the last 12 months: $2.06. Yield to market price: 5.1 percent. This holding company supplies electricity to customers in Michigan. In its nonregulated business, it develops and owns various energy products for institutional and industrial customers.

GPU, Incorporated (GPU)—Dividends paid the last 12 months: $2.12. Yield to market price: 5.1 percent. An electric utility holding company serving customers in the New Jersey and Pennsylvania area, GPU also has an interest in a British regional electric utility firm that serves over 2 million customers.

Frontier Corporation (FRO)—Dividends paid the last 12 months: $0.20. Yield to market price: 0.3 percent. This is a telecommunications company that provides local, long-distance, and wireless services. It serves Rochester, New York, and the surrounding area with local phone service and also owns small telephone companies.

Eastern Enterprises (EFU)—Dividends paid the last 12 months: $1.68. Yield to market price: 4.2 percent. EFU distributes natural gas in the Boston area. It also provides barge transportation services. A subsidiary is a leading carrier of coal and other dry bulk cargoes on inland waterways.

CINergy Corporation (CIN)—Dividends paid the last 12 months: $1.80. Yield to market price: 5.8 percent. This holding company supplies electricity and natural gas in the southwestern portion of Ohio and parts of Kentucky and Indiana. It also has an interest in a British regional electric company.

Central and Southwest Corporation (CSR)—Dividends paid the last 12 months: $1.74. Yield to market price: 7.8 percent. A utility holding company, CSR serves domestic customers primarily in the southwestern United States. It also has customers in southeastern England.

ONEOK, Incorporated (OKE)—Dividends paid the last 12 months: $1.24. Yield to market price: 3.8 percent. This company engages in natural gas utility operations in Oklahoma. It distributes gas to customers in Oklahoma, including the major cities of Tulsa and Oklahoma City. It also has a wholesale distribution operation.

Peoples Energy Corporation (PGL)—Dividends paid the last 12 months: $1.96. Yield to market price: 5.1 percent. PGL operates natural gas utilities in Illinois and serves customers in Chicago and the northeastern part of the state. It also provides heating and cooling services to Chicago buildings.

NICOR, Inc. (GAS)—Dividends paid the last 12 months: $1.56. Yield to market price: 4.0 percent. This holding company is one of the largest U.S. natural gas distributors. Its service area encompasses most of the northern third of Illinois, excluding Chicago. It also transports containerized freight between Florida and the Caribbean.

Niagara Mohawk Power Corporation (NMK)—Earnings over the last 12 months: $0.67. NMK supplies electricity and gas to cities in western and northern New York and some parts of southern Ontario. It owns nuclear units as well as fossil fuel steam plants and hydroelectric plants.

Northern States Power Company (NSP)—Dividends paid the last 12 months: $1.45. Yield to market price: 6.2 percent. Northern States supplies electricity and gas to customers in sections of Minnesota, Wisconsin, Michigan, and North and South Dakota. It also operates a gas marketing company that provides products and services.

PP&L Resources, Inc. (PPL)—Dividends paid the last 12 months: $1.00. Yield to market price: 3.2 percent. This holding company supplies electricity to homes and businesses in central-eastern Pennsylvania. Some of the larger cities served are Harrisburg, Allentown, Bethlehem, Lancaster, and Scranton.

New Century Energies, Inc. (NCE)—Dividends paid the last 12 months: $2.32. Yield to market price: 6.3 percent. This energy holding company has operations in six domestic states: Colorado, Texas, New Mexico, Wyoming, Kansas, and Oklahoma. It also brokers electricity and gas.

Constellation Energy Group (CEG)—Dividends paid the last 12 months: $1.68. Yield to market price: 5.7 percent. This electric and gas utility provides electricity and gas to over 1.5 million customers in central Maryland and the city of Baltimore. It is also involved in energy marketing and services.

Reliant Energy (REI)—Dividends paid the last 12 months: $1.50. Yield to market price: 5.4 percent. A leading international energy services company, REI's retail group consists of three natural gas utilities and one electric utility. The company's wholesale group provides wholesale trading and marketing services.

Source of earnings estimates: Zacks Investment Research.

B

THE ELECTRONIC INDEX INVESTOR AND TRADER RESEARCH SOURCE

WEB SITES

As I stated previously, the stocks in the indexes and averages are subject to change at any time, and they do. For instance, stocks in the S&P 500 index change at the rate of about one a month. To see a current listing, check the Web site of the average or index you're interested in. Here is a partial list of sites:

DIA: www.averages.dowjones.com/home.html

WEBS: www.websontheweb.com

QQQ: www.nasdaq-amex.com

SPY, MDY, Sector SPDRs: www.standardandpoors.com

BROKER SOURCE

Following is a listing of Internet brokers and discount brokers offering Internet services. Of special interest is the research offered and the charge, if any, for research. *Basic* refers to outside research services. *Both* includes the firm's own research. Check with the firm of your choice by visiting their Web site or calling their toll-free number.

Firm	Phone Number	Research	Web Page Address
AccuTrade	800-494-8946	Basic	www.accutrade.com
American Express	800-297-8800	Both (fee)	www.americanexpress.com /direct
Andrew Peck	800-221-5873	No	www.andrewpeck.com
Barry Murphy & Co.	800-221-2111	Standard (fee)	www.barrymurphy.com
Bidwell & Co.	800-547-6337	Standard	www.bidwell.com
Brown & Co.	800-822-2021	No	www.brownco.com
Bull & Bear Sec.	800-262-5800	None	www.ebullbear.com
Burke Christensen Lewis	800-621-0392	Standard	www.bdnet.com
Bush Burns Securities	800-821-4800	Both	www.bushburns.com
Charles Schwab	800-435-4000	Both	www.schwab.com
Downstate Discount	800-708-3543	Standard	www.edreyfus.com
East/West Securities	800-475-3400	No	www.eastwestsec.com
Fidelity Brokerage	800-544-8666	Standard (fee)	www.fidelity.com
Freeman Welwood	800-729-7585	Standard	www.freemanwelwood.com
Jack White & Co.	800-233-3411	Standard	www.jackwhiteco.com
Max Ule	800-223-6642	Both	www.maxule.com
Muriel Siebert	800-872-0711	Standard	www.siebernet.com

Firm	Phone Number	Research	Web Page Address
NationsBanc	800-926-1111	Standard (fee)	www.nationsbank.com
Newport Discount	800-999-3278	No	www.newport-discount.com
Norwest Brokerage	800-433-0738	Standard	www.norwest.com
Perelman-Carley Assoc.	800-444-5880	No	www.pcastocks.com
Quick & Reilly	800-672-7220	Standard (fee)	www.quick-reilly.com
R.J. Forbes Group	800-488-0090	No	www.forbesnet.com
Regal Discount	800-786-9000	Standard	www.eregal.com
Scottsdale Security	800-619-7283	No	www.scottrade.com
Scudder Brokerage	800-700-0820	Standard (fee)	www.scudder.com
Seaport Securities	800-732-7678	Standard	www.seaportonline.com
Sherry Bruce State Dis.	800-222-5520	Standard	www.state-discount.com
Summit Financial	800-631-1635	Standard (fee)	www.sfsg.com
T. Rowe Price Discount	800-638-5660	Both	www.troweprice.com
Trade-Well Discount	800-907-9797	Both (fee)	www.trade-well.com
TradeStar	800-961-1500	No	www.tradestar.com
Wachovia Investments	800-922-9008	Standard (fee)	www.wachovia.com
Waterhouse Securities	800-934-4443	Standard (fee)	www.waterhouse.com

Active traders who hesitate to depend on an online broker during big-volume days usually look for firms that offer broker-assisted trades. Here is a list of firms that offer live brokers.

Firm	Phone Number	Research	Web Page Address
A.B. Watley	888-229-2853	Standard	www.abwatley.com
AFTrader	888-682-4973	Standard	www.aftrader.com
Active Investor	888-781-0283	No	www.preftech.com
Ameritrade	800-669-3900	No	www.ameritrade.com
Bidwell Express	800-547-6337	No	www.bidwell.com
Charles Schwab	800-435-4000	Both	www.schwab.com
CompuTel Securities	800-432-0327	Standard	www.computel.com
First Flushing Sec.	888-988-6168	No	www.firstrade.com
J.B. Oxford	800-946-1776	Standard	www.jboxford.com
GFN Investments	800-354-7429	No	www.gfn.com
InternetTrading.com	800-696-2811	Standard (fee)	www.internettrading.com
InvestEXpress On-line	800-392-7192	No	www.investexpress.com

Firm	Phone Number	Research	Web Page Address
Investrade	800-498-7120	Standard	www.investrade.com
Mr. Stock	800-470-1896	Standard	www.mrstock.com
National Dis. Brokers	800-888-3999	Standard (fee)	www.ndb.com
Net Investor	800-638-4250	Standard	www.netinvestor.com
Soverign Securities	888-882-5600	Standard	mydiscountbroker.com
Trading Direct	800-925-8566	No	www.tradingdirect.com
WIT Capital	212-253-4400	Standard	www.witcapital.com
Wall Street Discount	800-221-7990	Standard	www.wsdc.com
Wall Street Elect.	888-925-5783	Both	www.wallstreete.com
Wall Street Securities	847-509-8600	Standard	www.WebStreetSecurities.com

Source: American Association of Individual Investors

THE REVOLUTION IN EXCHANGE SHARES IS JUST GETTING STARTED

Barclays Global Investors recently filed for new products that it plans to offer early in the year 2000. All of these products must be approved by the SEC, which makes the availability of the products uncertain and the timing inexact. But new classes of securities will be coming, whether these products or others not yet announced, or, perhaps, not even yet planned.

As always, these new classes of securities offer opportunity as well as risk. As the numbers of index products increase, knowledgeable investment advice will be needed to help guide traders and investors.

Following is a partial list of Barclays Global Investors proposed new products.

Standard & Poor (S&P) 500 Value; S&P 500 Growth

S&P 600; S&P 600 Growth

S&P 400; S&P 400 Growth; S&P Value

S&P 1500 Growth; S&P 1500 Value

S&P Euro (or Euro-Plus)

Russell Top 200; Russell 200 Growth; Russell 1000; Russell 2000 Growth; Russell 2000 Value; Russell 3000; Russell 1000 Value; Russell MidCap

Dow Jones (DJ) US Small Cap; DJ US MidCap; DJ Basic Materials Sector; DJ Consumer Cyclicals Sector; DJ Consumer Non-Cyclical Sector; DJ

Energy Sector; DJ Financial Sector; DJ Industrial/Independent Sector; DJ Technology Sector; DJ Utilities Sector

U.S. Advanced Technology Sector; U.S. Internet Industry; Global Leisure/ Entertainment; U.S. Healthcare Industry; Global Home Building and Furniture; U.S. Real Estate Industry; U.S. Chemicals; Global Telecommunications Industry; Global Pharmaceutical Industry

INDEX

Abbott Laboratories (ABT), 199
Account structures, 20
Active managers, 2, 4, 16
Active markets, 70, 71
ACWI, 144
Adobe Systems, Inc. (ADBE), 238
Adolph Coors Co. (RKY), 205
Advanced Micro Devices, Inc.
    (AMD), 239
AES Corporation (AES), 242
Aetna, Inc. (AET), 194
AFLAC, Inc. (AFL), 205
Agency trades, 37
Air Products and Chemicals, Inc.
    (APD), 186
Alberto-Culver (ACV), 204
Albertsons, Inc. (ABS), 201
Alcan Aluminium, Ltd. (AL), 186
Alcoa (AA), 185
All-or-none (AON) order, 73, 75
Allegheny Teledyne (ALT), 187
Allergan, Inc. (AGN), 204
Allied Signal, Inc. (ALD), 227
Allstate Corporation (ALL), 218
ALLTEL Corporation (AT), 241
ALZA Corp. (AZA), 205
Amerada Hess Corporation (AHC),
    216
Ameren Corporation (AEE), 242
America OnLine, Inc. (AOL), 232

American Electric Power Company,
    Inc. (AEP), 242
American Express Company (AXP),
    218
American General Corporation
    (AGC), 221
American Greetings Corp. (AM), 196
American Home Products (AHP), 199
American International Group, Inc.
    (AIG), 218
American Stores (ASC), 202
American Telephone and Telegraph
    Company (T), 231
Ameritech Corporation (AIT), 242
Amgen, Inc. (AMGN), 233
AMR Corporation (AMR), 208
Anadarko Petroleum Corporation
    (APC), 216
Andrew Corporation (ANDW), 238
Anheuser Busch Co., Inc. (BUD), 199
Aon Corporation (AOC), 223
AON order, 73, 75
Apache Corporation (APA), 216
Apple Computer, Inc. (AAPL), 238
Applied Materials, Inc. (AMAT), 233
Arbitrage, 35
Archer-Daniels-Midland (ADM), 203
Armstrong World Industries, Inc.
    (ACK), 213
Asarco, Inc. (AR), 192

Ashland Incorporated (ASH), 216
Ask price, 32
Asset allocation, 52, 86
Associates First Capital Corp.
    (AFS), 218
Atlantic Richfield Company (ARC),
    217
Australia, 154, 157
Austria, 154, 158
Author, 137
Autodesk, Inc. (ADSK), 238
Automatic Data Processing, Inc.
    (AUD), 234
AutoZone, Inc. (AZO), 211
Avery Dennison Corp. (AVY), 186
Avon Products (AVP), 203

Baker Hughes, Inc. (BHI), 217
Ball Corporation (BLL), 191
Banc One Corp. (ONE), 218
Bank of New York Co., Inc. (BK), 218
BankAmerica Corp. (BAC), 219
BankBoston Corporation (BKB), 222
Barber, Brad, 65
Barclays Global Fund Advisors, 6,
    144, 251
Bard (C.R), (BCR), 204
Barrick Gold Corporation (ABX),
    186
Barron's, 16

Basic Industries Select SPDR (XLB), 88, 158–192
Basket of stocks, 40, 146
Battle Mountain Gold (BMG), 192
Bausch & Lomb (BOL), 204
Baxter International, Inc. (BAX), 201
BB and T Corporation (BBT), 222
Bear Stearns (BSC), 226
Becton, Dickinson (BDX), 203
Behavioral finance, 10, 64–68
Belgium, 155, 159
Bell Atlantic Corporation (BEL), 240
BellSouth Corporation (BLS), 240
Bemis Co., Inc. (BMS), 190
Best Buy Corporation (BBY), 207
Bestfoods (BFO), 201
Bethlehem Steel Corp. (BS), 191
B.F. Goodrich Company (GR), 239
Bid price, 32
Bid/ask size, 33
Biomet (BMET), 205
Black & Decker (BDK), 211
BMC Software, Inc. (BCCS), 235
Boeing Company (BA), 233
Bogle, John C., 7
Boise Cascade Corp. (BCC), 191
Boston Scientific (BSX), 203
Bottom-up approach, 141
"Boys Will Be Boys" (Odean/Barber), 66
bp, 21
Briggs & Stratton Corporation (BGG), 228
Bristol Meyers Squibb Co. (BMY), 198
Brokers:
    active investors, 80
    active traders, 80, 81
    discount, 76, 77
    full-service, 77, 78
    information sources, 81
    long-term investors, 79
    mixed-bag category, 79, 80
    names/web addresses, 249–251
    online, 79–81, 249–251
Brown-Forman Corp. (BF.B), 205
Browning-Ferris Industries, Inc. (BFI), 228
Brunswick Corporation (BC), 213
Buffet, Warren, 108
Bulletin-board stocks, 69, 70
Burlington Northern Santa Fe (BNI), 207
Burlington Resources, Inc. (BR), 216
Buy stop, 72

Cabletron Systems, Inc. (CS), 238
Campbell Soup Co. (CPB), 200

Canada, 155, 160, 161
Canceling an order, 71, 76
Capital Group, 142
Capital One Financial Corporation (COF), 224
Cardinal Health, Inc. (CAH), 201
Carnival Corp. (CCR), 192
Carolina Power & Light Company (CPL), 242
Case Corporation (CSE), 228
Cash-secured put, 46
Cash sweep, 51
Caterpillar, Inc. (CAT), 227
CBS Corp. (CBS), 193
Cendant Corp. (CD), 193
Centex Corp. (CTX), 212
Central and Southwest Corporation (CSR), 244
Ceridian Corporation (CEN), 239
Champion International. Corp. (CHA), 187
Charles Schwab Corporation (SCH), 79, 80, 220
Chartists, 31
Chase Manhattan Corp. (CMB), 218
Chevron Corporation (CHV), 214
Chubb Corporation (CB), 222
CIGNA Corporation (CI), 220
Cincinnati Financial Corporation (CINF), 226
CINergy Corporation (CIN), 244
Circuit City Stores (CC), 211
Cisco Corporation (CSC), 231
Citigroup (C), 219
Clear Channel Communications, Inc. (CCU), 193
Clorox Co. (CLX), 203
Closed-end funds, 20
Closing time, 32
Coastal Corporation (CGP), 216
Coca-Cola Co. (KO), 198
Coca-Cola Enterprises (CCE), 203
Colgate Palmolive Co. (CL), 200
Columbia Energy Group (CG), 217
Columbia HCA Healthcare Corp. (COL), 193
Comcast Corp. (CMCK), 193
Comerica Incorporated (CMA), 222
Companies (see Lists of stocks)
Company changes, 17, 20
Compaq Computer Corporation (CPQ), 231
Computer Associates International, Inc. (CA), 234
Computer Sciences Corporation (CSC), 235
Compuware Corporation (CPWR), 233

ConAgra, Inc. (CAG), 201
Conseco, Incorporated (CNG), 223
Consolidated Edison Company of N.Y., Inc. (ED), 241
Consolidated Natural Gas Company (CNG), 217
Consolidated Stores Corp. (CNS), 213
Constellation Energy Group (CEG), 245
Consumer Services Select Sector SPDR (XLV), 88, 192–197
Consumer Staples Select SPDR (XLP), 88, 197–206
Cooper Industries, Inc. (CBE), 228
Cooper Tire and Rubber Company (CTB), 213
Corning, Inc. (GLW), 227
Costco Companies (COST), 207
Costs/fees, 21–23
Countrywide Credit Industries, Inc. (CCR), 225
Covered call, 43
Crane Company (CR), 228
Creation process, 40, 41
Creation units, 40
Crown Cork and Seal Company (CCK), 187
CSX Corporation (CSX), 208
Cummins Engine Company, Inc. (CUM), 228
CVS Corp. (CVS), 200
Cyclical/Transport Select Sector (XLY), 89, 206–214
Cyprus Amax Minerals Co. (CYM), 192

Dana Corporation (DCN), 229
Danaher Corporation (DHR), 229
Darden Restaurants, Inc. (DRI), 197
Data General Corporation (DGN), 239
Datek, 80, 81
Day trading (see Electonic trading (e-trading))
Dayton Hudson (DH), 206
Deere & Company (DE), 229
Dell Computer (DELL), 231
Delta Air Lines (DAL), 209
Deluxe Corp. (DLX), 196
Developed markets, 142
Diamonds (DIA), 14, 95–103
    cash settlement, 102, 103
    DJIA, 95–99
    DJIA listed companies, 96, 97
    LEAPS, and, 100–103
    out-of-the-money puts, and, 101, 102
Dillard's, Inc. (DDS), 212

Discount broker, 76, 77
Discover, 80
Dividends, 28, 148, 149
DJIA, 95–99
  (*See also* Diamonds (DIA))
DLJ Direct, 79
Dollar General (DG), 211
Dominion Resources, Inc. (D), 243
Dover Corporation (DOV), 229
Dow Chemical (DOW), 185
Dow Jones and Company (DJ), 195
Dow Jones Industrial Average, 95–99
  (*See also* Diamonds (DIA))
Downtick, 29
DTE Energy Company (DTE), 243
Duke Energy Corporation (DUK), 241
Dun and Bradstreet Corp (DNB), 195

E*Trade, 81
E-trading (*see* Electonic trading
  (e-trading))
EAFE, 142, 144
Easter Enterprises (EFU), 243
Eastman Chemical Co. (EMN), 188
Eastman Kodak Company (EK), 234
Eaton Corporation (ETN), 229
Ecolab, Inc. (ECL), 187
Edison International (EIX), 241
Efficient market theory, 64
EGG&G, Inc. (EGG), 239
E.I. DuPont de Nemours (DD), 185
Electronic Data Systems Corpora-
  tion (EDS), 233
Electronic trading (e-trading), 69–82
  active markets, 70, 71
  basics of making a trade, 78
  brokers, 76–81 (*See also* Brokers)
  canceling an order, 71, 76
  information sources, 82
  market openings, 75
  misconceptions, 75, 76
  order flow, 76, 77
  OTC bulletin-board stocks, 69, 70
  pink sheets, 69
  quick quote option, 78
  types of orders, 71–75
Eli Lilly and Company (LLY), 198
Emerging markets, 142
Emerson Electric Company (EMR),
  227
Energy Select Sector SPDR (XLE),
  89, 214–217
England (United Kingdom), 155,
  180–182
Englehard Corp. (EC), 189
Enron Corporation (ENE), 215
Entergy Corporation (ETR), 243
Equifax, Inc. (EFX), 237

Equitizing cash, 36, 51–53
Exchange index securities, 13–30
  account structures, 20
  arbitraging against risk, 42, 43
  company changes, 17, 20
  creation process, 40, 41
  dividends, 28
  expense ratio, 21–23
  liquidity, 33
  marginability, 29
  market makers, 39, 40
  option/equity strategies, 46–49
  order flow, 76, 77
  redemption process, 41, 42
  short selling, 29, 30
  smaller blocks, trading in, 33–35
  specialists, 37–39
  stock investing, and, 62
  taxes, 26–28, 49
  trading flexibility, 24–26
  transfer agent functions, 23
Expense ratio, 21–23
Exxon Corporation (XON), 214

FDX Corp. Holding Company
  (FDX), 209
Federated Department Stores (FD),
  208
Fees, 21–23
Fidelity Investments, 79, 80
Fifth Third Bancorp (FITB), 220
Fill-or-kill (FOK) order, 74, 75
Financial Select Sector SPDR
  (XLF), 89, 218–226
First Data Corporation (FDC), 234
First National Mortgage Association
  (FNM), 220
First Union Corporation (FTU), 220
Firstar Corporation (FSR), 221
FirstEnergy Corporation (FE), 243
5/50 rule, 144
Fleet Financial Group, Inc. (FLT), 220
Fleetwood Enterprises, Inc. (FLE),
  213
Fluor Corporation (FLR), 229
FMC Corp. (FMC), 190
FMC Corporation (FMC), 232
FOK order, 74, 75
Ford Motor Company (F), 206
Foreign investing (*see* WEBS)
Fort James (FJ), 203
Fortune Brands (FO), 203
40 Act, 13, 106
Foster Wheeler Corporation (FWC),
  228, 230
FPL Group, Inc. (FPL), 240
France, 155, 162, 163
Franklin Resources (BEN), 223

Freddie Mac (FRE), 219
Freeport McMoran Copper Gold
  (FCX), 191
Front-running, 143
Frontier Corporation (FRO), 243
Fruit of the Loom, Inc. (FTL), 213
Full-service broker, 77, 78
Futures, 32, 36, 53, 54

Gannett, Inc. (GCI), 193
Gap, The (GPS), 206
Gateway 2000, Inc. (GTW), 236
Gender differences, 66, 67
General Dynamics Corporation
  (GD), 236
General Electric (GE), 227
General Instrument Corp. (GIC), 237
General Mills (GIS), 204
General Motors (GM), 207
Genuine Parts (GPC), 209
Georgia Pacific (GP), 186
Germany, 155, 164
Gillette Company (G), 199
Golden West Financial Corporation
  (GDW), 225
Good-til-canceled (GTC) order, 73
Goodyear Tire & Rubber (GT), 209
GPU, Incorporated (DTE), 243
Great Atlantic and Pacific Tea Com-
  pany (GAP), 205
Great Lake Chemical (GLK), 189
Growth stocks, 99
GTC order, 73
GTE Corporation (GTE), 241
Guidant Corp. (GDT), 201

H & R Block, Inc. (HRB), 195
Halliburton Company (HAL), 215
Harcourt General (H), 210
Harnischfeger Industries, Inc.
  (HPH), 230
Harrah's Entertainment, Inc. (HET),
  197
Harris Corporation (HRS), 239
Hartford Financial Services Group
  (HIG), 222
Hasbro, Inc. (HAS), 211
Healthsouth Corporation (HRC), 195
Hedge against losing jobs, 59, 60
Hedge funds, 61, 62
Hedging strategies, 57–61
Hercules, Inc. (HPC), 189
Herlmerich and Payne (HP), 217
Hershey Foods (HSY), 204
Hewlett-Packard Company (HWP),
  230
Hilton Hotels Corp. (HLT), 196
H.J. Heinz Co. (HNZ), 201

Home Depot (HD), 206
Homestake Mining Company (HM), 190
Honeywell, Inc. (HON), 228
Hong Kong, 154, 165
Household International, Inc. (HI), 221
HRC Manor Care, Inc. (HCR), 196
Humana, Inc. (HUM), 196
Huntington Bancshares, Inc. (HBAN), 226

IKON Office Solutions, Inc. (IKN), 239
Illinois Tool Works, Inc. (ITW), 227
Immediate-or-cancel (IOC) order, 74, 75
IMS Health, Inc. (RX), 193
In the money, 44
Inco, Ltd. (N), 190
Index managers, 2, 16, 17
Indexes (see Exchange index securities)
Indexing:
  advantages, 2–6
  evolution, 6–10
Individual investors, 36, 37
Industrial Select Sector SPDR (XLI), 89, 226–230
Information sources, 82, 151, 247–252
Ingersoll-Rand Company (IR), 228
Intel Corporation (INTC), 231
International Business Machines Corporation (IBM), 230
International diversification (see WEBS)
International Flavors & Fragrances (IFF), 205
International Paper Company (IP), 185
Internet web sites, 81, 249–251
Interpublic Group of Companies, Inc. (IPG), 194
Investment Company Act of 1940, 13, 106
IOC order, 74, 75
Isaacman, Max, 137
Italy, 154, 166
ITT Industries (IIN), 210

Japan, 154, 167–171
Jefferson-Pilot (JP), 223
Johnson and Johnson (JNJ), 198
Johnson Controls, Inc. (JCI), 227
Jostens, Inc., 197
J.P. Morgan & Company, Inc. (JPM), 221

Kansas City Southern Industries, Inc. (KSU), 207
Kaufman & Broad Home Corporation (KBH), 213
Kellogg Co. (K), 201
Kerr-McGee Corporation (KMG), 217
KeyCorp (KEY), 222
Kimberly-Clark Corp. (KMB), 200
King World Productions, Inc. (KWP), 197
KLA-Tencor Corp. (KLAC), 237
Kmart Corporation (KM), 209
Knight Ridder, Inc. (KRI), 196
Knowledge trap, 67
Kohl's Corporation (KSS), 208
Kroger Co. (KR), 201

Laidlaw, Inc. (LDW), 212
LEAPS, 100–103
Lehman Brothers Holdings, Inc. (LEH), 225
Limit order, 71, 73, 75
Limited, The (LTD), 210
Lincoln National Corporation (LNC), 224
Liquidity, 33, 108
Listed index securities (see Exchange index securities)
Lists of stocks:
  DJIA, 96, 97
  Nasdaq 100 (QQQ), 131–134
  S&P MidCap 400 (MDY), 114–125
  select sector SPDRS, 183–245
  WEBS, 157–182
Liz Claiborne (LIZ), 212
Load, 20
Lockheed Martin Corporation (LMT), 234
Loews Corporation (LTR), 223
Long Term Capital Management, 67
Longs Drug Stores (LDG), 204
Lottery spin, 67
Louisiana Pacific Corp. (LPX), 190
Lowe's Companies (LOW), 206
LSI Logic Corporation (LSI), 237
Lucent Technologies, Inc. (LU), 231

Maintenance funds, 29
Malaysia, 155, 172, 173
Male perception of superiority, 66
Malkiel, Burton G., 7
Mallinckrodt Incorporated (MKG), 204
Management fee, 21
Marginability, 29

Market makers, 35, 38–40
Market-on-close order, 74, 75
Market openings, 75
Market order, 71, 73
Marking to market, 53–55
Married put, 6, 92, 93
Marriott International, Inc. (MAR), 195
Marsh & McLennan Companies, Inc. (MMC), 221
Masco Corp. (MAS), 208
Mattel, Inc. (MAT), 210
May Department Stores (MAY), 206
Maytag Corporation (MYG), 210
MBIA, Incorporated (MBI), 225
MBNA Corporation (KRB), 221
McDermott International, Inc. (MDR), 217
McDonalds Corporation (MCD), 192
McGraw-Hill Co., Inc., 194
MCI Worldcom (WCOM), 231
MDY, 14, 113–127
  (See also SPY)
Mead Corporation (MEA), 188
Media One Group, Inc. (UMG), 192
Medtronic, Inc. (MDT), 199
Mellon Bank Corporation (MEL), 221
Mercantile Bancorporation, Inc. (MTL), 224
Merck and Co., Inc. (MRK), 197
Meredith Corp. (MDP), 197
Meriwether, John, 67
Merrill Lynch and Company, Inc. (MER), 219
Mexico, 155, 174
MGIC Investment Corporation (MTG), 226
Micron Technology, Inc. (MU), 235
Microsoft Corporation (MSFT), 231
MidCap SPDRS (MDY), 14, 113–127
  (See also SPY)
Milacron, Inc. (MZ), 230
Millipore Corporation (MIL), 240
Minimum order, 74, 75
Minnesota Mining and Manufacturing Company (MMM), 227
Mirage Resorts, Inc. (MIR), 197
Mobil Corporation (MOB), 214
Momentum traders, 31, 140
Monsanto Co. (MTC), 185
Moore Corporation, Ltd. (MCL), 240
Morgan Stanley, Dean Witter, Discover & Company (MWD), 219

Morton Intl. (MII), 188
Motorola, Inc. (MOT), 232
MSCI, Inc., 143
MSCI indexes, 143, 145
  (*See also* WEBS)
Munger, Charles, 109
Mutual funds, 13, 20, 21

NACCO Industries (NC), 230
Naked, 45–49
Nalco Chemical Co. (NLC), 190
Nasdaq 100 (QQQ), 15, 129–136
National City Corp. (NCC), 219
National Semiconductor Corp.
  (NSM), 237
National Service Industries, Inc.
  (NSI), 230
Navistar International Corporation
  (NAV), 229
Netherlands, 155, 175
Network Appliances, Inc. (NTAP),
  207
New Century Energies, Inc. (NCE),
  245
New products, 251, 252
New York Times, The, 16
New York Times (NYT), 195
Newell Company (NWL), 210
Newell Rubbermaid (NWL), 211
Newmont Mining Corporation
  (NEM), 188
Nextel Communications, Inc.
  (NXTL), 235
Niagara Mohawk Power Corpora-
  tion (NMK), 244
NICOR, Inc. (GAS), 244
NIKE (NKE), 208
Noise, 64, 139
Nordstrom, Inc. (JWN), 210
Norfolk Southern (NSC), 207
Northern States Power Company
  (NSP), 244
Northern Telecom Ltd. (NT), 232
Northern Trust Corporation (NTR),
  222
Northrup Grumman Corporation
  (NOC), 237
Not-held order, 74, 75
Novell, Inc. (NOVL), 237
Nucor Corp. (NUE), 187

Occidental Petroleum (OXY), 215
Odean, Terrance, 65
Omnicom Group (OMC), 194
ONEOK, Incorporated, 244
Online brokers, 79–81, 249–251

Online trading (*see* Electonic trad-
  ing (e-trading))
Open-end funds, 20
Options, 6
  basics, 43–45
  cash-secured put, 46
  DIA, and, 101, 102
  listed index securities, and, 46–49
  married put, 6, 92, 93
  naked, 45–49
  rules/specifications, 47
  select sectors SPDRS, and, 90–93
Oracle Corporation (ORCL), 233
Order flow, 76, 77
Orders, types of, 71–75
OTC bulletin-board stocks, 69, 70
Out of the money, 44
Overconfidence, 66
Overtrading, 65, 66
Owens Cornings, Inc. (OWC), 212
Owens Illinois, Inc. (OI), 187

P/BV, 153
P/E multiples, 152
P/S, 153
PACCAR, Inc. (PCAR), 230
PacifiCorp (PPW), 243
Paine Webber Group, Inc. (PWJ), 218
Pall Corporation (PLL), 229
Parametric Technology Corporation
  (PMTC), 238
Parker Hannifin Corporation (PH),
  229
Paychex, Inc. (PAYX), 235
PE Biosystems Group (PEB), 238
PECO Energy Company (PE), 240
Penney (J.C.) (JCP), 207
Peoples Energy Corporation (PGL),
  244
PeopleSoft, Inc. (PSFT), 238
Pep Boys Manny Moe and Jack
  (PBY), 214
Pepsico Inc. (PEP), 199
Pfizer, Inc. (PFE), 198
PG&E Corporation (PCG), 240
Pharmacia and Upjohn, Inc. (PNU),
  200
Phelps Dodge Corp. (PD), 189
Philip Morris Companies, Inc.
  (MO), 198
Phillips Petroleum (P), 215
Pink sheets, 69
Pioneer Hi-Bred Intl. (PHB), 202
Pitney Bowes, Inc. (PBI), 234
Placer Dome, Inc. (PDG), 189
PNC Bank Corporation (PNC), 221
Polaroid Corporation (PRD), 238

Portfolio optimization, 17
Potlach Corp. (PCH), 192
PP&L Resources, Inc. (PPL), 244
PPG Industries, Inc. (PPG), 185
Praxair, Inc. (PX), 186
Premium, 43
Price/earning (P/E) multiples, 152
Price-to-book-value ratio (P/BV),
  153
Price-to-sales ratio (P/S), 153
Principal trades, 37
Privatization, 140
Procter and Gamble Co. (PG), 198
Progressive Corporation (PGR), 223
Proposed new products, 251, 252
Provident Companies, Inc. (PVT),
  225
Providian Financial Corporation
  (PVN), 223
Public Service Enterprise Group,
  Inc. (PEG), 242
Pulte Corporation (PHM), 214
Put, 92

Quaker Oats (OAT), 202
QQQ, 15, 129–136

Ralston Purina (RAL), 202
Random Walk Down Wall Street, A
  (Malkiel), 7
Raychem Corporation (RYC), 236
Raytheon Company (RTN), 234
Redemption process, 41, 42
Reebok International (RBK), 214
Regions Financial Corporation
  (RGBK), 223
Reliant Energy (REI), 245
Republic New York Corporation
  (RNB), 225
Revolution, 1
Reynolds Metals Co. (RLM), 188
Risk:
  arbitraging, and, 42, 43
  currency, 148
  foreign markets, 141
  SPY, 112
  transactions, 55–57
Rite Aid (RAD), 202
RJR Holdings (RJR), 205
Rockwell International Corporation
  (ROK), 235
Rohm and Haas Company (ROH),
  187
Rowan Companies, Inc. (RDC), 217
Royal Dutch Petroleum (RD), 214

R.R. Donnelley and Sons Co.
(DNY), 195
Russell Corporation (RML), 213
Ryder Systems, Inc. (R), 212

S&P futures, 32, 36, 53, 54
SAFECO Corporation (SAFC), 226
Safeway, Inc. (SWY), 200
Sara Lee Corp. (SLE), 200
SBC Communications, Inc. (SBC),
240
Schering Plough Corp. (SGP), 198
Schlumberger, Ltd. (SLB), 216
Scientific-Atlanta (SFA), 236
Seagate Technology, Inc. (SEG), 235
Seagram Company, Ltd. (VO), 193
Sealed Air Corporation (SEE), 187
Sears, Roebuck and Company (S),
206
Sector selection, 85, 86
(*See also* Select sector SPDRS)
Securities and Exchange Commission (SEC), 29
Select sector SPDRs, 14, 15,
85–94, 183–245
basic industry (XLB), 88,
185–192
consumer services (XLV), 88,
192–197
consumer staples (XLP), 88,
197–206
cyclical/transportation (XLY),
89, 206–214
energy (XLE), 89, 214–217
evolution, 86, 87
financial (XLF), 89, 218–226
importance of sector selection,
85, 86
industrial (XLI), 89, 226–230
options, 90–93
taxes, 94
technology (XLK), 90, 230–240
twofold strategy, 87, 88
utilities (XLU), 90, 240–245
Sell stops, 72
Sempra Energy (SRE), 242
Separate accounts, 20
Service Corporation Intl., 194
Settlement, 53
Shared Medical Systems (SMS), 197
Sherwin-Williams (SHW), 209
Short selling, 29, 30, 73
Sigma Aldrich Corp. (SIAL), 188
Singapore, 154, 176
Single issue rule, 144
SLM Holding Corporation (SLM),
224

Smaller blocks, trading in, 33–35
Snap-On, Inc. (SNA), 212
Solectron Corporation (SLR), 235
Sonat, Incorporated (SNT), 215
Southern Company (SO), 241
Southtrust Corporation (SOTR),
218
Southwest Airlines (LUV), 209
Spain, 156, 177
Specialists, 33, 35, 37–39, 147, 148
Springs Industries, Inc. (SMI), 213
Sprint Corp. FON Group (FON),
232
Sprint Corp. PCS Group (PCS), 234
SPY, 14, 105–127
global realignment, 110–112
liquidity, 108, 109
MidCap SPDRs (MDY),
113–127
risk, 112
stock selection process, 109, 110
turnover rate, 111
weighting, 112
St. Jude Medical (STJ), 204
St. Paul Companies, Inc. (SPC), 224
Stanley Works (SWK), 212
Staples, Inc. (SPLS), 208
State Street Corporation (STT), 222
Statman, Meir, 67, 68
Stock market pundits, 64
Stock orders, 71–75
Stocks (*see* Lists of stocks)
Stop limit, 72, 73
Stop-loss order, 72
Stop order, 72, 73
Strike price, 44
Summit Bancorp (SUB), 224
Sun Microsystems (SUNW), 233
SunTrust Banks, Inc. (STI), 220
Supervalu (SVU), 205
Suretrade, 80
Sweden, 155, 178
Sweep arrangement, 51, 52
Switzerland, 155, 179
Synovus Financial Corporation
(SNV), 225
Synthetic index, 55
Sysco Corp. (SYY), 202

Tandy Corporation (TAN), 210
Tax considerations:
advantages of listed index securities, 26–28, 49
select sector SPDRs, and, 94
tax planning, 56
wash sales, 94
Technicians, 31

Technology Select Sector SPDR
(XLK), 90, 230–240
Tektronix, Inc. (TEK), 239
Tellabs, Inc. (TLAB), 233
Temple Inland, Inc. (TIN), 188
Tenent Healthcare Corp. (THC), 194
Tenneco, Inc. (TEN), 186
Texaco, Inc. (TX), 216
Texas Instruments Incorporated
(TXN), 232
Texas Utilities Company (TXU), 241
Textron, Inc. (TXT), 226
The Gap (GPS), 206
The Limited (LTD), 210
The Southern Company (SO), 241
Thermo Electron Corp. (TMO), 236
Thomas & Betts Corporation
(TNB), 236
3Com Corporation (COMS), 233
Time Warner, Inc. (TWX), 192
Times Mirror Co. (TMC), 196
Timkin Co. (TKR), 191
TJX Companies (TJX), 208
Top-down approach, 141
Torchmark Corporation (TMK), 225
Toys "R" Us (TOY), 211
Trading flexibility, 24–26
"Trading Is Hazardous to Your
Health" (Odean/Barber), 65
Transamerica Corporation (TA), 224
Transfer agent functions, 23
Transitions, 55–57
Tribune Co. (TRB), 194
Tricon Global Restaurants, Inc.
(YUM), 195
Trustee, 40–42
TRW Incorporated (TRW), 236
Tupperware Corporation (TUP), 214
Turnover rate, 65
TV market pundits, 63, 64
24F2 fee, 22
25 percent single issue rule, 144
Tyco International Ltd. (TYC),
226

Underperformance of managed
accounts, 2–4
Unicom Corporation (UCM), 242
Uniliver NV (UN), 199
Union Carbide (UK), 186
Union Pacific (UNP), 208
Union Pacific Resources Group,
Inc. (UPR), 215
Union Planters Corporation (UPC),
225
Unisys Corporation (UIS), 235
Unit investment trust, 13

United Healthcare Corp. (UNH), 194
United Kingdom, 155, 180–182
United Technologies Corporation (UTX), 232
Unocal Corporation Delaware (UCL), 215
UNUM Corporation (UNM), 224
Uptick, 29
US Airways Group, Inc. (U), 211
U.S. Bancorp (USB), 220
US WEST Communications Group (USW), 241
UST, Inc. (UST), 202
USX-Marathon Group, Marathon Oil (MRO), 215
USX U.S. Steel Group (X), 190
Utilities Select Sector SPDR (XLU), 90, 240–245

Value stocks, 99
Vanguard 500 index fund, 22, 23
V.F. Corporation (VFC), 209
Viacom (VIA.B), 193

Wachovia Corporation (WB), 220
Wal-Mart Stores (WMT), 206
Walgreen Co. (WAG), 200
Wall Street Journal, The, 16
Walt Disney (DIS), 192
Warner Lambert Co. (WLA), 199
Wash sales, 94
Washington Mutual (WM), 219

Waste Management International (WME), 226
Waterhouse, 79
Watson Pharmaceuticals, Inc. (WPI), 198
Web sites, 81, 249–251
Web Street, 81
WEBS, 15, 16, 137–182
    analyzing foreign markets, 150–153
    concentration problems, 145, 146
    constant monitoring, 146, 147
    creation/redemption process, 42
    currency risk, 148
    developed vs. emerging markets, 142
    dividends, 148, 149
    economic factors, 151, 152
    evolution, 142, 143
    expense ratios, 149
    5/50 rule, 144
    information sources, 153
    lists of stocks, 157–182
    MSCI indexes, 143, 145
    portfolio optimization, 17
    profit potential, 141
    ratios, 152, 153
    risks, 141
    single issue rule, 144
    specialists, 147, 148
    stock values, 152, 153
    symbols/countries, 15, 16

time differences, 147
when to sell, 153
Wells Fargo and Company (WFC), 219
Wendy's International, Inc. (WEN), 196
Westvaco Corp. (W), 189
Weyerhaeuser Company (WY), 185
Whirlpool Corporation (WHR), 211
Williamette Industries, Inc. (WLL), 188
Williams Companies, Inc. (WMB), 215
Winn-Dixie Stores (WIN), 202
Worthington Industries, Inc. (WTHG), 191
W.R. Grace and Co. (GRA), 191
Wrigley (Wm.) Jr. (WWY), 202
W.W. Grainger, Inc. (GWW), 237

Xerox Corporation (XRX), 232
XLB, 88, 158–192
XLE, 89, 214–217
XLF, 89, 218–226
XLI, 89, 226–230
XLK, 90, 230–240
XLP, 88, 197–206
XLU, 90, 240–245
XLV, 88, 192–197
XLY, 89, 206–214

Zero-plus tick, 292

ABOUT THE AUTHOR

Max Isaacman is a Registered Investment Advisor and a nationally known financial journalist with *The San Francisco Examiner*, *Personal Investing News*, and other publications. Over a 30-year career, he was a stockbroker with Montgomery Securities, a manager and partner of SG Cowen, and an account executive at Merrill Lynch. You can learn more about Isaacman at his website—xchangesec.com—or contact him directly at exch13@aol.com.